# BLACK WEALTH

# THROUGH

# BLACK

# ENTREPRENEURSHIP

by Robert L. Wallace

*Duncan & Duncan, Inc., <u>Publishers</u>*

*Duncan & Duncan, Inc., Publishers*
2809 Pulaski Hwy., Edgewood, MD 21040

Editorial process: Staff of Duncan & Duncan, Inc.
Photography: Isaac Jones, Isaac Jones Photography

Library of Congress Catalog Card Number: 92-74274

Wallace, Robert Lee,
Black Wealth Through Black Entrepreneurship

1. African-American business enterprises 2. New business enterprises 3. African-
Americans - Economic conditions 4. Success
Index, Bibliography, Glossary, Appendix

ISBN 1-878647-09-1

Fourth printing
9 8 7 6 5 4

# DEDICATION

The author respectfully dedicates this book to the memory of Reginald F. Lewis, deceased chairman of TLC Beatrice International. A man who showed young black entrepreneurs that no one can define their level of success but them. He showed the world that African-American entrepreneurs **can** win.

May God of Abraham and Moses receive his spirit and may he find peaceful rest under the eyes of the Creator.

# ACKNOWLEDGMENTS

**Dr. Martin** Luther King, Jr., once said that we are who we are because of someone or something. We are what we are because of our parents, our schools, our environment, our education, and our experiences.

The writing of *Black Wealth Through Black Entrepreneurship* is the culmination of a life time of learning, listening, watching, analyzing, compromising, and taking action. Let me make a fragile attempt at acknowledging a few of those who made the writing of this book possible.

Above all, I'd like to thank God for sending His son, Jesus Christ, to earth so that I might have a chance to enjoy eternal life. I thank God for sending His servants to help me during those times of trouble and for showing me that despite the changes and vicissitudes of life, His love will abide.

To my mother, Irene, and my deceased father, Daniel, thank you for keeping the family together through some of the toughest times one could imagine. Thank you for introducing me to God, for loving me, for teaching me the value of a good education, and for not walking away when it would have been easy to do so.

A tremendous debt is due to my grandfather, Curry. For more

than one-half a century, my grandfather worked as a porter on the B&O Railroad. Thank you Grandfather Curry for sharing all your stories with me about working on the railroad and how you and your peers from the Brotherhood of Sleeping Car Porters courageously confronted the racism that so firmly griped America during that time. If you only knew how much those stories have motivated me and encouraged me throughout the years. I'm also grateful to my uncles Eugene, Walter, and Robert for providing me stellar examples of how to be a man.

To my four sons, Bobby Jr., Joshua, Collin, and Jordan, you've been my inspiration to finish this book even though I often felt like giving up. You boys are our future. You will be the business leaders of tomorrow and as long as God continues to give me a strong mind and body, I will always be there for you.

My brothers Richard, Ronald, Randy, and Raymond also played a long-term role in the evolution of this book. Although we never enjoyed much of the "good life" as poor black kids in the projects, we remained strong and resisted the temptations to succumb to the evils of drugs, alcohol, and petty crime. A special thanks to Randy for finding a way to feed us on a $10 per week budget and to my brother Raymond for being there when I needed him.

To my extended family, the Green's, and the "Home Boys in the Hood" - Kenny, Big Wayne, Elroy, Lee Bone, Johnny, Qui Qui, Kai Kai, Leonard, Sweet Baby Bruce, Mad Max Dalton, Butterball, David, and the rest of the gang. We've all had our setbacks in life, but despite what they tell us, we can win.

A warm thank you to the three ladies who transcribed all of my interview tapes and edited the initial versions of my manuscript - Celest Lucas, Lori Cohen, and Iris White. All of you deserve credit for bringing my ideas to life.

Even with all of the support I received, none of this would have happened had it not been for the Amos Tuck School of Business at Dartmouth College and the Minority Business Executive Program (MBEP) sponsored by the school. Thank you to the many MBEP graduates who took the time to speak with me on the topic of minority entrepreneurship and economic empowerment, particularly the graduates whose case studies I used in this book. I am particularly indebted to Ron and Cynthia Thompson and Del and Lula Mullens for caring and for being my role models. A heart-felt thanks goes to Paula Graves, the program director for MBEP, who provided me with all kinds of information on the program, its history, and its participants.

I have also benefited greatly by counsel from former Congressman Parren J. Mitchell. Mr. Mitchell, a life-long advocate for minority business rights, reviewed my manuscript in its very early stages and encouraged me to complete the project because he saw value in what I was saying. His encouragement brought back life into my endeavor.

A special thank you to my instructors who helped me liberate the man inside me, Ms. Gwendolyn Brown of Cherry Hill Junior High School, Mr. Greg Sanford at Polytechnic Institute, Dr. Jacob Abel at the University of Pennsylvania, Dr. Hector Guerrero, Dr. Ken Baker, Dr. James Brian Quinn, Dr. Len Greenhalgh, and Dr. Dean Kropp from the Tuck School of Dartmouth College.

Finally, although it all started with God, it ends with my best friend, my wife Carolyn. Ever since our days as students at the University of Pennsylvania, her commitment to me has been unwavering. As I repeatedly drained our family savings to either capitalize the numerous businesses that we started or to fund the cost of flying across the country to interview people for this book, not once did Carolyn complain or second-guess me. When things got tough and I became discouraged, she was there to pick me up, brush me off, and set me on my way again. She deserves the most credit for the successful completion of *Black Wealth Through Black Entrepreneurship.* God bless you Carolyn, and I love you.

# TABLE OF CONTENTS

## Part 5: Where Do We Go from Here?
## A Strategic Analysis

## APPENDIX

# FOREWORD

**For** more than twenty years, I have supported the idea of developing and enhancing minority entrepreneurship by legislation and by advocacy. During that time, and continuing today, I have sought to give advice and counsel to recently launched and existing minority firms. I have often told them they should expect to lose money the first year, break even the second year, and make a profit the third year. Robert L. Wallace, author of *Black Wealth Through Black Entrepreneurship,* writes about minority entrepreneurs from across the country, some of whom have made a profit during their first year of business, thus contradicting my advice. Some have consistently plowed their profits back into their businesses and have ultimately become very successful.

Wallace shares the successes and challenges of these bold entrepreneurs with candor, humor, insight, and admiration. All of these accounts result in fascinating reading and provide abject lessons for would-be entrepreneurs, fledgling businesses, and well-established firms.

He has written this well-researched and informative book, which is really a story about the acquisition of power. He holds that, "The triad of power consists of three integral lattices: ethnic rooting (cultural pride), political power, and economic strength." He points out, "Consequently, until blacks and other minorities obtain the wealth and economic power commensurate with their numbers and proportion in the overall population, they will never gain full membership into the American 'club.'" This is a tenable hypothesis to which I heartily subscribe.

Wallace is a Mechanical Engineer (University of Pennsylvania) and holds a Master's degree in Business Administration from the Amos Tuck School of Business, Dartmouth College. In his work, it is clear that he has successfully probed into the psychology of minority business persons. In Part 3, he analyzes the twenty traits found in successful black business persons. The owners I have worked with have at least half of those traits. One such person was experiencing dire circumstances in his third year of business. As we concluded our meeting, he said, "I'm not going to let this get me down. I'm good, I know it, and I will make it." Wallace believes that, "No matter the ordeal, minority business persons need to have the foresight to take what appears to be a hopeless situation and convert it into a promising and exciting opportunity." He echoes this same idea when discussing Trait #10, using an intriguing approach - "The Conversion of Saul to Paul."

A political revolution has taken place in America during the last two or three decades. We have seen an unprecedented number of blacks elevated to high positions in public service, including black city council persons, state legislators, mayors, congress persons, a black governor, and a black female member of the United States Senate.

Wallace admonishes, and properly so, that this new political power must be used as an integral tool to help blacks achieve economic justice in America. Former Mayor Marion Barry must not be judged only by the accounts of his personal weaknesses. He also must be judged by his successful use of political power for the economic enhancement of minority business opportunities in the District of Columbia. He implemented a sheltered market plan for minority businesses that enabled them to gain 37% of city contracts. Another example cited by Wallace is the aggressive use of political power by Mayor Maynard Jackson, which resulted in lucrative opportunities for minority businesspeople in the expansive construction of the Atlanta Airport.

*Black Wealth Through Black Entrepreneurship* comes at a time when advances for minority businesses have been slowed and at a time of great frustration for many entrepreneurs or would-be entrepreneurs. The decision by the U.S. Supreme Court in the case of *Croson v. the City of Richmond*, the uncertainties in the American economic system, and unfortunate national trends to eliminate black concerns from the national agenda are issues of grave concern in the minority business community.

Wallace's book is not only instructive and replete with sound business advice. It is also inspirational. He inspires when he writes, "Despite these challenges and the difficulties that face the community, African-Americans must remain optimistic about the ultimate outcome of this fight. *Keep your head to the sky* means that you ultimately believe in the final morality of the universe. It means that no matter how dark and pessimistic the community's economic condition may seem, you must maintain the faith that if you continue stepping up to the plate and swinging at the pitches, ultimately you will hit a home run and win the game! This is the faith that must carry the community until economic justice is a reality. God bless and *keep your head to the sky!*"

Parren J. Mitchell
Former Congressman of Maryland, 7th District.
Former Chairman of Congressional Small Business Committee.
Current Chairman, Minority Business Enterprise Legal Defense and Education Fund, Inc.

# PREFACE

**People** often ask why I have become so emotionally involved in minority business development and African-American economic empowerment. I find the question somewhat humorous because, although most assume I went through some planned and scientific process to arrive at that point, it was actually an emotional event that triggered the advent of my mission.

My impetus for pursuing this topic began as I was making the transition from engineer to businessman. After relinquishing a career at DuPont and beginning graduate business studies at Dartmouth College, a casual last trip home to visit my family before venturing off to business school seemed appropriate. While there, I purposely wandered down to the neighborhood shopping center, where I often hung out as a boy, to say hello to some old buddies. To my dismay, I observed that the majority of the stores, which were once owned by Jewish-Americans, were now owned by Asian-Americans. Instead of there being the logical business transition from Jewish-American merchants to African-American merchants, the transition entirely excluded the people living within the community. Once again, control of our economic destiny had been wrestled away from us and ended up in the hands of a "foreigner." Devastated, I vowed that as long as there was breath in my body, I would do whatever I could to make some contribution to my community's economic well-being. I pray that my work in this book will serve as one of those contributions.

The challenges facing the black community reach far beyond its tenuous economic position. A closer inspection of black America's position would lead most people to the same frustrating conclusion that Dr. Martin Luther King, Jr., reached decades ago. He concluded that it appeared that of the good things in life, black folks enjoyed only a fraction of that of whites, i.e., good jobs, decent housing, quality education, and reasonable life expectancy.

Conversely, of the bad things in life, blacks are over-represented, i.e., disproportional percentage of people living below the poverty level, inferior education system, victims of high crime, drug abuse, etc. Clearly, the centuries of harsh and inhumane treatment of people of African descent have taken a terrible toll on their descendants and have allowed the creation of two separate and woefully unequal societies, one black, the other white.

Despite such harsh and adverse conditions, black Americans have done an amazing thing - they have survived and in many cases thrived! While most groups would have crumbled under such debilitating conditions, blacks have overcome every obstacle put in their way. While most people would have developed a deep and lingering hate for other groups that sought to bring about their destruction, blacks have consistently, over the centuries, shown an abiding willingness to forgive and trust others - sometimes to their own detriment.

The challenge facing the black community and other minority communities now is to re-direct this "superhuman" goodwill and capacity to survive into constructive programs that will elevate the economic strength of the community and promote economic empowerment to all of its citizens who want it.

This book attempts to take a second look at the term "black power" from a different perspective. Yes, black power is important because the underlying premise of this book is that before any ethnic group in America will be taken seriously, respected, and allowed to prosper to any degree in the mainstream, that group must first solidly build the essential triad of power within their respective communities. Until this triad of power is properly constructed, African-Americans and others will continue to be at the mercy of the powerful.

*Robert L. Wallace*

# ABOUT THE AUTHOR

**Robert** L. Wallace, business consultant, entrepreneur, and President of The BITH Group Holding Company, is a native of Baltimore, Maryland. He is one of five sons and was an honor graduate from the Baltimore Polytechnic Institute. He later attended the University of Pennsylvania and the Amos Tuck School of Business at Dartmouth College, where he earned his Bachelor's of Science degree in Mechanical Engineering and Applied Mechanics and his Master's of Business Administration, respectively.

With engineering degree in hand, Robert practiced engineering for five years for the DuPont Company before attending Dartmouth College to conduct graduate studies in business and entrepreneurship. After graduate school, he joined IBM's Engineering Scientific and Industrial Marketing Unit, where he provided expertise to Fortune 100 companies in systems integration and business strategy. Five years later, Robert left IBM and co-founded the SDGG Holding Company, The Atlantis Leasing Company, and The Ivy Group Consultants. He is married to the former Carolyn Green and is the proud father of four sons.

Robert conducts workshops and lectures across the country on the issues of economic empowerment and the criticalness of accelerated business formation within the African-American community.

# INTRODUCTION

**My** research indicates that the triad of power consists of three integral lattices: ethnic rooting, political prowess, and economic strength. Some European ethnic groups, such as the Jews, have shown a remarkable ability to build all three elements concurrently with great success. However, it required a major civil rights movement for African-Americans to cultivate political strength and deep ethnic pride. Later, the Voting Rights Act of 1965 guaranteed blacks the right to cast votes in local and national elections. Since these major events, the political landscape has never been the same.

Unfortunately, the strengthening of the economic component of the triad languished as the economic parity gap between black and white America widened. Full integration into the mainstream cannot be consummated until the triad is closed and complete. Consequently, until blacks and other minorities obtain the wealth and economic power commensurate with their numbers and proportion to the overall population, full membership into the American 'club' will never be achieved.

Part of the reason I think African-Americans haven't been as active in the entrepreneurial fervor in this country is that many blacks view the process of business formation as having formidable barriers of entry, which also causes a certain degree of suspicion.

One of the most painful and embarrassing situations faced by the African-American community is why more blacks don't support black-owned businesses. Having been on both sides of the table on this issue and having researched this matter with both consumers and business owners, the concerns and misunderstandings that each have for the other are clearly understood. During the numerous workshops and presentations conducted on black entrepreneurship and its impact on the community, I often ask the above question. The answers that are usually provided include:

1) Business is not conducted in a comfortable and wholesome environment.
2) Products and services are inferior.
3) Products and services are not priced competitively.
4) Owners are not courteous and fail to show their customers respect.
5) It is difficult to identify which businesses are owned by blacks.
6) There are few black businesses that provide the goods and services demanded by the black community.

Although all six answers are serious and require our immediate attention, it is answer #6 that is probably the most critical and yet the most difficult to accomplish in the short-term, which makes it the focus of this book. Why are black businesses not better represented in the business community? How do black entrepreneurs survive and even thrive in a hostile environment? What makes them special? What is the impact of black entrepreneurs on the economic development of the black and minority community?

This study was done to share with the minority community's aspiring entrepreneurs the experiences of down-to-earth minority businesspeople and to provide some meaningful guidelines for getting started. By learning from the experiences of these businesspeople, the probability of accelerated business formation within the African-American community will be enhanced.

The majority of the businessmen and businesswomen who

participated in this study are small business owners who are graduates from the Minority Business Executive Program, which is annually hosted by the Amos Tuck School of Business Administration at Dartmouth College. While attending the Amos Tuck School of Business, I worked as a program facilitator with the faculty who developed the program and was fortunate enough to assist in organizing, administering, coordinating, and participating in the program from 1983 to the present. During this time, I met and confided in hundreds of minority business owners. I've listened to very interesting stories and learned some lessons that are not taught at business schools. It is my intent to share these stories and lessons with you so that you too can benefit from the experiences of this impressive group of entrepreneurs.

Entrepreneur graduates from the Tuck program are by no means limited to only African-Americans. Each year, an illustrious group of Hispanic, Native-American and Asian business owners become graduates of the program. Some of the original participants in this study were members of the above ethnic groups and provided provocative insights on the subject of minority economic empowerment. However, after beginning my task and realizing the enormity of it, I found it prudent to scale back my scope to include a smaller subset of minority Americans. I chose African-Americans because they are the largest and oldest minority group and the most visible. The analysis provided here however, can be indirectly substituted for any ethnic group in America.

All "would-be" entrepreneurs, owners of fledgling businesses, well-established existing business owners, and people with formal and informal educational backgrounds will find *Black Wealth Through Black Entrepreneurship* to be a valuable reference guide dealing with issues, answers, and experiences to some of the most troublesome business problems faced by African-Americans and other minorities. You could be a plumber, carpenter, security guard, janitorial worker, child care specialist, auto mechanic, retailer, truck/bus driver, beautician, engineer, doctor, lawyer, office worker, manager, or already in business. *Black Wealth Through Black Entrepreneurship* will help you to chart a course toward the successful creation of a business you can be proud of and one that may be passed down to your children.

To assist "would-be-entrepreneurs" and others to focus on business ownership, the findings in my study are presented in an "hour glass" fashion. This approach allows me to review the issues of black wealth, black entrepreneurship, and black economic empowerment first from an aggregate community perspective and then at an individual level. Once the community and individual findings are discussed, the final chapters move from an individual look at the issues to one that again encompasses the community as a whole.

The early chapters of the book review the current economic status of black America and attempt to expose the indelible link between black economic progress and black America's performance within the entrepreneurial players in our country. This link is further established through a discussion of the power model, which explains why the black entrepreneur is so critical to the well-being of the community and to the successful pursuit of black economic empowerment.

As this analysis moves from a group level to an individual level, chapters begin to show how the experiences of black and minority entrepreneurs can be leveraged to benefit the "would-be entrepreneurs" by the use of case studies. These case studies are included to provide real life experiences about many facets of business development from a minority perspective. The studies are dispersed throughout the book and include men and women from across the country. Each entrepreneur highlighted has a fascinating story to tell. Case studies illustrate the dynamics of business development from a personal level and extrapolate the common success factors of this distinguished group. These personal experiences and identified traits can be used by those who desire to go into business and those who are already in business for use as checkpoints to assist them in their business development efforts.

The last chapter presents a strategic blueprint for building a larger and more active black entrepreneurial base, which will ultimately fortify the power triad of the black community and accelerate the realization of black economic empowerment.

More than a quarter of a century ago, Malcolm X eloquently summed up the spirit of this book when he said:

> The old order must be completely destroyed and replaced with new political and economic systems that allow blacks and whites to share power equally...We never can win freedom, justice, and equality until we are doing something for ourselves.

It is my hope that my work will excite the "would-be-entrepreneurs" to step out, take a chance, and allow the entrepreneurial juices to flow. After reading this book, I hope you will be convinced that although business formation can be a slow, difficult, and frustrating process, it can also be exciting, fun, and rewarding. God bless and let's get busy!

Throughout this book, the personal pronouns he and she are used interchangeably. Also, the words African-American and black are used synonymously.

*Robert L. Wallace*

**PART 1**

# THE BLACK ENTREPRENEUR AND THE BLACK COMMUNITY

*Why the African-American Community Needs Black Entrepreneurs Now!*

**One** of the reasons this book has been written is to address the lack of significant progress in the development of business formation within the African-American community. Most of the small corner stores located within many black communities are owned and operated by people who live outside of the community. Once again, neighborhood dollars are being removed from circulation within the community and finding their way into other local economies.

In reviewing this situation, it becomes painfully obvious that the basic problem facing the black community is that it lacks significant power to have a direct and sustained impact on its own destiny.

## Black Political Power - Has It Helped Blacks Economically?

Certainly no one can argue that blacks have won significant political rights in the last thirty years, which has greatly empowered the African-American political machine. The changes in the political power structure of the black community are sometimes manifested in the number of American cities that are currently managed by black chief executives. As shown in Exhibit 1-1, not long ago, four of the five largest American cities were being managed by African-American mayors.

**Exhibit 1-1. Black Mayors of Major Cities**

| Black Chief Executives of Major Cities | | | |
|---|---|---|---|
| Cities | Rank By Population | 1990 Preliminary Census Figures | African-American Mayor |
| New York | 1 | 7,033,179 | David Dinkins |
| Los Angeles | 2 | 3,420,235 | Tom Bradley |
| Chicago | 3 | 2,727,979 | Harold Washington (Deceased) |
| Philadelphia | 5 | 1,543,313 | Wilson Goode (Former Mayor) |
| Baltimore | 13 | 720,100 | Kurt Schmoke |

U.S. Bureau of Census, 1990

Even in cities where blacks do not enjoy a substantial numbers advantage, more and more whites are finding it more comfortable to vote for black politicians and to view them in leadership roles. Norm Rice, mayor of Seattle, Washington, and Michael White, mayor of Cleveland, Ohio, are proof that the racial politics of the past can be defeated. Even in cities not managed by someone of color, blacks and other minorities in those urban centers often wield a sizeable amount of political power.

Unfortunately, these outstanding political gains are overshadowed by statistics that show African-Americans lagging far behind white Americans in terms of housing, education, and economic status.

The increased racial intolerance visible in today's current events are dwarfed when compared to the economic performance of African-Americans in the workplace. A review of the economic status of the African-American workforce also may serve to spotlight the challenges facing African-Americans. Of the nation's 30 million black people (12.1% of the population), 13 million participate in the nation's workforce. Of these 13 million people in the workforce, 35 percent work in blue-collar jobs and almost one out of every four labor in service occupations. This ratio in service jobs is double that of whites in the same fields. Among the 39 percent who are white collar workers, only 17 percent of black males have the designation "professional, technical, manager, or administrator" as compared to 31 percent for white males.

Although opportunities for blacks within the lower paying jobs are few, among the top executive ranks the chances for advancement are almost nonexistent. Korn/Ferry, a prominent executive search firm, recently surveyed 1,700 senior executives across the country who earned an average of $100,000 per year. Of those executives, only three ( less than 1%) were black. In a Chicago study of 13,000 managers with the rank "department head" or higher, only 117 (again, less than 1%) were black.

These statistics confirm what minorities and females have known all along. There exists a "glass ceiling" for women and minorities in corporate America, above which they are prevented from moving, no matter how talented they are. Even those who make it to executive heights are usually placed in highly visible jobs, such as human resources and public relations, but are restricted from entering positions that lead to powerful, top level responsibilities.

## *The Triad of Power*

Why, with all the great victories won during the 1960s has the African-American community's economic prosperity, on all fronts, been so delayed? Can racism be used to justify all of the economic and social problems that still confront this community in such a big way? Clearly racism is a factor, but how much of a factor? I submit that there are other factors that are at least as critical as racism.

The biggest factor is that the African-American community has not yet completed the essential triad of power. This triad consist of ethnic rooting (pride), political power (prowess), and economic power. Yes, while blacks have been successful at rebuilding their culture to the point of being proud of their African heritage and the contributions their ancestors have made to the world, as well as the impressive political clout amassed, their performance at completing the third leg of the triad, i.e., economic empowerment, has been less than impressive.

Malcolm X, a man who's vision was probably too intense for his time, summarized the economic challenge that looms in front of the African-American community when he said:

The man who tosses worms in the river isn't necessarily a friend of the fish. All the fish who took him for friend, who thinks the worm's got no hook in it, usually end up in the frying pan.

In deep disgust, Malcolm would later comment, "I watched brothers entwining themselves in the economic clutches of the white man, who went home every night with another bag of money drained from the ghetto."

Malcolm realized, long before most leaders of his time, that the key to social and economic parity and the accumulation of power was the achievement of economic self-reliance. He viewed prosperity as the ultimate equalizer. As a member of the Black Muslims, economic empowerment became the heart of his message to African-Americans. He knew that economic self-reliance would supply not only jobs and security, but also badly needed self-esteem and respect from the overall community.

When blacks complained about the slums they were forced to live in, Malcolm would scold them bitterly for their slave-like dependence on white America. He, like many of us today, felt that the need to develop businesses within the black community was of an urgent nature. Like mainstream America, he saw the ownership of property, whether that property was land or business, as a necessary requirement for any real freedom or independence. Malcolm's vision was to see blacks turn their neighborhoods into showcases of dynamic and exciting enterprises.

## Economic Performance of African-Americans

Since Malcolm last conveyed this strategy, the vision for economic self-reliance has been somewhat dimmed. The following pages provides a factual look at the current economic condition of African-Americans and confirms the seriousness of the matter.

## Economic Injustice

The 1980s was an especially disappointing time for blacks because although the country was booming during those "go-go" years, blacks benefited very little from the surge. In general, the 1980s were not very kind to African-Americans economically. Consider for a moment the following facts:

1) In 1979, the median family income for blacks was $8,858 less than for whites, a difference of more than 40 percent. 1987, that figure had risen to $14,176, and continues to show signs of expanding.
2) In 1980, black males earned $6,000 less than white males, and in 1987 the average difference had increased to just over $8,000.
3) Over 26 percent of white households had a median net worth exceeding $100,000, while only 4 percent of black households did.
4) Black ghetto poverty deepened, with a 49 percent increase in the number of blacks living in poverty in cities.

5) In 1989, one in seven black families had incomes above $50,000 compared to one in three white families.

A comparison of African-Americans' performance compared to white Americans' performance in the following areas will further dramatize the severity of the community's economic woes:

1) Unemployment
2) Mean Net Worth
3) Per Capita Income
4) Median Family Income
5) Persons Below Poverty Level (As Percent of Group)
6) Persons Below Poverty Level (Number of People)
7) Money Income Of Households

This comparison reveals a deep and pervasive economic gap between blacks and whites in our society.

**Exhibit 1-2. Unemployment Rates**

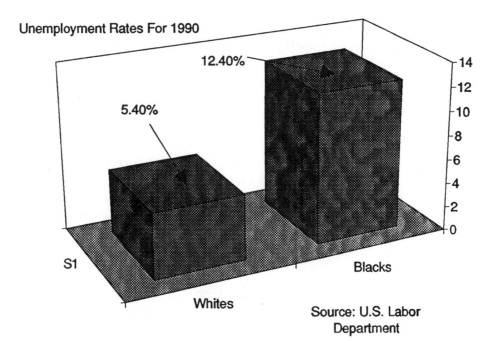

Unemployment Rates For 1990

12.40%

5.40%

S1

Whites

Blacks

Source: U.S. Labor Department

## Unemployment

The U.S. Department of Labor's Bureau of Labor Statistics reveals, as shown in Exhibit 1-2, that the unemployment rate in the black community was 12.4 percent in 1990 while the rate for whites was 5.4 percent. However, when one considers the significant number of part-time workers and workers who have become disillusioned about finding employment, the unemployment rate would probably exceed 20 percent. For black teenagers the unemployment rate often hovers between 30-40 percent. Traditionally, the black unemployment rate has fluctuated between 1.5 to 5.3 times that of whites.

## Mean Net Worth

Basically, net worth is the result of summing up all of your assets minus your liabilities. In other words, if you were to sell everything you owned, obtained the cash from this sale, then used the cash to pay off all of your bills, whatever is left would be your net worth (somewhat depressing, huh?). Most people build net worth by putting aside a portion of their earnings obtained from their jobs, into investments and savings accounts. Over a period of time these assets appreciate. Consequently, there is a strong correlation between income and net worth.

Based on the Federal Reserve Board's 1983 Survey of Consumer Finances, majority families, which have a median net worth of $39,135, are more than 10 times as affluent as black families. The median net worth of black families is $4,000. The latest data, Exhibit 1-3, from the U.S. Dept. of Commerce, Bureau of the Census, Household, Wealth and Asset Ownership, reveals that in 1989 the mean net worth for black America was $24,168 and $103,081 for white America. This translates into blacks having only one-fourth the net worth of whites.

One of the participants of this study put it best when he said that our community is basically in a "sharecropping" economic mode.

Black folks tend to live from paycheck to paycheck. If that paycheck was taken away, the little net worth available would be eroded rapidly, plunging the community further into poverty.

**Exhibit 1-3. Mean Net Worth**

**Mean Net Worth ( 1989 )**

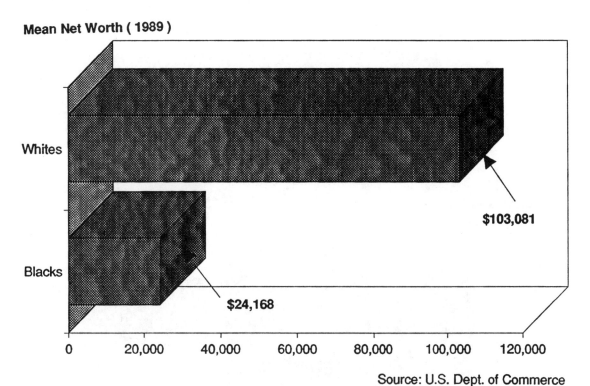

Source: U.S. Dept. of Commerce

## *Per Capita Income*

Per capita income is calculated by dividing the total aggregate money income by the total number of people in the target population. Basically it is the amount of income per person, for every man, woman, and child. Per capita income differs from family income because it includes the income of all persons, but family income is restricted to the income of related persons living in households.

According to the U.S. Department of Commerce, Bureau of the Census, the recent report (as of March 1989) on money, income, and poverty status in the United States reveals the following per capita income results for the three major groupings:

| | |
|---|---|
| All Races | $13,123 |
| White | $13,896 |
| Black | $ 8,271 |
| Hispanic | $ 7,956 |

Exhibit 1-4 shows that blacks continue to lag behind whites by $5,625 per person per year. Another way of stating these data is that every black family of four must earn approximately $22,500 more per year for blacks to achieve economic parity with whites.

**Exhibit 1-4. Per Capita Income (1989)**

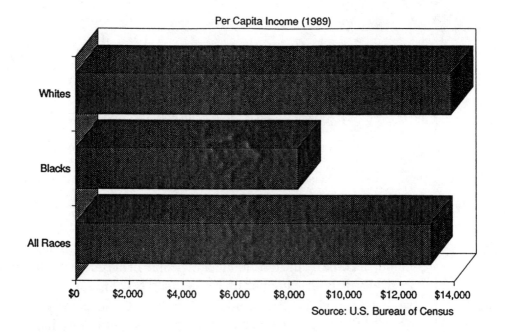

Per Capita Income (1989)

Source: U.S. Bureau of Census

## *Median Family Income*

The median income is an income level in which half of the households earn less than the median and the other half earn more than that income. The median family income is important because within the American society, the family unit remains the cornerstone of societal structure. Thus, economic information on the family unit often is a more realistic indicator of group performance. In 1989, as shown by Exhibit 1-5, the median family incomes of the three major groups were as follows:

| | |
|---|---|
| Blacks | $20,240 |
| Whites | $35,980 |
| Hispanics | $23,450 |
| All Races | $28,910 |

**Exhibit 1-5. Median Family Income**

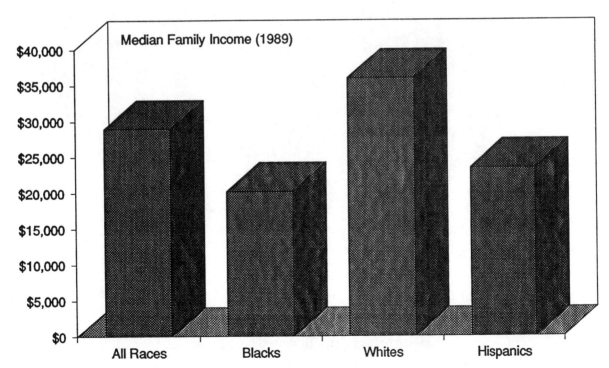

Source: U.S. Bureau of Census

These data indicate that the median family income for black families is 56 percent that of whites. However, when a comparison is made between median family incomes for married couples (two parents in the home), blacks fare much better in comparison to whites. In fact, the median family income of blacks increases to 78 percent that of whites in this comparison. For married couples the median family income is as follows:

Whites      $39,210
Blacks      $30,650
Hispanics   $27,380

**Exhibit 1-6. Percentage of Groups Below Poverty Level**

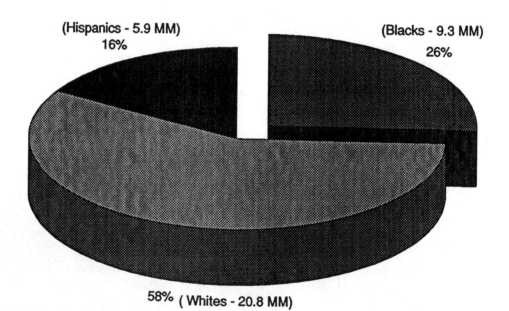

(Hispanics - 5.9 MM)
16%

(Blacks - 9.3 MM)
26%

58% ( Whites - 20.8 MM)

Source: U.S. Bureau of Census

*Persons Below Poverty Level (As % of Group)*

The poverty definition used here is adopted for official Government use by the Office of Management and Budget and consists of a set of money income thresholds that vary by family size and composition. Families or individuals with incomes below their appropriate thresholds are classified as below the poverty level. The poverty thresholds are updated every year to reflect changes in the Consumer Price Index. For example, the average poverty threshold for a family of four was $12,091 in 1988, $11,611 in 1987, and $11,203 in 1986. Average thresholds varied in 1988 from $6,024 for a person living alone to $24,133 for a family of nine or more members. The poverty rates for whites was 10.1 percent, blacks 31.6 percent, and Hispanics 26.8 percent.

**Exhibit 1-7. Number of Persons Below Poverty Level**

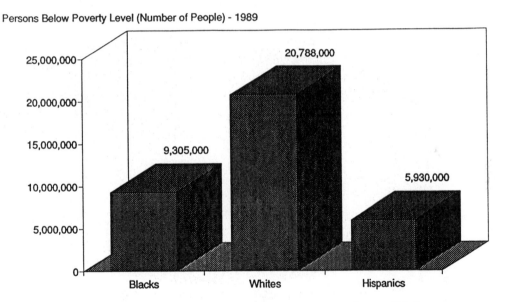

Persons Below Poverty Level (Number of People) - 1989

Source: U.S. Bureau of Census

As depicted by Exhibit 1-6 and Exhibit 1-7, blacks have consistently absorbed a disproportionate share of the poverty in this country. In 1980, 13 percent of all Americans lived below the poverty level. During the next eight years, the poverty level peaked at 15 percent during 1982 and ended up at 12.8 percent for 1989. During this same period, the percentage of blacks living under the poverty level peaked at 35.6 percent during 1982 and ended up around 30.7 percent in 1989. In this same year, the poverty rate was 10 percent for whites and 26.2 percent for Hispanics.

## Persons Below Poverty Level (Number of People)

One of the fallacies that some people like to perpetuate is that blacks and other minorities are the groups who are soaking up the social programs paid for with their tax dollars. As shown in Exhibit 1-7, this is not the case. In 1980, just as President Reagan was taking over the Executive Office, there were close to 30 million Americans living below the poverty level. Almost two-thirds of those people were white, while blacks and Hispanics made up a much smaller proportion. During the eight years of the Reagan administration, the number of people living below the poverty level increased to close to 35 million people, with all groups sharing in the increase. The total number of people living in poverty in 1989 by group were as follows:

| | |
|---|---|
| Whites | 20,788,000 |
| Blacks | 9,305,000 |
| Hispanics | 5,430,000 |

## Money Income of Households - Aggregate

Exhibit 1-8, illustrates the aggregate total of incomes from the three groups. These figures are compiled by multiplying all households by the amount of income they generated in 1989. Whites, due to their greater numbers, had a money income of approximately $3.0 trillion dollars per year, while blacks had an aggregate income of approximately $250 billion per year. Hispanics generated nearly $140.5 billion during the same period of time.

## *What Does It All Mean?*

As you can see from the summary of economic statistics, the African-American community faces a monumental challenge in realizing economic parity with mainstream America. Although some progress has been made there still exists a significant parity gap between blacks and whites and in certain instances, between blacks and other minority groups. If the African-American economy were to be isolated, it would become obvious that economic justice has not been realized within the black community, and urgent measures must be taken to rectify the situation. It is because of this urgency that the role of African-American entrepreneurs takes on a new and pivotal role in the community's survival and future development.

**Exhibit 1-8. Aggregate Incomes (1989)**

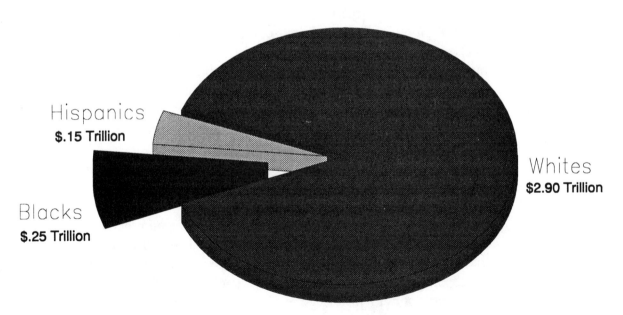

Hispanics
**$.15 Trillion**

Whites
**$2.90 Trillion**

Blacks
**$.25 Trillion**

Source: U.S. Bureau of Census

## The Creation of Wealth Building Power Within the African-American Community

With all this talk about power, one might rightly ask, what is power and how is it defined? There are some who assume that our numbers and political clout directly translate into power. If you view power in these terms, then it would be correct to conclude that because of our numbers, African-Americans do exert significant amounts of power, particularly in our urban centers. However, a majority in numbers does not always equate to equitable power sharing. Let's try to develop this concept of power sharing a bit further.

## Power Structure. What Is It?

Dr. Martin Luther King, Jr., once said that power is simply the ability to achieve purpose. For discussion purposes lets define power as the ability to have a direct impact on one's destiny or the ability to affect change. Although it is easy to define power, it requires a more thorough explanation to understand it and why it is essential to the survival of all ethnic groups. I believe it is much more accurate to view power in terms of a multi-dimensional structure. As shown by Exhibit 1-9, there are various components or members of the power structure.

Analogous to this depiction is the civil engineering involved in designing and constructing a high rise building. Before any walls are raised or roofs attached, the foundation of the building must be properly designed and constructed so that it can support the weight of the structure and help fortify it from the internal and external forces that will inevitably act upon the structure. Next, the walls are put up to support the roof and help translate the stresses from the roof to the foundation and to provide lateral support. The later stages of construction require that the structure, up to that point, is strong enough to allow the roofing component to be laid in place and fast-

**Exhibit 1-9. Power Structure Components**

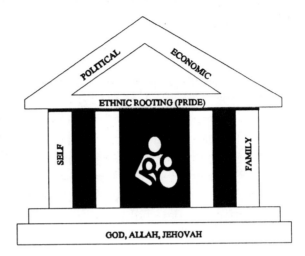

ened to protect the internal occupants and solidify the building's structural integrity.

Before any ethnic group can demand its rightful share of power in our society, like constructing a high rise building, it must first ensure that all components of the structure are in place and able to share their portions of the load. Every element of the structure must meet the specifications that are defined for it or ultimately the entire structure will fail. It is an all or nothing arrangement. The power structure cannot stand unless all power segments are strong and able to withstand the external and internal stresses that will inevitably act upon it.

If the analogy of the power structure were translated into individual or group terms, it might be depicted with the major components (power segments) as explained below:

- God (Spiritual)
- Self (Education)
- Family
- Ethnic Pride/Power
- Political Power
- Economic Power (Economic Justice)

I reiterate that if one of these segments is weakened, the entire structure becomes severely weakened and, if not strengthened, will ultimately cause the entire structure to collapse.

Let's try to analyze the status of black America's existing power base as it relates to the power model developed in Exhibit 1-9. The most critical component of the power structure is God (i.e., Allah, Jehovah, The Almighty, etc.) Without the God element, the group may prosper in the short-term, but will ultimately self-destruct. No one can question the rich, spiritually uplifting influence that God and religion has had on the black community. God is and always has been the glue that has held the African-American community in tact during the dark and sometimes uncertain centuries. It should come as no surprise that the civil rights movement in America was initiated, planned, orchestrated, and implemented from the pulpits of black America's churches.

Of course, some people will assume the opposite position, which suggests that the black community's reliance on religion and spirituality is what continues to hold the black community back. Some will ask the logical question - if God is our supposed foundation, then why did He allow our people to be persecuted? Although this is a fair question, I don't know the answer. What I do know is that it is a major miracle that black Americans are 30 million strong in America despite centuries of oppression and that black's belief in an eternal God is the major reason for the group's survival. African-American parents and grandparents believed that God was on their side, which provided them the moral high ground necessary for them to fight hard and persevere longer. Whether one views the glass as half empty or half full, it is clear that spirituality runs thick within the black community, and despite the many challenges, God remains the rudder of its collective ship.

Just as God is the foundation of the complete model defined in Exhibit 1-9, **self** is the basic element of the family unit. Self is important because unless each individual is strong enough to carry his own weight, the family unit and everything else will suffer. The strengthening of self requires that as individuals, we fortify our physical selves, our intellectual selves, and our spiritual selves.

As in mainstream America, black Americans have become better informed about their health and the importance of proper diet and exercise. The baby boom generation is especially interested in how it looks and how well it ages. This helps explain the booming diet and health club industries. Although the country as a whole continues to fight alcohol and drug epidemics across the nation, people (blacks included) are taking their physical bodies more seriously than ever before.

Intellectually and spiritually, despite formidable obstacles, blacks continue to advance and prosper. Although the number of African-Americans attending college has been on the decline in recent years, many young black people continue to successfully prepare themselves to assume leadership roles in the society. In the 1990s and beyond, we will continue to see more young black lawyers, engineers, doctors, and other professionals than ever before. Besides formal education, many young blacks are beginning to **teach themselves** about their ancestors' contributions to the world and what their own role should be in today's environment.

This desire for intellectual stimulation is manifested in many black youths embracing the teachings of Malcolm X. These once-maligned teachings of Malcolm X are now being studied with great vigor and enthusiasm by today's young people. This generation understands there are differences between blacks and whites and it is not necessary to feel inferior or to be uncomfortable with that fact. Although some blacks once hated the color of their skin, there is now joy in its individuality and uniqueness. The teachings of Malcolm X and other black leaders helped to orchestrate this change.

To continue developing the power structure model beyond God and self it is necessary to leverage these two elements to promote strong and cohesive **family units**. No other component of the black community have been more maligned by the media and scholars of this country than the black family. These critics often point to the supposed breakdown of family values, the abuse of lethal drugs, the spreading of fatal diseases resulting from irresponsible and licentious behavior, households that are managed by single mothers, rampaging gangs of youths who appear to have no guidance, out of control welfare dependency, and skyrocketing numbers of teen pregnancies, and concludes that all is lost for the black family.

Although these are indeed difficult challenges that must be addressed, these conditions are by no means unique to African-Americans and are in fact common to many of the ethnic groups who made their way from the under class to the upper class. Even as European-Americans began migrating to the cities near the turn of the century, their living conditions mirrored those of today's poor black urban dwellers. Consequently, it is my belief that because the obstacles we face are common to any group of people making the transition from the lower class to the upper class, the black community's overall family structure remains solid.

The fourth component of the power structure model is built upon the God foundation and undergirded by self and family. This fourth element is **ethnic rooting or ethnic pride**. Let no one fool you into thinking that this aspect of the power structure is insignificant. Having pride in one's heritage, culture, physical appearance, and overall contribution to society is necessary for survival in a competitive world. Unlike most ethnic groups, it took a major civil rights movement to galvanize the black community into one loud, angry voice that forever changed the way America looked at its citizens of color. The pride and direction generated from this movement solidified black America's realization that their destiny was connected to that of their brothers and sisters throughout the world.

The long and difficult civil rights struggle reaped numerous benefits for the black community, particularly in the areas of ethnic pride. No longer were African-Americans ashamed of their kinky hair. They started wearing Afros to accentuate it. No longer were they ashamed of their dark skin. "I'm black and I'm proud" became the battle cry for the younger constituency of the movement. The movement made blacks more comfortable with themselves and their contributions to the world in the fields of science, mathematics, engineering, health, agriculture, and every other aspect of civilization. This new-found ethnic pride soon spilled over into the political battlefield as the 1960s progressed.

The **political power** component of the power structure has been an overwhelming success for black Americans. This element of the structure is important because it allows blacks to help set the national agenda and enhances their ability to dictate what the distribution of the country's resources will be. Political power assures that blacks and any other ethnic group enjoy an equitable share of the "pie." Without this aspect of the structure, even noble and well-meaning deeds will be doomed for failure.

To chronicle the acquisition of political power by blacks is indeed a case study in perseverance and courage. With the passage of the 1965 Voting Rights Act, with its focus on the South, most legal barriers to full participation by blacks were removed. For example, three years after its passage, black voter registration in the state of Mississippi, a state then rampant with violence and racial injustice, increased from 6.7 percent to 60 percent. The new legislation opened the door for many of the disenfranchised voters to cast their votes - many for the first time in their lives.

This ground swell of political activity led to the election of new black political leaders at every level of government. White politicians, who once had the luxury of totally ignoring the black electorate, now were forced to court the black vote just as they did the white vote. Issues that concerned African-Americans moved up on the politicians' priority lists and onto the national agenda. Once on the agenda, these issues were often dealt with with a certain degree of urgency and seriousness. With the African-American's increase in numbers, the political landscape has been permanently changed. Blacks now manage the majority of the country's urban centers.

Of the top 15 largest cities in America, five are managed by black mayors and the number seems to be growing rapidly. An African-American, Douglas Wilder, was elected Governor of a southern state, for the first time since Reconstruction. In 1992, the state of Illinois elected the first black woman to the United States Senate. In the same year, black Americans overwhelmingly supported Governor Bill Clinton and in record numbers helped him defeat President George Bush in a landslide victory. Although there are some who would like to turn the political clock back on blacks, the community's political achievements to date cannot be denied.

However, what has been denied is the African-American's quest to share economic power with their European brothers and sisters. There were many who assumed that once political power was achieved, economic power would automatically follow. How wrong they were. It is impossible to overstate the importance of black economic power. It is one of the most important elements of the power structure model because without it the community remains at the mercy of the white power structure. Until this economic power component is strengthened, the entire power structure for black Americans will remain weak and tenuous. Thus, the remaining sections speak to the process of seizing economic power.

## Seizing Economic Power

Seizing economic power will not be as easy as it sounds. Naturally, questions will be asked: How do you seize economic power? How do you know when you have it? To begin with, what is meant by "seizing economic power?" Three criteria are as follows:

1) Close the economic parity gap between blacks and whites.
2) Accumulate significant wealth that is pervasive and lasting.
3) Control commerce and industry within the African-American community and increase the circulation rate of dollars within the black community.

## Closing the Economic Parity Gap Between Blacks and Whites

At first glance, the idea of closing the economic parity gap between black and white Americans in a reasonable time frame may seem quite formidable. However, the fact of the matter is, we already have the ability to completely erase the parity gap by using the resources within our own community. Consider the following:
1) As shown by Exhibit 1-10, each year the African-American

**Exhibit 1-10. Black Annual Revenue**

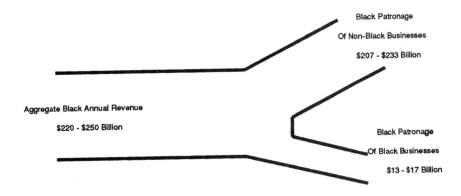

community earns approximately $248 billion (30 million x per capita income of $8,271). Of the total amount earned, on average the black community only spends 6.6 percent or $16 billion/year with African-American owned businesses. Consequently, the amount of dollars that run through our hands and into the hands of non-black enterprises without even circulating through the community once is about $232 billion.

2) As mentioned earlier, the per capita income for blacks as of March, 1989 was $8,271 and $13,896 for whites. The difference in per capita income is $5,625. This says that if we are to achieve economic parity using per capita income as a yardstick, then every black man, woman, and child would have to earn $5,625 more per year than what is earned now. For a family of four that works out to be $22,500 per family per year.

3) There are approximately 30 million African-Americans living in the United States, based on the 1990 census results.

Now, in Exhibit 1-11, let's take a look at what would happen to the parity gap if we spent larger percentages of our dollars with black-owned businesses. Look at what could happen if African-Americans allowed their dollars to turn over in their community just

**Exhibit 1-11. Estimated Changes in Per Capita Income Gap Between Blacks and Whites**

| Available Black Consumer Dollars Not Spent With Black Businesses | % Consumer Dollars To Be Spent With Black Businesses (estimated) | Current Per Capita Income Gap Between Blacks And Whites | New Per Capita Income Gap Between Blacks And Whites (With Increased Patronage Of Black Businesses) |
|---|---|---|---|
| $232 Billion | 50% ($116 Billion) | $5,625 | $-1,225 |
| $232 Billion | 69% ($160 Billion) | $5,625 | $242 (Higher than per capita income for whites) |
| $232 Billion | 90% ($209 Billion) | $5,625 | $2,842 (Higher than whites) |

a few times instead of less than once. In an ideal world, Exhibit 1-11, would be quite plausible. However, reality suggests the following flaws in the assumptions used to generate this illustration:

1) The additional dollars spent with an African-American business will not equate dollar for dollar into additional income for the owner or his workers. Obviously, a portion of the additional funds would be used to cover business expenses and cover the tax expense.

2) All employees working for African-American owned businesses may not be of African descent, thus additional funds would be diverted outside of the community.

3) Any additional dollars spent with black businesses may serve only to make rich blacks richer without the dollars being widely dispersed among the black population, thus reducing any positive impact that the shift of funds into minority businesses might have on the overall community.

Aside from the assumptions made, the example above was used

to illustrate a point. Basically, there is a tremendous amount that blacks can do on their own to gain economic parity, without any additional inflow from mainstream America. The critical point to remember here is that the power of the African-American dollar should not be underestimated; rather, it should be leveraged as much as possible.

## Accumulate Wealth And Control Commerce

As mentioned earlier, the two other requirements for seizing economic power are to accumulate wealth and to reclaim control of our local economies. The options at our disposal to achieve any one of these goals is pursuit of one or a combination of the following:

1) Excel in the private sector (e.g., work for IBM, Procter & Gamble, DuPont, NBA, NFL, etc.).
2) Excel in the public sector (e.g., work for the federal or local governments).
3) Capitalize on sin and suffering (e.g., sell drugs, alcohol, and get rich quick schemes).
4) Stimulate the formation of business development within the community.

### Excel In The Private Sector

Probably the first frontier that was attacked during the height of the civil rights movement was the entry of blacks and other minorities into America's corporate ranks. For years, women and minorities were denied access to this potentially lucrative environment because of their sex and skin color. With the introduction of affirmative action programs throughout corporate America, the very groups that were once denied the opportunity to participate in the board rooms, were suddenly invited in as "equal" players. Consequently, during the 1960s, we saw a large influx of women and minorities into the "good old boy networks" across the country. Or so we thought.

Although the civil rights movement opened the door for women and minorities, the opportunities that were hoped for have never really materialized. A year-long study of the employment and promotion practices of nine Fortune 500 companies, conducted by the United States Labor Department and released during the summer of 1991, concluded that "glass ceilings" do exist and that the ceiling is lower for minorities than for women. The Labor Department's study was based on surveys of businesses, a review of nine Fortune 500 companies as well as detailed independent research and discussions with representatives from management, women's groups, business and labor, and civil rights groups.

The report uncovered some startling, but not surprising, facts. Among them was the fact that only 16.9 percent of the 31,184 managers at the nine firms surveyed were female and only 6.6 percent were minorities. The study also found that most women and minorities who were in management were working in areas such as research, administration, and human resources. Of the 4,491 executive level managers (defined as assistant vice-presidents and above), only 6.6 percent were women and 2.6 percent were minorities. The report further concluded that companies need to do a better job of monitoring women and minorities for access to advancement opportunities, improve the monitoring of compensation policies and perquisites, and improve record keeping of affirmative action efforts.

Even for those who are able to break the glass ceiling, most people still live from paycheck to paycheck. Although we can live comfortable lives working in the private sector, chances are it will take a long time to accumulate enough cash to have a significant impact on the overall community or even to close the economic parity gap. Even as progress is being made through promotions and advancements, your white counterpart is also making advances just as frequently, if not more frequently.

Even if you are one of the few lucky ones who makes her way up, the current flurry of corporate acquisitions and mergers makes you especially vulnerable. People are no longer guaranteed lifetime employment. Therefore, even if you're a top performer, you could still very well become a victim of the reshaping of corporate America. Furthermore, when corporations slim down, typically the people in control of that task have a tendency to keep people who look, act, and think like them and axe those who have the misfortune of being "different" from themselves.

To compound this inequity even further, women and minorities can no longer depend on the Supreme Court or the federal government to protect their rights. There was a time when minorities who were unfairly treated in the corporate environment had the option of using the Federal Government to review the situation and decide on corrective actions.

Unfortunately, President Bush didn't see it that way. With the stroke of a pen, he vetoed the *Civil Rights Act of 1990*. This act was not about quotas as the Bush administration tried to convey. Instead, it was about economic justice in the workplace, which had long been denied to people of color. The law would have ensured only that those who continue to be victimized by the legacy of racism within the hallowed halls of corporate America would have the means to redress their grievances. A much watered-down version of the act was ultimately signed into law by the president. Consequently, with no pressure from the Federal Government (which I don't foresee changing any time soon), except for human decency, the corporate decision makers have no other incentives to be fair. Therefore, women and minorities will continue to assume a disproportional share of the cutbacks and have fewer opportunities to advance.

One of the other fallacies of the corporate dream is that after giving some company forty to fifty years of our life, the company will then take good care of us in our twilight years. My father thought that. Don't get me wrong - my father was a great man whom I loved and respected. However, he didn't make it very far in school. I believe he completed the 7th grade before he left school to work and help support his family. For more than fifty years, he slaved in the private sector at various blue collar jobs. Each morning he would leave at 4:30 a.m. to catch his bus and returned home hours after sunset. It didn't matter what the weather was, he religiously put in his twelve-to sixteen-hour days, never complaining and never missing a day.

Even when he got up in age and could hardly walk due to arthritis and other ailments, he continued to make that daily trek until one day his employer told him that they no longer needed his services and "asked" him to retire. Not having a job hit my father like a hammer. He started "freaking out." He shaved his head, became very irritable, and began to question his value to his family and to the general society. Unfortunately until that point, he had always measured his worth by the job that he was performing and how much money he was making. I wonder how many of us measure ourselves the same way? My father recently died with little money in his pocket, in spite of his more than one-half century of dedicated labor to someone else.

### Excel in the Public Sector

One area of the country that is supposedly recession proof is the Baltimore-Washington D.C. Metropolitan Complex. This complex includes Washington D.C., Baltimore, and the surrounding areas of Northern Virginia and Southern Maryland. The reason it is supposed to be recession proof is that the economy there is heavily fueled by the activity of the Federal Government. Theoretically, even in times of recession, the wheels of government continue to turn, fueled by our tax dollars and driven by the direction of Congress and the Executive Branch. Unlike the Federal Government, working for municipalities is not considered recession proof because the city's revenue streams are not as certain as the Federal Government's, and cities often trim their services in order to balance their budgets.

But like the private sector, working in the public sector can be treacherous and uncertain. The highly political and intricate bureaucracies that drive these organizations tend not to reward their most talented people. Creativity, drive, and outstanding performance are rarely rewarded. Instead, those who have the "right" political connections and who socialize with the right people generally move ahead and are awarded the lucrative opportunities. Besides, these public sector jobs do not pay exceptionally well, unless you're at certain GSA levels. Therefore, it becomes increasingly difficult to accumulate significant wealth in a reasonable period of time. Thus, the impact on the overall community is minimal.

### *Capitalize On Sin and Suffering*

Recently, the city of Washington D.C. has attracted a great deal of media attention due to the increased drug trafficking and the violent crimes that tend to follow the drug flow. It has been noted that many of these drug dealers, at least on the street level, are of African descent. Now, most people abhor the selling and use of drugs within the community, but lets put this issue into some sort of perspective.

With few exceptions, every ethnic group that migrated to the American cities during the turn of the century established their initial economic base in some form of illegal enterprise. During the Prohibition Era, many of your Irish, Italian, and Jewish "Mafias" created and conducted illegal bootlegging operations across the United States and Canada. Some groups even developed intricate prostitution, loan sharking, and drug rings in order to capitalize on America's flirtation with sin and suffering. Having accumulated significant cash through these illegal operations, these various groups were then able to "launder" these huge amounts of cash and use them to develop legitimate businesses within and external to their own ethnic communities.

Clearly, I'm not condoning this type of criminal activity, but I certainly can understand the lure of easy money. Unless someone has moral, legal, or ethical values that serve to prohibit them from engaging in this enterprise, it becomes an attractive business opportunity. Very few business opportunities exist today where an untrained, uneducated person can accumulate so much cash so quickly. This person can generate significant cash flow without having to consume capital in plant and equipment, utilities, medical plans, or burdensome salary and administrative costs. Besides, the return on investment for these type enterprises is phenomenal.

Of course, there are two problems with taking this "entrepreneurial" route. First, you will probably never get to enjoy the money. You will either die young or you will waste your life in prison. Second, these drugs are destroying our future - our young people. These two factors alone make this option highly undesirable.

### Accelerate Business Formation Within the Community

Without a doubt, the best way for us to accumulate wealth quickly and increase the circulation rate of our dollars within our community is through the rapid formation of businesses within our community. To accomplish this, we must start directing a greater number of our young people through the entrepreneurship channel. This will not only benefit the African-American community, but the overall American community.

As the United States struggles to remain competitive in an increasingly competitive global economy, America will have to rely more and more on the segment of the population that has historically been discriminated against (women and minorities). Reports show that by the year 2000, the workforce is expected to go through a major transformation. Instead of the majority of the workforce being white males, the majority of the workers will be women and minorities.

Although this new majority is great in numbers, it will be the least prepared and most poorly trained. Unless these groups are provided the skills that will give them the ability to contribute and to make a good living honestly, these young people ultimately will take to the streets.

Although estimates vary, most experts agree that as much as one-fourth of the United States workforce (approximately 28 million Americans) do not have a firm enough grasp on mathematics, reading, and writing  skills to perform basic job tasks. Business leaders are concerned that as the world becomes increasingly competitive and foreign countries like Japan begin to throw their weight around even more, the American workforce will not be literate enough to meet the challenge. American corporations currently spend a significant amount of corporate resources each year teaching their employees the basic skills that they should have learned while in grade school.

Many fear the problem will be further compounded by the year 2000 due to significant changes in the make up of the worker population. In years past, as the labor force grew rapidly due to the influx of the baby boom generation, corporations could take their pick of the best employees. Now, however, the next generation of workers is decisively smaller with a much different gender and color breakdown.

For example, women will makeup about 45 percent of all new workers and non-whites will hold 25 percent of all new jobs, up from 22 percent currently. White males will no longer be the majority group in the corporate environment (although decreased numbers don't always translate into decreased power).

Will white, male-run corporations continue to train and prepare these new people of color? What will be the vehicle for training these young, bright, but untested people? The Federal Government? I doubt it, particularly with the conservative, right wing direction that the overall population seems to be taking. Also the fact that the *Gramm-Rudman Law* will decree an overall reduction in expenditures, especially in the areas of human development.

Although the total burden cannot and should not be left with the African-American entrepreneurs, a portion of blacks will be responsible for training and preparing other blacks for the business opportunities that lie ahead.

Recently, an MIT researcher, Mr. David Birch, estimated that 80 percent of all new jobs are created by small and medium-sized businesses. These businesses will transcend all geographical and industrial boundaries. If this is true, then we need to make sure that we are represented adequately in those new business developments so that African-Americans have a fair shot at these new opportunities.

Certainly, our quest for economic equality in the 1990s and beyond will be realized best through the creation of wealth through accelerated business formation within the African-American community.

**Jacqueline Lester**
**Director**
**Human Relations, State of Missouri**
**St. Louis, Missouri**

St. Louis has been known as the gateway to the west. The city has even built the arch to remind people of this fact. As the city of St. Louis has grown in leaps and bounds, the business community has played an instrumental role in that success. In 1981, to ensure that minority and female owned businesses are connected into the business loop there, Jacqueline Lester, the Director of Human Relations for the State of Missouri, was given the mission of ensuring this participation. Jacqueline, a very vibrant and energetic woman, settles down in her chair to discuss the status of minority business in Missouri and throughout the United States.

*Suppliers*

Jacqueline feels that, in general, minorities are not getting cut into the major deals that are transacted. She states:

A mainstream business can go in to see a supplier and is able to negotiate a first rate deal in which both sides win. Minorities often times cannot. Although these cases are difficult to identify, some minority business owners have even encountered suppliers who increased prices to ensure that the minority business was unable to be competitive. As in the overall society, racism continues to play a crucial part in business - usually to the detriment of the minority business community. This racism clearly inhibits the ability of African-Americans and other minorities from dealing effectively in the business world.

## *Position*

The position that Jacqueline Lester holds is a common one that most states and municipalities maintain. In her case, Jacqueline's position was created under Executive Order 8227. Under this order, she was charged with directing the State's minority business efforts within all facets of government. This includes all goods and services, facilities, bonds, and stocks. Everything is inclusive in this executive order. Her primary focus is employment, and Jacqueline makes certain that minority businesses coming to the state are allowed and encouraged to participate in the bidding of all contracts. She usually takes a more progressive approach to her job and actively lobbies to assist minority businesses in getting contracts.

Jacqueline reports directly to Commissioner of Administration and the Governor. She assists minority businesses in interacting with the State Government and has been actively involved in this process for more than a decade. The strategy that she employs to facilitate better interaction among minority and majority businesses is one that places a heavy emphasis on training. Part of her strategy also entails conducting training seminars in all aspects of small business development.

To bring minority businesses and the private sector closer together, Lester has developed numerous creative vehicles for facilitating this interaction. Some of the vehicles include training seminars and trade fairs. All of the minority businesses are given an opportunity to display their goods and services and she invites other companies to view these businesses in hopes of creating more business.

## *Perspectives On The Challenges Facing Minority Businesses*

Having worked with a number of small minority businesses, Jacqueline feels there are challenges that need some attention. One of her main observations is that minority businesses need to pay closer attention to detail. This requirement is especially true in the areas of new business, business development, and contractual arrangements. In Jacqueline's words:

> They [minority businesses] too often lack good accounting skills, do not utilize the computer, and should develop better business plans. Minority businesses need to get better organized so that when they go to the bank, they've planned where they want to go financially. Another mistake is employing family members who don't understand business. When you hire family, often times there is not a real commitment and very often the family members do not understand the job.

Lastly, Jacqueline feels that minority businesspeople should acquire as much education as possible. Also, she advises businesses to make contacts, go to happy hour, take the time to meet people, and then go home. Go to the athletic club or join one. It may cost a lot, but that's where decisions are being made, she says.

## Competition

When you pursue a state contract, you need to be aggressive, says Jacqueline. Minority business people have to understand that they must get information, call people, and ask questions - that's what people are there for. If you don't get the information you need, go to the next level. Express an interest.

She believes that minority businesses need to be better informed. They need to know where to get better educated, where to go for help, and even what questions to ask. Another problem she has observed in the black business community is the need to network. Blacks have to be responsible for helping each other.

## Financing Minority Business

Most states have numerous programs for the financing of

minority enterprises. Jacqueline feels that if you can go through the state's system, you should also be able to handle a bank. As one would expect, the requirements are very stringent. One's ability to sell/market herself is essential for success. That's why you're always in sales regardless of what business you're legally in, Jacqueline explains.

Minority business people sometimes have difficulty courting clients, i.e., taking them to lunch, to dinner, or just general socializing. These business people need to know how to build relationships. With suppliers, we need to know how to drop by and develop contacts through developing relationships. A lot of minorities don't know how to do that. It's not what you know very often; it's who you know. It's a game, and you must play it to win.

Formerly a member of the Republican Committee, Jacqueline often would go to a meeting and observe that blacks were always on one side and whites on the other. After reaching a frustration saturation level, she'd say, "Is this a Klan meeting?" This comment would break the ice and allow people to come together. She continues:

> It's not racism necessarily all the time; it's strangeness, a lack of familiarity, people don't know where to go. We've had to learn about their culture; we live in their culture. But they haven't taken the time to learn about ours.

Jacqueline feels that blacks have learned a lot about whites, but whites haven't learned much about blacks.

## Peter Parham and Calvin Grimes, Jr.
## Grimes Oil
## Washington, D.C. and Boston, Massachusetts

Although Calvin Grimes, Sr., was selling oil since the mid to late 1930s, Grimes Oil officially began operating as a corporation in

1940. Through providing quality service, competitive pricing, and maintaining excellent visibility within the minority communities, Grimes was very successful in building and retaining a large and diverse residential customer base. He was particularly successful at developing the black residential market because prior to his movement into this business, the black consumer base was, for the most part, ignored by the major oil distributors.

For a long time, Calvin Grimes, Sr., refused to pursue the commercial markets for development of a commercial client base. Business in the residential sectors was going strong and showed little signs of slowing down. However, when the Small Business Administration's 8(a) program was initiated in the mid 1970s, Grimes saw an opportunity to develop a commercial customer client base that held the potential to surpass the residential client base that he had spent so many years nurturing. As Calvin Grimes, Jr., (Kern) began to assume more of the day to day management of the operation, Grimes Oil aggressively sought to develop its commercial clients and did so with much success.

Part of the reason Grimes Oil was successful at developing these new markets was because of the advice and entrepreneurial instincts of a marketing consultant, Peter Parham. Calvin was no stranger to Peter. Parham had known Kern all of his life and was very close to the Grimes family. One day while in Boston, Kern met with Peter to discuss ways in which Grimes Oil could begin to expand its market into other geographical locations across the country.

Kern believed that based on the size of Grimes Oil and the company's relative success to date, he would be well positioned to meet the fuel oil needs of major corporations and municipalities that sought to do more business with minority oil companies. Peter concurred with Kern's assessment and agreed to work for Grimes Oil on a retainer basis to help the company expand its market share beyond the Boston and New England areas.

Peter was so successful at accomplishing this task that Kern later asked him to join Grimes Oil on a permanent basis as vice-president of marketing. The markets that Peter engaged in included Washington, Boston, Philadelphia, New York, and New Jersey. Parham has his eye on an even bigger pie. He explains:

We have many cities where blacks hold positions of power and can make decisions that could favorably impact on black businesses. Unfortunately, there are not many black owned oil companies comparable to Grimes Oil to respond to these opportunities. What good is it to have legislators who might know that there's going to be an economic or business opportunity that could help the black community if you don't have the companies in place to take advantage of it? We've developed a strategy where we go into a place like Hartford Connecticut, identify the local minority oil company there that may only have one or two trucks and work with him to deliver on a $4 million job. We could bid on the job ourselves and subcontract a piece to him. The end result is that we get to go, he gets to go. That's part of what I'm doing.

Although Kern Grimes runs the company in a low-key fashion, it is by no means a simple "mom and pop" operation. Kern has been in business a long time and has built a strong organization that has weathered some severe storms over the years. The company faced one of the most difficult times after its graduation from the 8(a) program in the early 1980s when a decision was made to focus solely on its commercial client base at the expense of its residential base. Unfortunately for Grimes, shortly after the firm began focusing on its commercial clientele, conditions affecting the oil industry began to impact negatively on Grimes' business. As oil prices went into a spiraling decline and winters were consistently mild for a number of years, the demand for oil at a profitable price fell sharply. During that period, Grimes saw a significant drop in sales while his expenses remained the same or even showed slight increases. Within a short span of time, Calvin saw his margins being squeezed to a point where it was becoming increasingly difficult to service his debt.

Grimes Oil was able to weather these storms, in large part because of the company's reputation, the relationships it had built over the years, and the honesty and perseverance of Calvin Grimes, Jr. Another factor that made the company's survival possible was the corporate structure that Calvin had put in place prior to the troubled times. He had strategically dissected the business, attracted talented people, and placed them in strategic positions within the corporate structure. As Peter explains it:

> The sign of an educated man is not that he has it all up here, but that he knows where to go get it. A good administrator is one who can have good people around who know how to do a multitude of things. Both Kern and I have been successful at attracting good black people and helping them grow.

Despite Grimes' successes, there are those who still have complaints about the company. The oil business is a tough business with its high volumes and low margins. Consequently, business owners sometimes have to make tough decisions, which may not always be very popular. Clearly, Kern has had to make some difficult decisions of his own, which may explain why Kern Grime's contribution to the community is not unanimously recognized by its residents. Few understand the struggles he's forced to go through on a daily basis and most don't make the extra effort to even communicate their concerns. However, Kern seems to be unaffected by the miscommunication or even the jealousy that exists. He understands that he can't be all things to all people and he doesn't try to be.

## Financing

The fact that Grimes Oil has been in business for more than thirty years has helped the company attract the financing it needs. The company has developed an outstanding reputation in the Boston area and Grimes has been successful in developing a long-term, mutually beneficial business relationship with his major supplier. As it turns out, the oil company that supplied Grimes his oil also became his biggest financier. In the oil business, a distributor who has earned the trust of his supplier and who has established a good reputation can often use supplier credit to fund his transactions on a short-term basis.

In the case of Grimes Oil, the supplier also benefited from this flexible financing arrangement. Although Grimes Oil may be a small company, it provided a conduit through which the supplier could channel its product to the minority community. This client base is one of Kern's priorities, which results in suppliers knowing that he can deliver.

Kern has built such a good relationship with the oil companies because he is basically a very honest and hard working man. He has built the business to a point that he's responsible for moving over 35 million gallons of oil per year. He either is or is close to the largest New England client that Gulf Oil has.

## *Controlling Wealth*

Peter Parham agrees with a comment Rev. Jesse Jackson made when they were once traveling together: "I don't think that African-Americans understand how much wealth they have at hand." Too often blacks assume that mainstream America owns more than it really does. If blacks only learned to reciprocate in their business transactions, there would be a noticeable improvement in the number and quality of minority businesses in America. Peter recalls a particular situation:

Grimes Oil gets letters from development offices from black colleges around the country asking us to fund scholarships for their kids. Well, I went to the annual meeting for the Black College Association to give a presentation. I concluded by asking, "If you can write to Grimes Oil about scholarship money without even knowing him that well, then why can't you let us have the opportunity to bid on your oil contracts?" Rev. Jackson once challenged the administration of North Carolina A&T who were in the midst of a major building project, asking them if they were giving contracts to any black firms. We have to learn to utilize our own resources.

Kern Grimes also has urged local black groups to channel their wealth to the benefit of the black community. Peter once organized a meeting with black administrators of New England Colleges including MIT, Harvard, BU, and Northeastern to discuss how each of them could work together to benefit their institutions' students and the community. Peter doesn't mind that the school's minority programs expect some financial support from Grimes Oil but he asks in return that they support his efforts to compete on heating oil contracts from these same institutions. Grimes Oil now has established contracts with many of these schools. He continues to build long-term business relationships with the black administrators of each school.

Kern has consistently acted on the belief that the black community should control its own wealth. When Senator Brooke and Ron Homer opened up Boston Bank of Commerce, Kern took all of his money out of First National and put it into their bank. Grimes Oil is one of the main reasons that the Boston Bank of Commerce remains open. Although Grimes Oil was not financially involved when William Cosby and Julius Irving bought a major Coca Cola franchise through the Economic Justice Campaign, the company was a steadfast supporter of the concept and the campaign.

## Leveraging Financial Institutions

Peter contends that one of the most important things that the African-American community can do to build up black-owned enterprises in their community is to create black-owned and operated financial institutions. These institutions are much more sensitive to the needs and problems that face minority people. Peter adds, however, that the only way to make the government do what it should do to help create black financial institutions is by using our ballot and our political strength. Blacks should demand that their tax dollars be leveraged effectively to benefit their community. Peter hastens to add:

As long as we allow banking institutions to shut us out from the level where decisions are made, they will not be responsive to our needs. We might have a black person in a good job downtown, but if he does not pave the way for somebody else then we are missing the point. When a bank refuses to consider our loan application, rather than change banks, we often continue to maintain our savings and checking accounts with them. We have to fight this thing on many fronts.

Peter concludes that those people who have benefited from the community have an obligation to give something back. Returning value to the community is a responsibility that blacks must recognize. If resources are pooled, greater deals can be consummated. Unfortunately, Peter feels some black businesspeople are afraid of being open with one another and end up wasting a great deal of time. Black businesspeople need to look at themselves, be honest, and fix the things that need fixing.

## The Importance of African-American Businesses

Like many young men in today's African-American community, Peter never saw black businessmen when he was growing up, except for the funeral director. Because he didn't see anyone else, his subconscious eventually began to tell him that this was the only business option available to him. Peter learned differently as he grew older and became exposed to more situations. However, he still contends that African-Americans need to do a better job of teaching their children about business and how to start enterprises. More people need to do what Kern Grimes does for school-aged children. Grimes Oil produced a film that tells the Grimes Oil story. Depicting him as a minority businessman and showing how he runs his company, the film is shown in schools nationwide and has become so popular that Kern gets numerous requests for the film from colleges throughout the country.

## *Planning*

Peter often finds himself speaking before groups of young people and his message is always the same - prepare, prepare, prepare. Prepare to meet all of one's goals and dreams. Peter encourages young, aspiring entrepreneurs to engage in every avenue open to them. Academics is critical, but people need to remember that success with academics is only one element of success. Equally as important is a person's sense of responsibility, integrity, and willingness to get a start somewhere, anywhere. Peter quickly gets to the point:

> So many young entrepreneurs want to start at the top but usually it doesn't work that way. People need to spend more time volunteering and picking up as much free information as they can. There are certain things that don't change. I often see white kids starting out in the mail room in Washington, even those whose parents have money. Next thing you know they've moved up and are now administrative assistants or something even higher. Listen and learn; you might need the information to get a job. And most importantly, have a plan.

Peter also strongly urges those people who are already in business not to judge others in the community by the way they dress, where they were raised, or where they went to school. There is a wealth of talent in the community that needs only to be given a chance. Grimes Oil has had its chance and has done quite well with it.

# PART 2

# INTERNAL CHECKPOINTS FOR BUSINESS SUCCESS

## *Be Honest with Yourself. Why Do You Want to Do This?*

**After** graduation from business school, my wife, Carolyn, and I agonized over what our next adventure should be. I was fortunate to have many attractive job opportunities with reputable corporations at new and exciting locations around the country. However, after careful review, we decided to relocate to our home town of Baltimore, Maryland. As it turned out, coming home was a real blessing.

First, I could spend more time with my family and friends. Also, my parents were getting older, and my father's health was beginning to fail. Being home afforded me the opportunity to at last spend some special time with Mom and Dad. Second, at the risk of sounding corny, I have always dreamed of coming back home and making a contribution to my community. Maybe I could help keep kids in the old neighborhood from going astray. Unfortunately, there is a tremendous amount of talent that we're losing to crime and drugs everyday. Third, my interest in building business enterprises within the African-American community was stimulated by my experiences at Dartmouth, and what better location to get started than the Baltimore-Washington corridor. With both cities being managed by African-American mayors and the region's large and active black middle class, it seemed an ideal place to put down business roots.

As Carolyn and I started to reacquaint ourselves with our family, old friends, and all the changes that had taken place, I soon realized that I was not the only one who had a strong interest in developing the business infrastructure within the African-American community. What a pleasant surprise!

With all of these potential business partners, I thought my mission of building coalitions and formulating partnerships would be easy. My excitement quickly turned to dismay when I found that most of these people were not really serious about pursuing viable business opportunities. Further investigation revealed that many of them naively thought they could quickly start a business, accumulate significant wealth, and retire on a private Caribbean island at the ripe old age of thirty. Their lack of commitment, planning, and genuine understanding of the nuances of business formation disturbed me for some time.

Business people are always asked, "Why did you go into business?" Based on the subjects of this study, I find that there is no one clear cut response to this question. People go into business for as many reasons as there are different types of entrepreneurs. Although the stories of Microsoft's William Gates and of Lotus' Mitch Kapor are well documented in today's press, the good fortune and success that they enjoyed at such young, tender ages is quite rare. It will probably be another ten to twenty years before another William Gates mesmerizes the business community. Then again, maybe not. It certainly is conceivable that you could be the next William Gates, but if you're not, don't be dismayed. There is still lots of money out here to be made by mere mortals.

Although most people are motivated by the idea of making large sums of money quickly, there are a few who want to start their businesses just for the challenge of it. Some people have very strong egos and feel that if anyone can be successful in business it certainly must be them. They shudder at the thought of working tirelessly for someone for fifty years only to be given a gold watch and then led off to pasture until their Maker calls them home. Their conviction and commitment remind them daily that they have all the smarts, ideas and energy to make their dream a reality. These people simply want the satisfaction of being able to say, "I did it!"

One group within the community who will be challenged by the building of enterprises is a group I've called the "soon-to-be-entrepreneurs." This group of professionals can be found in existing corporations, the Federal Government, or in various types of consulting firms. They're biding their time and patiently waiting for the right opportunity before they make their move. At the proper moment, they will emerge onto the business scene and make names for themselves.

These "soon-to-be-entrepreneurs" are motivated to participate in the creation of successful business enterprises that benefit the community because they understand the correlation between strong economic development and social economic parity in our society. They learned the "Golden Rule" of American economics a long time ago, which says, "He who owns the gold, rules."

Unfortunately, many people still don't understand the correlation between money and power and quite frankly, don't care. As a matter of fact, some entrepreneurs started their ventures out of sheer necessity. As revealed by the Dartmouth study, some of the business owners started their businesses because they needed another way to provide for their families. Due to circumstances outside of their control, entrepreneurship was the most logical and visible option for them at the time. They were not seeking wealth and fame. Their only desire was to make an honest and decent living. Having spent some time with these "reluctant entrepreneurs," I often have difficulty mustering up much sympathy for those unemployed people who drown themselves in self-pity. Anyway, believe it or not, the "reluctant entrepreneur" does exist.

Starting a business out of necessity is quite plausible and maybe even noble, but there are folks out there who actually desire to be entrepreneurs because it is the "hip" thing to do. During the "go-go" decade of the '80s, it became popular to start your own business or at least to say that you want to start one. You don't believe me? All right. I suggest that you conduct your own survey and use your family and friends as a sampling group.

I would bet my first born that if you were to ask them to articulate their long-term professional goals, embedded somewhere in the babbling would be the words "start my own business." It has been my experience that about 90 percent of the people you poll will say this. Let's face it, the '80s and '90s are the decades of the entrepreneurs. We're bombarded daily with stories of entrepreneurs - their successes and failures. Why do you think Donald Trump is constantly on the news even though the media claims he's now facing possible financial ruin? People like to hear and read about what old Don is up to.

Unfortunately, most people in your casual survey may lack a clear understanding of business and the business savvy necessary to make a venture successful. Most will be without a sound plan or strategy that would allow them to set that dream loose on the world. For them, the idea of owning a business is just a thought that languishes on the thresholds of their imaginations. One of the purposes of this book is to reveal the reality of going into business to people who may not be closely in touch with this phenomenon.

The point of this discussion is to convey the importance of understanding why you want to go into business. The source of your motivation is just as important to your long-term success as the quality of your idea or the persuasiveness of your business plan. Your reason for pursuing a venture ultimately will help to dictate which markets you attack. Going into business because it's the "hip" or "slick" thing to do is not slick; it is sick. Be careful. Going into business for the wrong reason could actually ruin your life.

## Internal Success Actualization

Internal success actualization is defined as the situation in which the would-be entrepreneur has completed the steps necessary to prepare herself for the rigors of various business endeavors. The ability to achieve these internal success requirements is basically within the control of the individual and is often independent of external events or forces. This pyramid of internal success requirements includes the following:

**Exhibit 2-1. Internal Success Actualization**

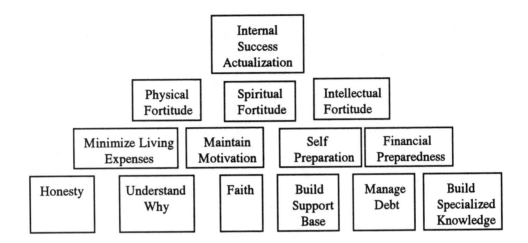

## *Getting Your Life Together*

After having assessed your reasons for going into business carefully, the next step is to "get your house in order." A house that is not in order cannot and will not stand. You have to be strong if you're to have any chance of making this journey successfully. Your checklist for getting your house in order should at least include the following set of tasks:

- Building Your Spiritual Fortitude
- Facing The Enemy Within and Defeating Him
- Building Your Physical Fortitude
- Self-Preparation
- Learning How to Stay Motivated
- Obtaining Specialized Knowledge in Appropriate Areas
- Preparing Yourself Financially
- Establishing a Strong Support Base
- Taking the Leap of Faith and Starting a Business Despite the Odds

## *Building Your Spiritual Fortitude*

With few exceptions, the entrepreneurs profiled had successfully established "working relationships" with their Creator and remained in touch with their spirituality. This divine relationship provided them protection when their enemies had surrounded them and there was no way out. However you perceive your God, you will need His power to guide you through the tough times, to sustain you when you're in the valley, and to humble you after you've scaled the mountain tops. There is power in knowing your God. Use this power to your advantage.

The second most important aspect of getting your house in order is loving and drawing close to your family. The majority of the entrepreneurs in the case studies did not enjoy the luxury of having family members who were familiar with the business environment. Consequently, the family was unable to assist them with specific business matters. However, what the family lacked in understanding the business was more than compensated for in the amount of love and support it showered on the struggling entrepreneurs. In most situations, the entrepreneur's spouse contributed the lion's share of the love and support.

One's spouse is especially important when starting a business. A "good" man or woman beside you can often mean the difference between success and failure. Most of the entrepreneurs interviewed had strong spouses who strengthened them when they grew weak and motivated them when they became discouraged. Although I espouse the institution of marriage, if matrimony is not in your plans, then make sure that you have a mate who will support you, love you, and share in your successes and your failures. Money or success is no fun unless you have someone you love with whom to share it.

However, whatever you do, don't try to start a business when your love life is on the rocks. There exists only a finite amount of energy with which you're blessed. If the majority of this energy is consumed finding, courting, and nurturing multiple love relationships, then what energy is left to build an enterprise? In his book *The Art of Loving,* Erich Fromm states, "The deepest need of man, is the need to overcome his separateness, to leave the prison of his aloneness. The absolute failure to achieve this aim means insanity..." History is replete with examples of how the love of a mate has spurned many men and women to great and wonderful things. Seek this love, capture it, and then harness it to do great things for you.

## *Facing the Enemy Within and Defeating Him*

A strong argument could be built to suggest that African-Americans have been the most oppressed ethnic group in the history of this country. But, in spite of all the damage external oppressors have inflicted upon blacks, I submit that the most vicious oppressor is the one that lives on top of our shoulders. The system in which we live has been so effective at attacking our self-esteem that it has made us believe that we cannot acquire and grow businesses like our mainstream counterparts do. Our society has left us with such an inferiority complex that we are often afraid to make mistakes or even to "engage" in business transactions. Some fear that white America will ridicule us and use the experience to confirm their often quoted thoughts about our supposed inferiority.

Before you can seriously entertain the idea of becoming an entrepreneur, you must first confront the enemy within you and defeat it. Successful minority entrepreneurs have become experts at battling the enemy within and bringing it to its knees. I'm convinced that the biggest reason African-Americans are not better represented in the entrepreneurial ranks is because they think they cannot be successful. Never be afraid to fail. Take every opportunity to engage. Vince Lombardi summed it up best when he said, "Success is not in never falling, but in rising every time you fall."

## *Building Your Physical Fortitude*

Physical and mental fitness would appear to be an obvious

attribute of maintaining the order of one's house, but too often it is overlooked by anxious and impatient would-be entrepreneurs. Ralph Waldo Emerson once said, "The first wealth is health." One of the Hispanic members of this study shared a story with me about his young bride and how it took her some time to accept the importance of exercise and good health.

As young newlyweds, they argued excessively about the amount of time he spent at the gym working out. Like most young brides, she felt that her new husband should be spending more time with her and less time in a dark and damp gymnasium. What she failed to realize at the time was that getting exercise for him was not a luxury but in fact a necessity! These brief interludes at the gym allowed him to release his stress, clear his mind, and remain focused on the business. This Hispanic brother rationalized that in order to function efficiently, his body needed a good work out just as it needed food, water, and love.

Exercise is a part of our well-being. Any of you who are athletes or former ones can probably attest to the existence of a "natural high" experienced after a good workout. Numerous studies have shown that when your body is in this state, you are sharper and much more alert. This "high" produces significantly more creativity, and there appears to be a higher level of consciousness. Those of us who are physically unfit tend to lack energy, drive, perseverance, and endurance. With few exceptions, every entrepreneur I interviewed looked healthy, vibrant, trim, and in shape. Many confessed to having some type of regular workout routine - from aerobic classes to a daily walk around the local park.

## Self-Preparation

Before any business can be successful, its owner or leader must prepare himself to handle the multiple situations that can arise. We've already talked about getting close to your God and about building up your support base. Now, let's talk about building you up!

When I took the entrepreneurship course while attending the Amos Tuck School of Business, I had an unique opportunity to "break bread" with a few venture capitalists who were evaluating our business projects. Having strong entrepreneurial ambitions myself, I wanted to pin these folks down on how they evaluate a business deal. One day, I thought, I'll be financing my business so now is a good time to better understand how the venture capitalist business works.

Prior to my meeting with these venture capitalists, I had always assumed that these guys experienced orgasms from studying slick spreadsheets and rosy cash flow projections. However, I was terribly wrong. For the most part, the most important criteria used in evaluating a deal were the people behind the deal. One venture capitalists with whom I became friends often said, "I don't bet on the horse; I bet on the jockey!"

My two business partners, Eliot Powell and Jerome Sanders of SDGG Holding Company, often reminded me of this fact as we made the rounds on Wall Street in our attempt to put together financing packages for our acquisitions. It may be difficult to believe, but the majority of venture capitalists focus on the people, and not just the ideas or business plan. They clearly are more concerned with the education, work experience, integrity, and realism of the management team than with cash flow projections.

One venture capitalist went on to say that integrity and honesty ranked highest on his list. In other words, having a willingness to face the facts, admit when you're wrong, and accept the advice of others is critical. The road to entrepreneurial success is full of sharp turns and steep inclines. It takes an extremely confident person to tolerate this uncertainty, admit mistakes, and at the same time, keep traveling down the road. This same self-confidence is what forces the "soon-to-be" entrepreneur to say good bye to their prestigious positions in corporate America - health plans, profit sharing, and everything else. This blew me away! I had misunderstood completely the make up of a typical venture capitalists and what their hot buttons were. This experience confirmed my present belief about the importance of building yourself up. But, how does one build himself up?

First, let me get something off of my chest. There was a time when I felt that in order to be a successful entrepreneur, you first had to go to a good school and earn a respected degree. Well, I'm not so sure that I totally agree with that philosophy any longer. Although some of the subjects of these case studies had impressive academic credentials, the majority had humble academic beginnings. To their credit, many of the participants in the study had gone back to college to obtain degrees after starting their businesses. However, there were also some who were very successful with no college degrees at all!

There are some who suggest that having a respected degree from a top-tier school is the worst thing that an aspiring entrepreneur can do. The theory goes that these schools turn out highly paid bureaucrats instead of thirsty entrepreneurs. I must say that there may be some truth to this theory.

I'm reminded of a conversation I had with a young entrepreneur who had started a plastics injection business in Michigan. This young man had impeccable academic credentials - a B.S. in engineering and an M.B.A. from Harvard. He shared with me that before he attended B-School he had contemplated going into a number of different businesses - from opening a barber shop to starting his own engineering company. At that time, he hadn't learned all the latest and greatest in spreadsheets, cash flow analysis, market strategy, net present values, and so forth. Consequently, although he was a "dumb" engineer, he would not hesitate to pursue a deal purely based on rough financial projections and "gut level feelings."

Unfortunately, after earning his M.B.A. from Harvard, he observed that every deal that came across his desk had to be taken through a number of algorithms that look at projected business growth, market analysis, cash flow projections, and other criteria that he was taught in business school before he'd make a move. In essence, he had become what I've termed "M.B.A. spooked." This term means that you analyze a deal so thoroughly that you eventually convince yourself that the risks are too high for you to proceed with the idea.

It doesn't matter how "sweet" a deal is, if you analyze it long and hard enough you can always find reasons it won't work. Instead, you need to focus on the reasons it will work! Although I don't condone blind pursuit of business deals, most successful entrepreneurs agree that it is possible to overanalyze a deal. For all of you hot-shot M.B.A.s out there, don't let yourself become "M.B.A. spooked."

There is another side to this prestigious education theory. If you're a minority person, having the proper academic credentials as "feathers in your cap" will help your cause. Unfortunately, there are many business leaders in positions of power who will only listen to black entrepreneurs if they come to the table with certain credentials. One of the business owners in the study said, "If you want your kids to be entrepreneurs, don't send them to Ivy League schools. These types of schools will only turn them into highly paid corporate Dobermans." Although most would agree that our young people do face the risk of being blinded by the corporate glitter, having certain credentials will make it easier for them to get through the door and at a minimum listened to.

You are probably asking yourself how much education is needed before venturing out on your own. At the risk of sounding contradictory, it is suggested that you obtain as much as you can as quickly as you can. The point I made previously is that you don't want your education to blind you. The Lord gave us all natural mechanisms that assist us in making good and logical decisions. Don't ignore those natural mechanisms (insight, gut level feeling, hunch, dream, etc.,) and totally rely on primitive tools of analysis taught by mere humans. As long as you can remain committed to an idea and plan, you should get training from a good school and obtain the best business training that you can acquire. If you already know what business you'd like to get into, try obtaining a degree in that area. Specialized knowledge is critical to success.

Build up as many potent weapons in your personal arsenal as possible. A M.B.A. from a prestigious university is a good weapon to have. Another benefit the M.B.A. gives you is that it strengthens your self-confidence. One of the most debilitating problems that our community faces is a shortage of confidence. If you are told and shown enough times that you are worthless, pretty soon your subconscious mind, if not your conscious mind, will believe it.

## *Learning How to Stay Motivated*

Staying motivated will be one of the most difficult things for you to do during your quest to get started. People's interest or intensity of purpose in a project usually follows the normal distribution curve. When people first start their ventures they're extremely excited and full of energy as shown by the steep incline in the early stages of the project. Over time though, as the burdens and problems of making their ventures realities confront them, their energy and excitement start to wane.

As shown by the schematic in Exhibit 2-2, at some point in time their interest peaks and then falls dramatically. Your interest curve is especially vulnerable if you're one of those people trying to start a business while remaining a full-time employee for someone else. It will seem almost impossible to do both jobs well. Also, with the pressures of a mortgage, a demanding spouse, civic responsibilities, child rearing, and the usual problems of life, you could become severely stressed.

This additional stress caused by your attempt to get your business off the ground will generally result in frustration, anxiety, and disillusionment. It is during these times that it becomes essential for you to inject "excitement points" into your efforts. African-American entrepreneurs who excel understand the importance of these excitement points. As shown in Exhibit 2-2 by points a, b, and c, excitement points serve to generate for you a new interest curve to take over when your prior one peaks.

Excitement points are unique to the individual. Whatever excites you to the point at which you become re-focused and re-committed to achieve your goal is considered an excitement point. These excitement points could include buying a new sports car, joining a new organization of entrepreneurs, benefiting from divine intervention via a dream or a real life experience, talking quietly with your God, receiving a vision, or reading an outstanding book. The idea here is that you need to understand what excites you to the point that it forces you to occasionally re-generate your interest curves and inject those excitement events into your life on a regular basis.

**Exhibit 2-2. Excitement Points**

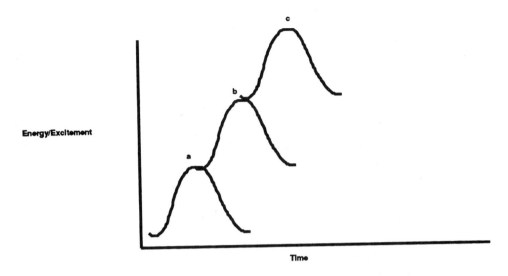

## *Obtaining Specialized Knowledge In Appropriate Areas*

To prepare yourself for future entrepreneurial action, I'd be remiss if I failed to mention the need to develop specialized knowledge in some area. If you looked at the successful entrepreneurs in our society, you would find that the majority started their empires by providing a needed product or service; or, they possessed the creativity to produce brilliant ideas that could be sold easily for profit. One effective way to gain this knowledge is to pursue a job in an area in which you would like to one day start a business.

In terms of the study of the alumni of Dartmouth's Minority Business Executive Program, there is a strong correlation between the industry these people worked in prior to staring their businesses and the type of firms they own. Ron and Cynthia Thompson have a railroad car manufacturing business in Illinois. For years, Ron worked in Washington D.C., studying the conditions and direction of the railroad industry in the United States. This experience provided Ron with a better appreciation for this industry and, consequently, he was able to capitalize on opportunities in this area.

Walter Hill, co-founder of ECS Technologies, a systems integration and value added reseller for IBM in the Baltimore-Washington area, initially worked for Westinghouse Electric Corporation for close to ten years before starting his firm. While employed by Westinghouse, one of his main responsibilities was to acquire many of the essential electronic components and computer systems used in the manufacture of radar systems. While in that capacity, he learned the technical details of the components, made contacts with key vendors in the industry, and began to develop an appreciation for the opportunities in this field. When he and his partner, Eillen Dorsey, left their jobs to start their business, they both brought with them a clear set of marketable skills, valuable customer contacts, sufficient technical competence, and good market foresight.

Clearly, if you have a good idea about which industry you'd like to compete in, try to obtain a job in that industry. By allowing someone else to pay the cost of training you, you minimize your investment in training once you start your business, thus reducing your initial capital requirements.

## Preparing Yourself Financially

Not a day passes that I don't discuss with someone somewhere the idea of starting a small business. Many of my cohorts in the information processing industry have dreams of building their own businesses but few have taken the initiative to make the dream a reality. Probably the biggest excuse that I hear is that they lack the proper funds needed to adequately capitalize the business. Indeed, this is probably the biggest stumbling block of most small business owners and aspiring business owners. However, this obstacle is no excuse for not working on your plan.

This issue of lack of funds certainly didn't stop many of corporate America's most successful CEOs. Do many of you get your taxes filed by H&R Block? Well, consider the fact that Henry Block and his brother Richard started preparing tax forms for clients around 1954. The initial financing came from a $5,000 loan from one of his family members. The rest of the funding came from internally generated funds, thanks to the many customers who swarmed over Henry and his brother for tax assistance. During fiscal year 1986, H&R Block grossed more than $600 million with business generated from 8,800 offices nationwide.

Someone more new to the entrepreneurial scene is Joshua Smith, founder of Maxima Corporation, headquartered in Rockville, Maryland. Mr. Smith was once executive director of the American Society for Information Science. While in that position, he observed that most enterprises were unprepared to manage their information processing requirements. He also noticed that the marketplace was greatly fragmented.

Unlike IBM, most of the companies in the computer industry either sold hardware, software, or some form of services (e.g., installation, maintenance, etc.). There were very few institutions that could do it all. With about $15,000 of his own money, Mr. Smith ventured out, started the Maxima Corporation, and hasn't looked back since. Maxima's revenues skyrocketed from just over $300,000 in fiscal 1979 to more than $27 million in 1985! What makes Mr. Smith different from you or me?

Wait! Don't start thinking that all of the success stories are in the computer and high tech industries because that's not the case. Consider for a moment Ms. Leone Ackerly. Ms. Ackerly purchased a few cleaning supplies in 1973 and began cleaning houses. The initial supplies cost her less than $10 but she was able to parlay this idea into a nationwide franchise called Mini-Maid International of Marietta, Georgia. In 1986, her 111 franchises cleaned up with $11 million in sales.

You do not always need a significant amount of cash to start your business. In fact, too much cash might be harmful! Experts say that an abundance of cash tempts people to start enterprises that are bigger and more complex than they can handle. Mr. Geoffrey Kessler, a small business consultant based in Los Angeles said that starting out with little money makes an initial flop easier to recover from. "It's like riding a bicycle on the sidewalk; if you fall down, you can keep trying until you get it right. But if you start out on the freeway, there's no room for mistakes." Mr. Kessler has also observed that business owners working with little capital are forced to be more innovative when considering several solutions to a problem. As strange as it sounds, I agree with him, and with one or two exceptions, all of the business owners in the Dartmouth Case Study started off rather humbly.

Don't worry. I'm not trying to kid myself. I realize that even with minimal capitalization requirements, we're expected to provide some cash to help fund the enterprise. Unfortunately, for many of us, coming up with even a few thousand dollars to bring life to a worthy venture is a formidable task. Based on the information I've compiled, I have some suggestions that may help to alleviate this problem.

## Manage Debt and Accumulate Cash

This concept may sound simplistic, but the first thing you need to do is evaluate your present financial situation. The evaluation can be completed by yourself or a financial planner. In my household, I run the operation like it was a business. Although I consider myself the Chief Financial Officer, my wife, Carolyn, is actually the Chief Executive Officer (my boss).

I think my wife is amused by how seriously I take my role but she lets me have my little kicks anyway. Just as in a business, my role in "Wallace Family, Inc." is to maintain the financial posture of the entity, respect and take care of its workers (my wife and kids), and turn a profit for the shareholders (accumulate capital for college educations, exotic vacations, and lucrative business ventures). As CFO of your family, you need to understand the resources your family has at its disposal and the results achieved by their use. The type of information needed to effectively leverage the assets may include:

· Operating information
· Management accounting information, and

· Financial accounting information

Believe it or not, a considerable amount of information is required to conduct the day-to-day operations of the home. Expenses have to be met, amounts owed must be known, up-to-date status on asset base must be maintained, and the well-being of your loved ones must be constantly monitored. To assist me in carrying out this task, I often rely on the management accounting skills I obtained while attending business school. For those M.B.A.s reading this, you may recall that management accounting information is used to control, coordinate, and plan.

Controlling the finances of a family is not an easy task, as many of you can probably attest. One entrepreneur who owned a small manufacturing company in New England, shared the story about his lovely wife who did many things well, but who left their checking account in ruins! He jokingly recalled that his wife was one of those people who writes a million checks and consistently forgets to make the entries in the checking log. Consequently, when evaluating their financial position at any point in time, his records might indicate that he had more cash in the bank than he really did. After she had done this enough times, they decided to put a system in place that alerts her to when she makes that mistake and encourages her to act in a way that is consistent with the family's overall goals and objectives. Their system sometimes acts as an attention getter, signaling when problems that require investigation and possibly action exists.

Just as important as control is coordination. Clearly, every component of a household must work in unison to achieve its objectives. This implies that communication between the various members (you and your spouse) must be open and frank. If I, for example, come up with new guidelines and objectives, they must be communicated to my wife, otherwise her actions may be detrimental to the achievement of our goal. Someone in your household must take responsibility for this role and become semi-fanatical about making it work. Household bills must be scrutinized continuously and innovative ways developed to minimize them.

Coordination without planning is useless. Planning is the

process of deciding what action should be taken in the future. One important form of planning is called budgeting (sound familiar?). Budgeting is the process of planning the overall activity of your household for a specified period of time. Most people budget on a monthly basis. My wife and I integrate the various needs of all members of the family such that all assets are effectively leveraged. Planning often involves making difficult decisions, such as: Do I really want to go into business? Am I willing to make the sacrifices necessary for the business to succeed once it has started? Do I really need to get this Mercedes-Benz now?

Usually the process of maintaining operating information on your household finances through control, coordination, and planning, positions you well in dealing with outside financial institutions. If you've ever borrowed money from any financial house, you know what I mean. As far as your financial condition is concerned, every aspect of your financial posture is reviewed. Just like potential stockholders of a corporation need certain information about a company to help them decide if they want to invest, most banks want similar information about you!

## Prepare a Personal Financial Statement

Even before you decide what business to pursue, your first step is to construct your personal financial statement. In most situations, a financial statement serves two purposes. The first purpose is to provide you a clear and honest picture of your financial status and to help you pinpoint any financial weaknesses you may want to strengthen before approaching potential investors. The second purpose is that it is usually required when negotiating with investors, business brokers, or potential sellers.

Typically, your financial statement should be broken into two major parts; a balance sheet composed of your assets and liabilities, which shows your net worth; and an income-expense statement, which gives a picture of your cash flow. Some statements also include information about you, your family, and your past credit performance. You should state (if it's true) that you've never been through bankruptcy court and have no suits or judgments against you. In the business and science sections of most libraries, you will find examples of how a personal financial statement should be structured.

In general, the bank or other lender wants information that will show that your financial position is sound, and that there is a high probability that the loan will be repaid when it comes due. The more successful you are at controlling your expenses, increasing your asset base, and enhancing your net worth, the better positioned you'll be to launch your venture.

## Minimize Living Expenses

People who were raised in lower income environments usually have difficulty when it comes to minimizing their living expenses. To be honest about it, this phenomenon is prevalent among anyone who has not had an opportunity to benefit from America's wealth. Usually, when the only contact you've had with the niceties of American life is through television or the pages of a magazine, the first chance you get to splurge, you do so. This phenomenon is not unique to one race. It includes poor white people as well as poor people of color. People in this group find it exceedingly difficult to postpone the good life until the struggling venture has paid off significant dividends. They want the good life now!

Why does this tend to be the case? Clearly, there are numerous reasons. To start, a large number of minority Americans were probably raised in environments where everyone struggled daily to survive and very few enjoyed the conveniences and pleasures that many of their mainstream counterparts took for granted.

One of my fraternity brothers who started his own software business recalled his days growing up in the inner city of Chicago. There were times when his family went for longs periods without heat or running water. Even when the water was on, the system could not deliver enough hot water to satisfy the needs of his large family. Boiling water, pouring it into a basin, and washing from that basin was their primary method of bathing. Showers were unheard of in his neighborhood during that time.

This young man escaped the projects when he attended a predominantly white high school, where he lettered in three sports. To him, the best part of participating in sports was the fact that he got a chance to get a hot shower each day. The rest of the guys took hot showers for granted, but not this grateful young man. For him, it was an emotional event because he was not use to this luxury and found out that he really enjoyed it! Today, this young man will not even look at a house unless it has lots of showers.

This person's experience is a good example of how some us overcompensate for what we lacked as children. The point is that when you're forced to live in a way that prevents you from enjoying many of the privileges that most Americans take for granted, you'll go right out and recreate that object or experience that you've desired for so long the first opportunity that you get.

Another reason that struggling people have difficulty minimizing living expenses is because of their need to convince the world that they have more than they really do. Have you ever noticed how some rich people fanatically try to down play their wealth (at least some of them). They often wear the same old jeans and button down oxford shirt day after day. They seem to place very little emphasis on the clothes they wear, often preferring to be seen in well-worn garments. Some even prefer to drive around in old, out-dated automobiles that most of us would hate to be seen in. Usually, contrary to what they would have you believe, these people may have vast holdings of real estate and other assets and enjoy a very high standard of living invisible to the public eye.

The subjects of this study have made it crystal clear that, if you want to get into business, there is no getting around the fact that you have to accumulate some cash for starting capital. Most agree that the way to do that is to cut expenses as much as possible by minimizing your standard of living. However, if you're committed, your sacrifices today will pay big dividends for you tomorrow.

This idea of postponing the "good life" reminds me of a story told to me by one of the small business owners interviewed for this study from southern California. The individual told me of one of his childhood friends who had this philosophy that since you don't know what's going to happen to you tomorrow, you should really live it up today. Why save for tomorrow when there is no guarantee that you'll be living tomorrow?

As fate would have it, this man lived for a long time, but in his latter years was forced to struggle daily to meet his basic human needs. Many people in our community espouse to this type of philosophy - in my opinion, too many. No, the future is not promised, but there comes a time when you just have to believe in your longevity and plan for the future.

## Establishing A Strong Support Base

This section on self-development and self-preparation for your upcoming entrepreneurial venture is one of the most important. Here I address the importance of surrounding yourself with trustworthy and intelligent people as you strive to create and build your enterprises.

In his book titled, *Think And Grow Rich*, Napoleon Hill discusses in great detail the benefits of surrounding yourself with great minds. He labels this group as a "mastermind" group and delineates the criteria for choosing members. Mr. Hill explains that there are two characteristics of the mastermind principle, one of which is economic in nature and the other is psychic. From an economic standpoint, the benefits are quite obvious.

When you surround yourself with brilliant minds, you have a unique coordination of knowledge, spirit, effort, and direction that works in harmony to help achieve some common goal or objective. Although the psychic component of the mastermind principle is more difficult to appreciate, it is nevertheless a powerful part of this pair. Mr. Hill later suggests that whenever two strong and sincere minds come together for a common cause, there exists a part of the human energy element that is spiritual and that those spiritual energies somehow go through some form of metamorphosis that in essence creates a third mind. Every single minority business owner in this study in some way or another had a group of friends with whom they confided for ideas and support.

Not only must you surround yourself with good minds, you must also associate yourself with other budding entrepreneurs. There is no doubt that you are a product and a reflection of your environment. If you are consistently around young professionals whose goal in life is to climb the corporate ladder and be a corporate executive, then there is a good probability that you'll assume the same ambitions and desires. If your running buddies are into drugs and alcohol, then you'll probably start trying drugs and indulge in excessive drinking

However, when you're constantly around aspiring or established businesspeople, a synergy is created and you become a part of it. You begin to start thinking like a businessperson, looking like a businessperson and even feeling that you are already a business owner. Each level of excitement catapults you to another, until your vision of business ownership becomes reality. In most cases, just the fact that you have a personal relationship with an existing business owner removes much of the mystery usually associated with being an entrepreneur, causing you to take the attitude that *if she can do it, so can I!*

Once you've gotten your brain trust group together, which I hope will consist of intelligent, trustworthy, conscientious entrepreneurs and soon-to-be entrepreneurs, you then need to weed out all of your dead end relationships and sever the connection. Why is this important? The answer is simple. When you start putting your plans together for your venture and ultimately start it, you will need all the time and support that you can get!

There are only so many hours in a day and days in a week, and you'll need all of that to accomplish your goals while maintaining your sanity. You don't need to waste your precious time with folks who are insincere, selfish, weak minded, and lacking direction and drive. Learn quickly how to identify and isolate these relationships and move quickly to terminate them.

While you're severing dead relationships, whatever you do, strengthen the good ones that you have. The people in your life who are important to you and whom you love should be told that. Tell them how much you love them and how important they are in your life. Whether it is your wife, husband, father, mother, brother, sister, or pal, they need to know how much they mean to you. Nearly every person in this study articulated this critical fact at some point. Many of them reiterated the fact that when you go into business, your family and friends go in with you. You'll need their love and support, so work to strengthen those relationships now, before you start.

## *Taking the Leap of Faith and Starting a Business Despite the Odds*

I realize that I've just taken you through an enormous amount of information in my attempt to make sense of the detailed information collected from the participants of my study. I trust that the previous chapters have encouraged you enough that you're excited about starting your venture in spite of the odds.

In discussing entrepreneurship with minority and mainstream folks, the most difficult part of getting into business is determining what type of business one wants. Naturally, there are many options, i.e., consulting, which requires very little capitalization; manufacturing, which requires high capitalization; or other businesses in between. You will have to take your best guess, given the information you have, and choose an area. Even if it turns out to be the wrong choice, you'll be that much closer to finding the right option for you.

**Jimmy Herndon**
**Metrolina Knitting Mills**
**Charlotte, N.C.**

As we strained to talk over the loud noise of the knitting machines, the heat generated by the machinery started to make it very uncomfortable walking inside the factory. However, Jimmy Herndon, owner of Metrolina Knitting Mills, was quite comfortable and even appeared to enjoy the heat, the dust, and the loud clanging of metal rubbing against metal. When the first lot of gloves produced by the machines dropped into the loading basket, Jimmy carefully inspects the color, the stitching, and the quality of the material before he allows the product to be boxed, loaded, and shipped to the United States Army. After motioning the packer to proceed with packing the goods, Jimmy makes eye contact with another machine operator across the floor and advises him to replace the spent spool of fabric with a fresh one to help maintain production continuity.

With all machines running full steam, Jimmy smiles and motions to the operator to be careful while running the machine during the next shift. As he walks back to his office to make more marketing calls, Jimmy acknowledges how he almost missed the opportunity to go into business due to the well-intentioned advice of his former manager at Celanese Corporation.

## *Going for It*

In 1978, against the advice of his manager at Celanese Corporation, Jimmy accepted the challenge and decided to go into business for himself. At the time, his manager, although well-intentioned, warned him he was crazy to attempt such a venture. Years later, after Jimmy had proven that he could be successful running his own business, his supervisor returned and confessed that he envied what Jimmy had done and would have tried it himself if he had been a few years younger.

Jimmy admits that the first few years were quite difficult. However, Jimmy easily justifies his decision:

At age 28, I had that burning desire and felt I didn't have anything to lose. That's the way you have to think of it. I could have gotten a job. It's not life and death. If you fail, get yourself together, get a job, get a better business plan, try again. Persistence produces opportunity. You can have all the discrimination in the world; if you have a made up mind, you're going to make it.

Like many minority business start-ups though, Metrolina Knitting Mills experienced severe cash flow problems that almost ruined the business before it ever got off the ground. During this difficult period, Jimmy was forced not only to work his business, but he also had to work two other jobs on a part-time basis. His wife, who has been supportive of him from the very beginning, continued to work a full-time job while Jimmy tried to build and expand Metrolina's customer base. To add more complexity to an already complex situation, Jimmy and his wife had recently become the proud parents of two new babies and had serious doubts about their ability to juggle all of these commitments. Quite often, when Jimmy found himself alone, he would ask himself the questions, "Why am I doing this? Why did I become so excited about owning my own business?"

## *In the Beginning*

The southern accent that gives Jimmy away every time he speaks can be somewhat misleading. Jimmy was born in Kings Mountain, North Carolina, but raised in Newark, New Jersey. The men in Jimmy's family had a history of venturing out on their own in spite of seemingly insurmountable odds. Jimmy's father, although he didn't possess much formal education, became a talented automobile mechanic who developed and ran a successful automobile repair business right out of his backyard.

Jimmy's grandfather was also an entrepreneur even though it was extremely difficult for a black man during that period to own and operate a business. Yet, his grandfather became a successful farmer and landowner early in the century. His mother, who had no entrepreneurial ambitions, was a domestic and cleaned house for many local families. Like Jimmy's father, his mother did not possess much formal education but she was an exceptionally wise woman who often encouraged and led Jimmy to attack life, rather than use whatever handicaps he had as excuses. Like black mothers throughout history, she taught her son to strive for his dreams.

Similar to most rural families of that time, Jimmy's family was quite large. Being the sixth child of seven, Jimmy learned the importance of fighting for what you want and the potential benefits of working hard. While attending high school, he often worked multiple jobs after school so that he could save enough money to help take care of his family and to provide a nest egg for him after he went off on his own.

Jimmy was introduced to the textile industry at a very young age. One of his first jobs at sixteen was at a local sweater-making mill. Although the job paid pennies and was quite dangerous, Jimmy developed a love for manufacturing and the textile industry in general. He often worked far beyond his scheduled hours so that he could learn as much as possible about the manufacturing process and what opportunities there were for young men like himself. Convinced that this was the career he wanted to pursue, Jimmy later set out to further prepare himself for this challenge by pursuing formal education to supplement the invaluable experience he gained by working in the mills.

After careful research, Jimmy chose two schools that he thought would prepare him for his chosen career - New York Fashion Institute of Technology and the North Carolina Vocational School. At the time, he had no idea how he would pay for this education but he had already committed to making it happen and continued to move forward anyway.

Years later, with degree in hand, Jimmy's short-term goal of starting a career in the textile industry was realized. The Celanese Corporation offered him a position as a textile technician. Jimmy's responsibility in this job was to help solve difficult technical problems surrounding the manufacture of textiles. Jimmy naturally excelled in this environment. He approached all of his technical challenges with great resolve and dedication. He often worked late into the night, unwilling to quit before a solution to a problem was found.

Even though Jimmy showed great promise and strong dedication to his employer, as with most large corporations, talented minority members and women often bump up against "the glass ceiling" - a seemingly invisible barrier to the advancement of anyone who is not white and male. Therefore, it was no surprise that Jimmy, although fortunate to have many challenging opportunities at the lower levels of the hierarchy, decided to take the "leap of faith" and build his own textile business.

## *Financing*

Jimmy's euphoria instantly ran into reality when he attempted to capitalize his business. Starting the business was one thing, but trying to get it financed was another. Even with all of the experience and education that Jimmy had amassed, he had little experience with handling the accounting and finances of starting a business. A quick learner, Jimmy compiled a rough analysis of how much he would need to get the business started. His first analysis revealed that he would need approximately $100,000 to capitalize the business adequately. His estimate was based on the following assumptions:

| | |
|---|---|
| Leasing of Equipment: | $30,000 |
| Bldg. Lease | $15,000 |
| Materials | $10,000 |
| Utilities | $ 4,500 |
| Working Capital | $20,500 |
| Wages and Admin. (himself) | $20,000 |
| | $100,000 |

Jimmy felt that he could come up with approximately $50,000 of the capital he needed. The remaining $50,000 he figured he could borrow from a local North Carolina bank. As is the case with most minority, initiated ventures, when Jimmy first approached the bank, even though he had a well-developed business plan and a very workable strategy, the bank rejected his application.

Undaunted, Jimmy sought assistance from the Small Business Administration (SBA). Before the SBA could be of any assistance to him though, he learned that he couldn't just approach one bank and with one rejection solicit help from the SBA. The SBA informed him that he was required to approach numerous banking institutions to acquire the loans. If he was rejected by all of the banks, the SBA might be able to assist him. As instructed, Jimmy resumed his search for funding by applying for a loan from five different banks. As expected, Jimmy was rejected five different ways.

With rejection letters in hand, Jimmy revisited the SBA, who, after an exhaustive study of Jimmy's background and character, agreed to guarantee the loan from one of the local banks that Jimmy had approached. After a long and drawn-out process, Jimmy obtained a loan for $72,000, more than he had estimated, but as it turned out, the additional funding helped him manage the business through some scary times.

To handle his first orders, which involved manufacturing hats for junior high schools, high schools, and some of the local colleges, Jimmy realized that he needed to make a capital investment to purchase specialized machinery. As his orders from large corporations started to multiply, the corporations wanted him to use the same type equipment that his academic customers were requiring him to use. Jimmy says:

> Getting a contract is one thing, but you have to have an economic plan. You can't put together a loan application unless you have diligently compiled your financial projections. I looked at all aspects of my financial position and had the information documented. You definitely need an accountant to keep you abreast of what's going on.

The accountant proved invaluable when he was faced with his next round of financing. It became necessary to obtain additional equipment that was radically different from the machines for which he had budgeted. Forced to return to the SBA for help, Jimmy, much smarter now about using the government agency, convinced the SBA to guarantee his loan again to purchase the equipment. This time around it was easier to get the loan, and Jimmy purchased the machine and was in business.

Jimmy learned quickly that no matter how well one plans for anticipated cash requirements, he will usually be wrong. This theory was certainly true in the case of Metrolina Knitting Mills. Through his diligence and creativity, he was quite successful early on in attracting customers and consummating contracts for his business. Unfortunately, the vigorous business activity also meant a substantial increase in his need for working capital. Jimmy estimated his total requirement during that peak business phase to be more than $100,000.

This additional funding estimate assumed that he would have customers who refused to pay on time or at all and other unforeseen production problems that would require an immediate injection of cash. Jimmy was able to raise the funds by obtaining various lines of credit from the banks he had done business with in the past, and who knew him and his business better.

## Getting Customers

Jimmy initially got business from an organization that worked through a large corporation - a development council. The corporation had signed an agreement to do business with minorities. From this, Jimmy was able to meet Burlington Industries, an aluminum company in Pittsburgh that proved to be a great customer and one with which Jimmy could build a long-term relationship. He was also successful at generating business leads through the many trade shows he attended throughout the country. He warns prospective entrepreneurs that even though one can be successful at generating business and building long-term business relationships, the process is a slow and often frustrating one. Jimmy concedes that had it not been for his wife, son, and daughter helping him to find and generate business, he would not have been as successful as he was.

Business for the very near future looks bright for Metrolina Knitting Mills. Although Jimmy employs seven people full-time now, he sees significant growth on the horizon, which would require him to bring on additional help quickly. Jimmy, however, admits that he prefers slow growth versus rapid growth. During rapid growth periods, some businesses get behind and end up losing control of the business. In a slow growth situation, Jimmy feels he has more time to make the right decisions and is not forced to make quick and potentially damaging ones.

Jimmy anticipates that his sales will increase briskly each year. His marketing strategy includes continuing to attend as many trade shows as possible, go after the industrial uniforms market more vigorously, and increase his advertising budget so that he can maintain a presence in most  key industries.

## *Business Ethics*

Jimmy succinctly puts the issue of business ethics into the proper perspective:

It's important to always deliver the goods and services asked for by clients. If you have a problem, let them know. Most customers are more than willing to work with you. The proper ethics are essential. In my view, being ethical means being honorable, reliable, and resourceful. Your reputation via word of mouth can be broad and encompassing; therefore, you must protect it at all times.

Proper business conduct, in Jimmy's opinion, also entails giving something back to the community in which you do business. Any businessperson who just takes and takes will not be in business very long. Besides, most communities expect the businesses in their areas to contribute to solving local problems. Jimmy is quite active in his home of Charlotte, North Carolina. He is a member of the Board of Directors for the City of Charlotte, the Salvation Army, and the Boy Scouts of America. Providing these groups time, money, and leadership is how Jimmy does his part in making his community a pleasant place for all people to live.

## Perfect Fit

The textile industry was a perfect fit for Jimmy. He advises all people to start a business they know something about. Jimmy encourages young entrepreneurs to start where they are. If they're currently working in a particular industry, try getting your business started in that same industry. Jimmy doesn't think that any business person should go into business and tread on unfamiliar turf:

You have to be knowledgeable of your business, understand the technical problems, and be able to solve internal problems. It saves you money. You also can really talk to your clients and explain things to them when you understand the business.

## Spiritual Power

In life there are things that you can control and other things that you cannot control. Your job is to try to control as much as possible all those things that you have the power to control. Once you've done your job, you have to leave the other issues up to God (or whoever you believe in). Jimmy was unwavering in his faith in God and how he relies on this strength to get him through the tough times and to help him keep the good times in perspective. Regular worship and diligent prayer helps keep Jimmy a major player in the game.

## *Starting Again*

Jimmy admits that if he had to start over again, the industries that he would focus on are the food and clothing industries. Pursuing manufacturing or some type of service in these industries would be an exciting and potentially rewarding venture. Regardless of the kind of business though, Jimmy is quick to add that solid financing, detailed knowledge about your chosen business, persistence, caring, and good employee relations are important if you plan on being a long-term player instead of a short-term one. He advises:

First, you have to convince your customer that you're honest and know what you're doing before he'll be willing to give you business. You need detailed knowledge to win and maintain customers over the long run. Persistence - keep on keeping on. Understanding - understand your customer needs and your own needs."

## Earl Chavis
## Chavis Tool & Company
## Lamar, South Carolina

It has often been said that going into business with someone is like getting married. Like marriage, it requires that all people involved maintain a certain amount of trust and commitment among themselves. When the trust factor breaks down, then all parties involved need to re-evaluate whether they should continue with a venture or not.

Early in 1976, Earl Chavis, CEO of Chavis Tool & Company, was confronted with this very dilemma. A few years earlier, Earl, bristling with confidence and optimism, left Rockwell International to form his own machine tool company in South Carolina. At the time, Earl was very low on cash, but had a surplus of experience, credentials, and creative ideas. One day while in church, Earl started a conversation with one of the church members concerning the company that Earl was contemplating starting. To Earl's surprise, the man appeared very excited about the deal and even suggested that maybe he could help provide some of the financing. Earl could not believe his ears. His prayers had been answered, or so he thought.

After further discussions with the man and determining that he was quite serious, Earl and his new partner decided to create a partnership in which each man controlled 50 percent of the stock. The initial agreement between the two was that Earl would not have to put up much capital to start the company, but would instead contribute his leadership and expertise.

Initially, the arrangement between the two men was like a match made in heaven. The two got together and developed a strong business plan identifying their markets, equipment needs, and what type of building they would need to house all of the equipment. After more detailed discussions with their advisors, they decided to rent a 6,000 square-foot warehouse and to contract with an equipment leasing company to lease the necessary machinery.

From dealing with the leasing company, Earl soon learned an important lesson. That is, if you have a strong financial statement, you can borrow money as often as you like and as much as you like. In financing equipment acquisitions, it became apparent to him that you could actually acquire equipment without having to put any cash down. Because Earl's partner had millions of dollars in personal net worth, he had no difficulty getting the banks to loan the team money. The fact that his partner was white and well connected in the small South Carolina town didn't weaken their position either.

By the end of the first year of operation, Earl's small business was doing about $250,000 in sales and was on the verge of experiencing exponential growth in the coming year due to the anticipated award of lucrative government contracts. Unfortunately, huge cash requirements are also a companion of rapid growth and Earl realized the company would need a quick cash injection to handle the additional business. At that time, Earl's partner was handling the company finances so whenever there was a cash requirement, his partner was the one to write the checks. When the firm ran low on cash, the partner would write checks from his own personal accounts - or so he was leading Earl to believe.

As the new contracts began filtering in, Earl started noticing that the customers were taking an unusually long time to pay their bills. This situation lasted for a few months before Earl became really concerned and started making calls to his friends in those companies. What he heard made him sick to his stomach. As it turned out, the companies were promptly paying their bills as they had agreed. The problem was that instead of depositing the checks into the corporate accounts, Earl's partner was depositing the funds into his personal account.

Earl was infuriated and later sought to bankrupt the firm so that he could bring an end to this business relationship as quickly and effortlessly as possible. Earl's partner denied any wrong doing and insisted that the company continue on its present course. Earl refused and, after finishing the contracts that he had agreed to complete, ended up liquidating the firm's assets. He called in the leasing company to take back the leased equipment and sold the building. Due to some outstanding debt that the firm was saddled with, Earl walked away from the liquidation debt free but penniless. Earl recalls:

> When I liquidated my business, the only income I had coming in was from my unemployment insurance. I went from earning $25,000 per year down to a fraction of that amount. The difficulty of my dilemma was further complicated because I had four kids who were still in school. After swallowing a little pride, I forced myself to apply for food stamps (I got $300 worth for $15) and used my unemployment income to feed my family and pay my mortgage. My family and I lived like this for about a year. I had nothing.

Earl was obviously very hurt by this fiasco. He felt cheated and violated. But as time passed, he began to realize that he had learned a tremendous amount from this experience. To his credit, he had started a business without investing a dime of his own money and had acquired brand new equipment to build his products. The experience had taught him that it was possible to start a business with very little of his money and still make it work.

## Starting Over Again

Undaunted by his most recent setback, Earl resolved to start his business again but this time he would do it his way - the right way. He began this time by studying programs that were available to help start minority firms. He contacted the SBA, identified the specific programs, and arranged numerous face-to-face meetings with the representatives of SBA to determine if and how they could help him. Unlike many of his counterparts at that time, Earl refused to rely completely on the SBA. While he was negotiating with them, he continued to pursue other options he had on the outside.

One lesson Earl had learned from his previous experience was that in order for him to make a product, he didn't have to do all of the manufacturing himself. He could use subcontractors to build a portion of the product and then he could provide the finishing touches. Rough calculations on the merits of subcontracting convinced him that he could in fact make money this way instead of doing everything himself.

This second time around, Earl also reconsidered how he would purchase his equipment and manufacturing space. Instead of buying brand new equipment Earl opted to buy used equipment at a significant discount. He was able to fix up the equipment himself at very little cost to his new company. For $1,000, Earl was able to buy all of the equipment he would need initially, even though he had to borrow the money from his brother-in-law because he was still broke. Earl was just as creative in his search for a building to house the equipment. He happened to know a friend in his lodge who had a vacant building available and convinced his friend to rent him the building for $25 per month. Once Earl began making money, he would increase the monthly rent to a level that was more realistic.

## *Leveraging Political Connections*

While Earl continued to build his business from the ground up, he also began building a strong working relationship with the SBA. Although he hadn't been successful in obtaining funding yet, he had completed all of the paper work and had met with most of the officials running the agency. After a period of time, Earl became frustrated and disillusioned with the SBA and its ability to help him. About this time, Earl heard about a SBA conference that was being held at Benedict College in South Carolina, which Senator Ernest Hollins would attend.

The intent of the conference was to convey to all of the small businesses in South Carolina that the SBA was sponsoring some very creative programs to stimulate small business activity in the state. Earl decided to attend the conference. To dramatize his frustration, he brought along all of the paper work that he had completed for the SBA before he could get any help. Earl tells the story:

So I stood up with a stack of papers this high under my arm and I stood out in the middle of the hallway. There were no whites in there, other than government officials. The majority of the people there were black. We don't have many Native-Americans left in South Carolina. I said, 'Senator, you said I have to do this and this and this and then the Small Business Administration would take over. Right?'
'That's exactly right!' he said.
I dropped the stack of papers on the floor and said, 'Senator, do you see all these papers I just dropped on the floor? This is all the paper work I've completed for the SBA. I have done everything you've said that I need to do and I still haven't gotten much help.'
The senator turned around and looked at the guy who was the director of the Small Business Administration and said, 'What's the matter with you people? This man has done everything he was supposed to do and you haven't done anything yet?' Senator Hollins then turned back to me and

instructed me to call the SBA office on Tuesday, and if they hadn't done anything by the following Monday, he would intervene. I thanked the senator, quickly picked up my papers off of the floor and quietly left the room.

After Earl's encounter with Senator Hollins, things started to happen very quickly at the SBA. The following Monday morning the SBA called Earl in for a meeting and helped him draw up the paper work for a $50,000 loan. In June of 1976, 18 months after he had applied, Earl finally received a check for $50,000, which he used as working capital to acquire inventory, pay utilities, and repair old equipment.

As the business began to expand, Earl's capital requirements also began to spiral upward. Early in 1980, Earl was awarded a Department of Defense contract to produce gun barrels. The contract was worth close to $1,000,000. Unable to meet this contract with funds on hand, Earl was forced to borrow $300,000 from a local bank that was guaranteed by the SBA. The $300,000 was only going to buy the raw material and the tooling. Earl's firm was forced to meet any other expenses. Shortly thereafter, Earl was forced to borrow another $100,000 from the same community bank. This time the funds were used for operating capital. Unfortunately for Earl, inflation took off about the same time he floated the additional debt and for some time he was saddled with high interest rates, diminishing his ability to service the debt.

## Defining the Customer Set

After making the additional loans, Earl turned his attention to firming up his customer base. Although much of his business was coming from the Federal Government, he did have some success generating customers from the private sector as well. A few of his private customers included General Electric, Cummins Engines, and Southeastern Steel Company. Earl claims that his success in attracting business from private companies was a combination of contacts, timing, and luck. As he explains:

> Once someone is in a key position with a company, while they may have to move, chances are they will continue in the same line of work. After you've been around for a while and you've worked at various companies you begin to know all the people in your profession. The fact that you see them socially and at various professional forums helps you keep track of their whereabouts. Consequently, everyone knew that I had been a technical director at Rockwell and A.B. Dick. After convincing potential customers of my ability to perform the task at hand, I usually was awarded the work.

## Defining the Correct Business Strategy

Chavis Manufacturing Company has been in business for more than twenty years. The sales volume generated usually falls under $10 million per year. Earl has taken the business to a critical point, and he must now decide what his next step will be:

> At my age, the question of what I'm going to do for growth is a difficult one. Regardless of what strategy we follow, there are a few things that we must do. First, we must upgrade all of our equipment to realize efficiency benefits. We are in the process of doing that. It is estimated that we'll spend somewhere between a half million to a million dollars in capital equipment improvement over the next few years. Now for us to elevate our shop to the point where we can consistently generate sales above the $5 million mark, we will have to invest in advanced equipment and new automation technologies. Right now, we are diversified. We can go in any direction at any time that we chose. We have many options.

Currently, Earl is purposely running the plant far below capacity. He is currently servicing a heavy debt load and doesn't have the capital to run the operation at full capacity. Part of his short-term strategy is to reduce his debt to more manageable levels before he initiates his next growth spurt. He also would like to re-evaluate alternative funding strategies, debt financing, and possibly factoring his receivables.

Earl has four children - two boys and two girls. However, only one of this children is actively involved in running the business. Earl manages basically all of the administrative functions, including financing, purchasing, office managing, buying, selling, and marketing.

Because Earl is over sixty years of age, he often debates whether he should commit the resources to move the business to the next level or should just turn over the reins to his son and take early retirement. He has already estimated that he would need to invest at least $500,000 in new equipment to have any chance of meeting his growth goals. The problem he faces is that he may have to put up more collateral than he's willing to commit in order to satisfy the banks. Earl is visibly concerned about investing for this growth and then having the bottom fall out. He cautions:

A business owner has to be careful. Let's assume that you've used every asset you own as collateral to acquire loans. As you continue to grow and expand you will probably find that you'll need additional funding. But what will you use for collateral? How are you going to get more money? What are you going to use to get money? That's what you have to watch out for - growth, fast growth.

## Advice to Young Entrepreneurs

Earl is quick to caution all young entrepreneurs to be sure to go into a business they know something about unless they are going into business with someone who has knowledge in the area:

> There is no time for on-the-job training. You have to know
> what you are supposed to do before you go out. If you are in
> school and you do not know what you want to do, take some
> business administration courses. A sound business back-
> ground provides you many options for pursuing business. An
> individual with good business training and a good business
> mind can be very beneficial to a business. For example, if one
> is an engineer, he could probably do the technical, administra-
> tive, and possibly the managerial work. One person fulfills
> more than one functional role.

Although most small businesses experience cash flow problems, Earl suggests that if you're going to have cash flow problems,
it's better to experience them early in the venture instead of later.
He's found that if you're smart, it's easier to survive when they hit
you early versus the later years. Earl adds:

> Throughout the booming 1980s, many businesses failed. In my
> opinion, the primary reason they folded was because the people
> were not familiar with and didn't know how to function under
> severe cash flow constraints. Too many have been taught to go
> to the bank and get whatever money they needed to solve the
> particular problem. In the 1980s, the rules changed. You
> couldn't go to the banks to get the money because they
> wouldn't give it to you! You had to learn how to run your
> business with less cash. I think as we move into the 1990s
> people will be a little more conservative and cash conscious.

The fact that Chavis Manufacturing is a minority firm has not
helped or harmed the company, according to Earl. To his chagrin,
some of his local competitors believe that because he is a minority
firm, his business gets better opportunities than theirs. Earl's
response to this prevailing sentiment is "bull crap."

I was given nothing! The minority status only helps you if it is used in the manner it was designed to be used. If you try to use it in some other form or if you try to circumvent it in some other way, you are dead. You are going to have all kinds of problems. Although the Federal Government has the 8(a) program for disadvantaged businesses and although I've participated in the program since 1977, I have not received a significant amount of business at this point. Unfortunately, the only time the public hears about the 8(a) program is when it's being abused. You've seen Wedtech all over the news. Those people stole millions of dollars. They abused the system and now it is costing me and other minority business owners. I have to pay for their greed.

Earl further cautions young businesspeople to maintain a low profile and some degree of humility. If you maintain a high profile that means there are more people who can take shots at you. Earl recommends that if you need that type of attention, let someone else do it for you. If what you're doing is that spectacular, then it will only be a matter of time before the public begins to notice.

Earl advises young entrepreneurs to remember that while they're building their businesses, they should do something for themselves and their families. In spite of difficult times, Earl was able to buy a farm in South Carolina and a beach front home for the summer. Earl will soon have the farm, his plant, his beach home, and his regular home paid off.

## Born to Be Proud

Based on Earl's impoverished childhood, it is a major accomplishment that he has accumulated and achieved so much in his lifetime. Born into the Cheraw Lumbee tribe in a small rural area of North Carolina, Earl was one of twelve children. He is proud of his Native-American roots and is quick to remind people that Native-

Americans of the Cheraw Lumbee tribe were once part of the great Tuscarora nation. This nation, which originated in what is now North Carolina, later populated the areas that are now called New York and Ontario, Canada.

Like many of the men of this nation, Earl's father was a farmer and performed sharecropping services for many of the rich, white landowners. All of the children were expected to help out on the farm, including Earl. However, Earl had bigger ambitions and often dreamed of going off to college. Thanks to his mother, Earl was given that chance. Even though she was illiterate, she understood the value of education and did all she could to ensure that her son would have it. She often reminded him that without education he couldn't do anything.

Responding to his mother's wishes, after completing his tour of duty in the Navy, Earl was able to attend college and earn his degree. With the Navy and college behind him, Earl married his Greek sweetheart and began his career. During his long and illustrious career, Earl worked for companies such as Western Electric, A.B. Dick, and Rockwell in various engineering, R&D, and management positions.

# PART 3

# EXTERNAL CHECKPOINTS FOR BUSINESS SUCCESS

**The** internal checkpoints for business success, which we discussed in the last chapter, were all tasks that you can accomplish with little or no assistance from anyone else. These are the tasks that you need to complete in order to prepare yourself individually. In contrast, this chapter summarizes the external checkpoints - those tasks necessary to take you from your dream to the reality of business ownership.

External checkpoints for business success are just as critical as the internal checkpoints for success. However, I have observed that people have more difficulty achieving the external checkpoints than they do the internal ones because they tend to have less control over the external world. The issues surrounding achieving the external checkpoints are often more complex and unpredictable. Nevertheless, any successful entrepreneur needs to work through the external checkpoints in order to establish a direct connection between the individual dream and the actual structure to support the dream. These checkpoints, as identified in the study, are as follows:

Step 1: Refine Vision
Step 2: Hold Your Head High and Count Your Blessings

Step 3: Live "Lite"
Step 4: Revisit Your Values
Step 5: Establish Proper Goals
Step 6: Establish a Proper Set of Rules
Step 7: Develop a Personal Mission Statement
Step 8: Perform S.W.O.T. Analysis of Self and Team
Step 9: Identify the Right Opportunity
Step 10: Start the "Sifting Process"
Step 11: Compile the Opportunity List and Compare
          to Your Values and Your S.W.O.T. List
Step 12: Execute, Execute, Execute

Like the internal building blocks of success, the building blocks for achieving the external requirements of success as shown in Exhibit 3-1, are mutually dependent.

**Exhibit 3-1. External Checkpoints for Business Success**

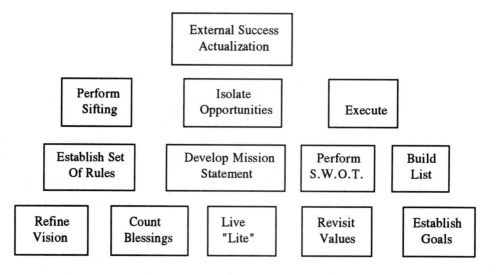

## *Refining Your Vision*

"Where there is no vision, the people perish..."
Proverbs 29:18

One of the giants of gospel music was James Cleveland. Although he recently passed away, he is often credited with popularizing large gospel choirs and identifying promising singing groups, mentoring them and exposing them to the public. Most people, like my mother who adored the man, probably failed to realize how much of a visionary James Cleveland was. In 1968, among other accomplishments, he founded the Gospel Music Workshop of America. The mission of this workshop was to bring together gospel talent from all over the country and to elevate gospel music to the same level of acceptance and respect as that given to jazz, classical, and modern music. The workshop now has more than 21,000 members and boasts having 200 chapters nationwide. One of James Cleveland's most formidable dreams was to build an accredited college for gospel music. Imagine that, an accredited college for gospel music majors. What vision!

One of the reasons Mr. Cleveland rapidly transcended his roots in the south side of Chicago to become an internationally recognized gospel musician was that he filled a very important need that many African-Americans and others shared. That is, the need to believe that in spite of the hatred, racism, poverty, and ignorance that still pervades our society, there is an omnipotent power in the universe that will change wrongs to rights and lies to truths. It's the belief that the inequalities of life are not permanent or final. If you listen to the lyrics of his songs, you will realize they all share the common mission of giving hope to oppressed people. We all thrive on hope so it should be no surprise that Mr. Cleveland's music has been a phenomenal success over the years.

In spite of his obvious success, many people considered him to be an average man with average looks and talent. How could an average man with average talent be able to realize such outstanding accomplishments? First, because he had such clear vision, he was able to accurately gauge his market and determine which goods or services he could offer to meet the demands of the public. Second, he surrounded himself with exceptionally talented people who helped him make things happen. In other words, Mr. Cleveland became quite successful at finding whatever resources he deemed necessary for accomplishing his objectives.

We can learn a lot from Mr. Cleveland by understanding these two principles. Mr. Cleveland's vision reminds me of something Michelangelo once said about dreams that are real in one sense but not in another. On one occasion when Michelangelo began to carve a huge block of marble, he declared that his specific aim was not to construct a masterpiece but to release the angel who was imprisoned in the stone. In other words, the beauty was already there. He didn't have to create it. There also exists an angel in the visions that each of us produce that we must work to release.

James Cleveland and Michelangelo took what appeared to be plain blocks of marble and released the angels inside. Their visions became the focus of what eventually evolved into something great. Vision is simply the manifestation to the senses of something that is yet to come. Vision is an interesting phenomenon. It never lets you go, and you can't let go of it. A clear vision provides motivation, stimulation, and exuberance.

All of the entrepreneurs involved in this study actually had started their businesses years before the businesses actually materialized. Their businesses started the first day they visualized their enterprises in their hearts and minds. Although the physical environment may have told them differently, their visions or dreams convinced them daily that their dreams were alive and well.

Most successful people will attest to the fact that there is a tremendous amount of power in vision. The vision created in one's mind has the power to control the physical senses. Those senses then proceed to work in unison to achieve the object of your vision. I'm sure that many of you yearn to start your own business but maybe you lack a clear vision of what that business should be. Well, don't despair. I hope this section of the book will propel you on your way to allowing that dream to become real.

The first step is to try a vision-generating exercise. The beauty of conducting this vision-generating exercise is that it doesn't require any capital or supreme intelligence to make it work for you. It is appalling how few people have visions or dreams. Unfortunately, those who do dare to dream are often long on dreams but short on money and strategies. Interesting enough, most of us unconsciously visualize daily the things that we desire and the qualities that we long to possess. These images are then transferred to our sub-conscious for further manipulation.

For those of you who are short on vision, let's play a little game. Stop what you're doing right now. Just stop. Put the book down (I know it's difficult to put the book down and continue with this exercise but do your best), lay your head back, close your eyes, and relax. Now, let your mind wander and fantasize about the future. Do you see a red Ferrari or Porshe 911 sitting in the driveway of your multi-million dollar estate? Maybe you see yourself relaxing on your farm in Virginia, surrounded by acres of lush forest on one side and a crystal clear lake stocked with fresh trout on the other side.

As you relax on your large rear porch, you catch a glimpse of your specially bred stallions roaming freely in front of the quaint country home that you and your spouse have built. As you look over your acreage, maybe the tall rows of corn slightly block your view of your distant apple orchard. Behind the house, you may have another garden that the kids labor in but that you enjoy watching grow as you sharpen your tennis game on the adjacent court.

Maybe your vision doesn't focus so much on material things. Your thoughts may be much more altruistic. You see yourself earning a great deal of money and then using that money to help uplift the downtrodden, feed the hungry, and provide shelter for the homeless. Can you feel the excitement and energy that focusing on your vision generates within you? Can you feel your heart start to beat a little more quickly?

Since you're reading this book, you undoubtedly desire or dream about being the president of your own business, feeling excited everyday about going to work and facing the challenges of running a small business. If you're like most of the subjects in this study, you'd also like to build an empire within and outside the minority community, using the resources of this empire to provide jobs and self-esteem to those members of our society who have been ignored and forgotten. Fantasizing a little further, you probably see your children inheriting a business that will give them a head start in life rather than them inheriting poverty, ignorance, and a perpetual dependence on unproductive welfare programs.

Sound crazy? Not really. Everything that you can see or touch first started out as someone's vision. Your business must also start out by your active visualization of your soon-to-be enterprise. By seeing this vision of yourself on a daily basis, you force the elements of your being to fall in line with this vision and make it real.

Whenever one is forced to confront the reality of his situation today and the uncertainty of his situation tomorrow, he will find that there are only two possible outcomes: either the reality of the present will destroy the dreams for the future or the dreams of the future will overshadow the reality of today. The present contains the reality of everyday life: your job, the household bills, college tuitions, and family issues. The future contains that vision of yourself that you'd like to make a reality. The ideal situation occurs when the vision is so strong and overbearing that it begins to take on a life of its own and quickly overshadows the problems and issues of the present. This second scenario is the one that I hope is taking place in your life because you'll never start the business if the vision isn't a powerful and convincing one.

Another perspective on the power of vision is the view that at any point in time prior to start up, your business is both present and not present. Let me explain. The business may not exist in terms of equipment, land, buildings, and people. It does, however, exist in the sense that it resides in your heart and mind as an inner spark that creates in you large doses of inner motivation and energy.

This motivation is what forces you out of bed to work on your business idea when everyone else is still sound asleep. It's the motivation that forces you out of the house on Sunday afternoons to pursue a certain business project instead of snoozing in your favorite chair. This vision-induced energy drives you hourly and daily to turn the focus of your vision into a reality. This spark allows you to overcome all adversity, regardless of what's put in front of you. Establish that vision, expand it, tailor it, let it take on a life of its own, and revisit it constantly.

## Holding Your Head High and CountingYour Blessings

Everyone has at one time or another experienced periods of depression, disappointment, and frustration. If you're like most people, you've probably had times in your life when everything seemed to go wrong no matter what you did. You've probably experienced failures that have shaken your confidence and made you question your value and self-worth. If you haven't had these experiences, you're either extremely blessed or not a very honest person!

Often, we spend so much time focusing on our shortcomings, our failures, our lack of material possessions, or our lack of cash that we become blind to the obvious blessings that we do enjoy. Blessings such as good health, a happy and healthy family, the ability to work and dream, food to eat, and a roof over our heads. I know how you feel because I'm guilty of this type of self-pity also. I too have wasted time focusing on the negatives instead of the positives. If we learn to count our blessings and maintain a positive attitude, then we begin to generate positive energy instead of the negative energy that is destructive and useless. The Father often reminds us through meditation, prayer, conversation and experiences that he does love us and that we're more blessed than we realize. One of the entrepreneurs who started a local area network consulting firm talked about a personal experience he had that shocked him back to reality.

One day, while working on an office automation project for a large east coast client, this young man decided that he had enough of his computer for the moment and decided to give himself a much needed break. It was a rainy, misty day with dark, low-lying clouds. He mentioned that business was not going well and that he hadn't seen the sun in a few days. The dampness outside made the already dirty streets look even dirtier.

As he secured his overcoat to protect himself from the cold rain, he caught a glimpse of a small vehicle coming down the street where he was standing. Initially, he couldn't discern what the strange looking vehicle was because it was raining and because the vehicle was still some distance away. Out of curiosity, he slowed his normally brisk pace to a casual walk, just to get a better view of this unusual contraption. As the vehicle came closer, he began to make out the details of the vehicle and its occupant.

What he saw completely shocked him. First, the weird-looking vehicle turned out to be a motorized wheelchair and sitting in it was what appeared to be a middle-aged black woman. But this was no ordinary woman. To begin with she had no legs. Not only that, although she had full use of her arms, she also suffered from some visual handicaps as well. With one arm holding an umbrella providing her some protection from the rain and the other arm working the controls of her motorized chair, this brave woman maneuvered her way through the rush hour traffic of downtown in the cold damp rain.

This young entrepreneur stood there looking stupid and dumbfounded. Luckily, the amazing woman had not seen him staring at her. After regaining his composure, he once again began his trek back to his client's office to resume his work. As he hurried his stride, he began to cry uncontrollably. He later admitted that he didn't mean to cry and he didn't want to cry. But for some reason he couldn't stop the tears from rolling down his cheeks. Embarrassed, the man quickly ducked into one of the alleys to get himself together before anyone he knew saw him. He was thankful it was raining because the rain helped to camouflage his tears and the confusion he felt.

As he leaned against the alley wall, he tried to figure out why he was crying. Suddenly, it dawned on him that he wasn't crying because he felt sorry for the woman - even though he did. He was crying because at that moment he felt so ashamed. Ashamed because in spite of all the blessings God had bestowed on him, he had failed to recognize them.

Another entrepreneur shared a similar story with me. After having lost a major contract to the competition, this young man was very depressed and down on himself. As he was leaving his office late one night, he happened to walk past a homeless woman who was sitting on a city bench leafing through her many shopping bags. She was a middle-aged woman with dark hair, brown eyes, and a slender build. Like most of us, this young man tried to avoid making contact with her because she looked ragged and filthy.

As he tried to escape her sharp glances, she beckoned to him, "Excuse me, sir. I've been sitting here most of the day and many people have walked by my bench but no one has bothered to stop and help me. I'm having a hard time right now and was hoping that you could lend me some change so that I could get a bite to eat."

Feeling guilty, the young man dug into his pocket for a dollar, walked over to the woman, and handed it to her. Looking somewhat surprised, the homeless woman smiled at him and said, "Thank you, sir."

As the young entrepreneur started to walk away, the woman said to him in a soft pleasant voice, "Sir, I have one more request to ask of you. I live on the streets and people who see me treat me like I'm a walking disease. If you don't mind, would you please give me a hug. It has been such a long time since someone hugged me I've forgotten how it feels."

Realizing what was happening, the man walked over and with no apprehension hugged the homeless woman. As their eyes met, they both flashed a smile at one another as if to say, "I understand." With no further delay, the woman gathered her shopping bags, the young man picked up his briefcase, and they both went their separate ways. As the man walked away, he suddenly had a much better understanding that in spite of all the daily problems he faced, there was still much to be thankful for. Let's move on.

## Living "Lite"

One more time. Keep your living expenses low so that you have enough free cash to engage in deals. Remember, you can move a lot more quickly and travel further if you travel "lite." Enough said on this matter.

## Revisiting Your Values

Ralph Waldo Emerson once said, "Nothing gives so much direction to a person's life as a sound set of principles." It is almost impossible to achieve greatness without a set of principles or values. Values are what make us what we are. With the exception of our souls, it is the only thing that separates man from the animal kingdom. Verbalizing one's values is significantly easier than writing them down. However, for your values to become integrated into your inner self and for them to control your destiny, they have to be written down. Once they're written down, they need to be reviewed on a daily basis.

Your values are your rudder in the voyage that is your life. Without values, your life is rudderless, and you will be tossed to and fro on the rough seas of life. You will have no direction and no purpose. Imagine, waking up when you're 65 years old and coming to the realization that you have accomplished nothing and your life was a waste. I shudder at the thought. However, you have time now to establish these values and let them guide you.

Values mean different things to different people. Values used in this analysis are those principles that guide our thoughts and actions. Each person's value set is different from another. However, there are usually common categories of values that everyone has a set of values in. These categories may include:

· Spiritual
· Physical
· Financial
· Emotional
· Intellectual

To give you an example of a set of values, the following outlines the value set used to guide me and my family:

·I love God and try to emulate the life-style of His son Jesus Christ.
·I love my family and provide for them financially, emotionally, and physically.
·I am financially independent and am not dependent on anyone for my financial well being.
· I seek excellence in all that I do or am associated with.
· I am physically healthy and strong.

Believe it or not, your values will dictate what type of business you will ultimately get into. For example, let's look at the drug business (I'm not talking about prescription drugs.) If you remove the emotional and ethical issues of this business, what you're left with is one of the most lucrative business opportunities of the 20th century. What other business allows you to make $100,000 a day profit with no major overhead, no research and development costs, a manageable payroll commitment, no unions, and no government taxation and restrictions? What other business can you invest in that doesn't require any education or special skills and that will allow you to live like the movie stars on television - big house, expensive car, and exotic vacations? Now be honest, if I told you about this business opportunity without telling you what the business was, how many of you would jump at the chance to become a part of this venture? Every single one of you would.

There are other businesses that may be very lucrative but conflicts with your value structure. I recall one incident when one of subjects of this book was approached by an old buddy of his who wanted the entrepreneur to become his partner and help him buy a local liquor store in New York. Business was very good at that particular store. The store was located on the corner of the one of the poorest and crime-plagued neighborhoods in the city. It was an African-American neighborhood, and market research revealed that the bar was always crowded. Even though the business was exceptionally profitable, the entrepreneur chose not to invest because his value system wouldn't allow him in good conscience to sell poison to the people of his community.

The only reason more of us don't enter into these money-making business opportunities is because of our value systems. Our values tells us that these types of businesses are evil, short-lived, and corrupt. Our values dictate to us that life is valuable, and we resist participating in any venture that serves to shorten it or cause it to go in the wrong direction. See how our values direct our actions?

## *Establishing Proper Goals*

It never ceases to amaze me how few people have goals. Most people wander through life aimlessly with no idea of a destination. What a tragedy. God only gives us a few hours per day, a few days per week, a couple weeks per year, and only a handful of years in a lifetime. Once that time has passed, there is no way that you can ever get it back. It is lost forever. The best way to use this time is to establish goals and commit yourself to them.

Like your values, your goals must also be visualized and ultimately written down and possess a time dimension. Your goals must be believable, clearly defined, and take on a life of their own. As with our values, we must learn to set goals for every aspect of our lives, particularly when you're working on starting your business. Set goals for **when** you'll identify what business you want to go into, how much money you want to make, how much growth you expect to realize, who your partners will be, and when and how you want to exit the business.

When setting your goals for business, it is suggested that you break down your goals into two major categories:

· Tactical Goals
· Strategic Goals

Strategic goals help you to set long-term goals and direction.

Tactical goals help you to achieve intermediate and short-term or daily direction. Both sets of goals are critical to the overall accomplishment of your dreams.

## *Establishing a Proper Set of Rules*

Early in this study, I started to realize that many of the business owners interviewed stressed the importance of having fun with your business. My entrepreneurship professor, Dr. James Brian Quinn, after discussing the details of writing business plans and obtaining financing for start-ups, often stressed the importance of having fun while building and running your business. He made us understand that once you commit yourself to the business, it would in essence become your life. Obviously, if you're not having fun, you'll ultimately hate what you're doing and your creativity will suffer.

One way to ensure that you have fun while starting your business is to compile a set of rules that will be used to gauge what types of businesses you can and cannot get into. For example, if one of your rules states that your business must not come into conflict with the laws of God, then you would not want a business that requires you to operate on the Sabbath. If one of your rules states that your future business must not proliferate the exploitation of poor and minority people, then you might think twice about being a slumlord or owning a corner liquor store. Whatever your values are in life, set up a governing set of rules and measure all business opportunities against them. Yes, you may end up discarding some financially attractive opportunities, but you will be at peace with yourself and with God.

## *Developing a Personal Mission Statement*

A mission statement simply articulates a specific task or set of tasks you are dedicated to carry out. In other words, after you've exerted tremendous effort and consumed significant resources, what things must be in place before you say, "My mission has been accomplished"? The mission statement should be concise and crisp and should clearly delineate what it is that you're out to get. It should also be worded in such a way that it can be easily memorized.

You may find that your mission statement is dynamic in nature, changing constantly to reflect variations in your desires and means. Don't be alarmed by all of this. It is normal. Be willing to make the appropriate changes and keep the statement fresh in your mind. If you're working with a group of people, the mission statement should reflect the wants and needs of everyone involved.

## Performing S.W.O.T. Analysis of Self and Team

Those of you who recently completed business school will probably recall the famous S.W.O.T. analysis, i.e., Strengths, Weaknesses, Opportunities, and Threats. This method is an excellent tool to evaluate the competitive position of any business. Although the majority of the business owners analyzed did not learn the formal technique for performing the S.W.O.T. analysis, most went through a similar exercise that provided the same results. Let's discuss this a little further.

Although mainly used to evaluate the competitive stance of businesses, S.W.O.T. is also a valuable exercise for the "would-be entrepreneur" when determining what kind of business to start.

To begin this analysis, look at yourself or your group very closely and assess honestly the strengths of that group. Do you have a strong technical background? Do you have the patent rights to a new technologically advanced product that no one else has? Are you well respected in your chosen profession and consequently have many contacts that may prove beneficial in helping support your business? Maybe you're young, talented, aggressive, hungry, eager, and persistent. These are all strengths that can be capitalized on during the early stages of business formation. Identify these strengths, whatever they are, and write them down.

For most people, articulating their strengths is much easier than identifying their weaknesses. No matter how difficult, understanding one's weaknesses is critical. Just as you did with strengths, look within yourself and/or your group of business partners and pick out the weaknesses that exist.

The first entry on most of your lists will probably be lack of funds. Right? Maybe you're young, inexperienced, and lack direction. Are your business partners in close proximity to you or are they scattered around the country? Are you in a business environment that is already saturated with small businesses and consequently competition is fierce? What about skill set? Does your group possess all of the business skills (e.g., accounting, business law, marketing) necessary to acquire and manage a growing business successfully?

These are just a few examples of what might be considered weaknesses in a typical S.W.O.T. analysis of yourself. Keep in mind that strengths and weaknesses are all relative. What may be considered strengths by one group or person may be perceived to be weaknesses by another.

Having gone through the exercise of identifying your strengths and weaknesses, now study them for a while. You now want to look at what opportunities exist that are consistent with those strengths and weaknesses. For example, if you have a great mechanical aptitude and love to tinker with automobiles, maybe an opportunity might be to open a neighborhood gas station that provides auto maintenance. If you're the best cook in the neighborhood and you enjoy cooking, turn that love into an enterprise and open up a neighborhood restaurant.

Let's assume that you're an engineer, have worked in corporate America for a few years, and have had numerous engineering assignments. You enjoy being an engineer, especially working in a manufacturing environment. You might want to look into the opportunity of owning a small manufacturing firm. But wait a

**Exhibit 3-2. S.W.O.T. Chart**

| STRENGTHS | WEAKNESSES | OPPORTUNITIES | THREATS |
|-----------|------------|---------------|---------|
|           |            |               |         |
|           |            |               |         |

minute. Under weaknesses you listed the fact that you're short on funds. Manufacturing businesses are highly capital-intensive enterprises, requiring in some cases a minimum of a couple $100 thousand dollars to get started and probably more. Consequently, strengths, weaknesses, and opportunity don't quite match.

Don't despair. This analysis doesn't mean that you can't start that manufacturing business. What the S.W.O.T. analysis reveals is that for you to realize this opportunity, you have to put a plan in place to overcome that weakness, in this case, the weakness of having no significant funds. One good thing about this exercise is that it keeps you honest!

Identifying opportunities may be the most difficult component of getting into business. Consequently, Step 9 will explore this topic in a little more detail.

The last step in the analysis is to identify the threats that would prevent you from realizing any of the opportunities that evenly match your documented strengths and weaknesses. Some examples of typical threats include rising interest rates, changing national economy, dynamic market conditions, uncommitted group members, and government restrictions. Look at potential threats very carefully and document them. Study carefully how these situations could affect your game plan for getting into business and surviving the early years.

When you've completed this analysis, you may end up with a chart that is organized like Exhibit 3-2.

## Identifying the Right Opportunity

As mentioned earlier, identifying the right opportunity is undoubtedly one of the most difficult aspects of getting into business. For this reason, more effort will be devoted to better understanding this requirement.

In a basic sense, opportunity is any good or service that satisfies a need so vital that people are willing to pay for that good or service.

**Exhibit 3-3. States With Largest African-American Populations**

| 1990 African-American Population Ranking | State | 1990 African-American Population |
|---|---|---|
| 1 | New York | 2,859,055 |
| 2 | California | 2,208,801 |
| 3 | Texas | 2,021,632 |
| 4 | Florida | 1,759,534 |
| 5 | Georgia | 1,746,565 |
| 6 | Illinois | 1,694,273 |
| 7 | North Carolina | 1,456,323 |
| 8 | Louisiana | 1,299,281 |
| 9 | Michigan | 1,291,706 |
| 10 | Maryland | 1,189,899 |

Source: U.S. Census Bureau

Identifying where those needs are is not extremely difficult. As with most academic exercises, identifying needs is done more easily on an aggregate sense. For example, study the national and international environment and pinpoint which industries are booming and which are dying. A day doesn't go by that you don't hear about the booming service industries and the dying manufacturing industry in our society. Be careful. Although these statistics may reveal the market dynamics of the overall society, there may still exist some gold nuggets there for minority businesspeople. This would be particularly true for industries in which minorities have been traditionally under-represented.

Speaking of identifying a niche in a seemingly dying industry, David Bing quickly comes to mind. You probably remember Dave when he played in the National Basketball Association. He electrified audiences with his outstanding basketball skills, relentless defense, and admirable team concept of the game. However, I'm sure that few people realize that after Dave's NBA career, he started a small business in the steel industry. Based on industry statistics, this market was quickly being taken over by foreign steel manufacturers. It appeared that American steel companies were unable to complete. Yet, Dave has successfully carved out a niche in this very industry and is doing well. Bing Steel ranked as one of the ten largest black businesses in *Black Enterprise* magazine's 1992 ranking.

## Starting the "Sifting Process"

Not only should you be interested in which industries are booming but also where the boom is taking place. Pay especially close attention to which areas are providing opportunities to minority businesspeople. It is probably a good bet that those cities with black mayors will at least provide minorities a fair chance at winning lucrative city contracts. Also, areas that have a high concentration of black and other minority people may provide a strong foundation on which to build a business. If nothing else, it may provide you a sense of comfort during the early days of your venture. For your information, Exhibits 3-3 and 3-4 lists some of the states that have sizeable African-American populations.

Beyond the state level, most cities, along with the federal agencies, have begun aggressive set-aside programs to assist minorities and women in starting businesses. Most cities have a list of goods and services that they contract out to small businesses. Obtain a copy of your city's list, go through it, and pick out goods and services that you might provide. Also, get a copy of your city's minority set-aside law, study it, and make sure that you understand how it works.

One word of caution. In choosing locations, don't get caught up in what I call "chocolate city magnetism." As was mentioned, it's a good assumption that in a city where minorities are in the majority, there exists a ripe environment for minority businesspeople. However, there are many places where there are relatively few minorities, yet there exist ripe opportunities for the taking. Many of these cities

**Exhibit 3-4. Top Ten States With Largest Percentage of African-Americans**

| Ranking Of African-Americans As A Percentage Of Total Population | State | Percent Of State Population (1990) |
|:---:|:---:|:---:|
| 1 | District of Columbia | 65.8 |
| 2 | Mississippi | 35.6 |
| 3 | Louisiana | 30.8 |
| 4 | South Carolina | 29.8 |
| 5 | Georgia | 27.0 |
| 6 | Alabama | 25.3 |
| 7 | Maryland | 24.9 |
| 8 | North Carolina | 22.0 |
| 9 | Virginia | 18.8 |
| 10 | Delaware | 16.9 |

are desirous of having minority businesses and can help make your investment there worthwhile. Therefore, don't write-off these places too quickly.

## Studying Your Daily Routine

Not a day goes by that you don't wish for a product or service that is not being provided. Or maybe the product or service that is available doesn't meet your quality expectations. I recall one day during my bill-paying depressions when I wished there was some company somewhere that would assume the task of paying my monthly bills (I thought of starting a business around this concept but I deplore paying bills too much). A few months later, I was flipping through *PC Magazine* and came across an ad of a new company

## Exhibit 3-5. The "Sifting Process"

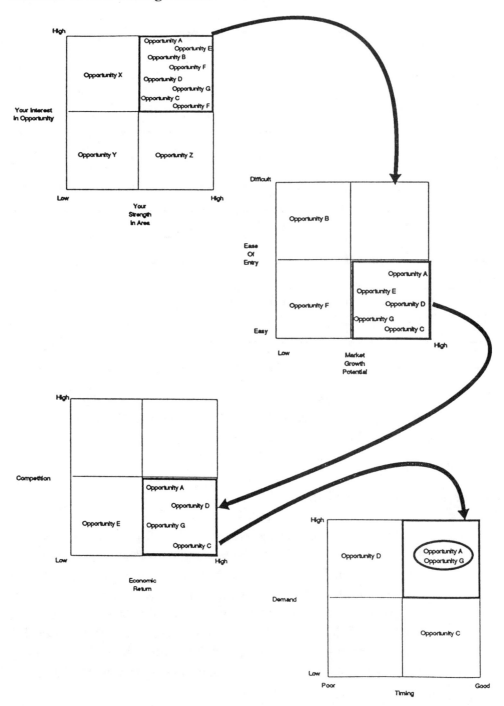

whose concept was to electronically pay bills for people. Some one had stolen my idea!

How many of you have had a great idea only to find later that someone else had the same idea? That person however, had the vision and guts to turn that idea into a lucrative business. Look around the minority community and see what goods or services people need. In most situations the majority businesses ignore the minority community completely when searching for a business location. When you go to a minority-supported shopping center, what types of stores would you like to see that are not presently there? The answers to these questions can provide some very good business opportunities.

It's amazing to me how many business opportunities the African-American community has actually created, but failed to capitalize on. Like most of you, house parties were very big when I was growing up. It seemed like every Friday or Saturday someone would host a party and everyone would "get nice" first and then enjoy the party. This was a time when we would show each other the latest dances and occasionally try to sneak a kiss with your favorite girl (or boy). Usually, the host would replace the normal light with a red or "psychedelic" light to provide the proper ambiance.

While we were jamming the night away, some white guy, 3,000 miles away was creating a movie about an Italian kid who was to become the king of urban dancing. They even had the audacity to go to Australia to hire a white band to produce the sound-track for this musical movie. You've probably guessed by now who those people were. The Italian kid was John Travolta, the group from Australia was the Bee Gees, the movie was *Saturday Night Fever*, and the missed business opportunity was the creation and economic exploitation of the disco craze.

To make matters worst, the music used was typically created by African-Americans and their dances were just an imitation of what they saw on "Soul Train." As a matter of fact, it was a black man from the Soul Train family who spent weeks showing John Travolta how to dance like a brother! Although discos are no longer as popular as they were during the 1970s, mainstream America made fortunes from this business concept. How many blacks do you know who owned discos or made any significant money off of this short-lived craze? Very few.

### What About Where You Work?

Interestingly enough, the majority of the entrepreneurs ventured into businesses in which they had some prior experience. Wherever you work, keep your eyes open for what goods and services these organizations are spending money on. Observe the small businesses that are currently filling these needs and find out what aspects of these businesses your company is unhappy with. Understand these weaknesses. If you ran that business, could you do a better job?

Even if you find that there is a large number of small businesses providing similar products, how many of them are minority owned and run? There may still be opportunities in that environment for minority businesspeople.

### Start the Sifting

Once you've compiled a healthy list of opportunities, start sifting through them using the model shown in Exhibit 3-5. This model will allow you to screen opportunities quickly and visually. Evaluate each option based on the criteria shown on each of the axes. Place the opportunities in one of the four quadrants, collect the ones from the most favorable quadrant, and then run them through the next matrix. By the time you're finished the fourth matrix, you should have narrowed down your choices.

## Compiling the Opportunity List and Comparing It to Your Values and Your S.W.O.T. List

You've just been provided with a couple of ideas about how you can begin to generate your opportunity list. Our society is rich with ways in which you can identify good business opportunities: your daily routine, dynamic market conditions, your job, the Sunday newspaper, and your friends and neighbors. By now, your list should be quite extensive, but the more difficult part becomes prioritizing these opportunities and then comparing these opportunities to your personal S.W.O.T. analysis and determining if these opportunities allow you to accomplish your mission.

On a single sheet of paper or in your log book, begin to write down the business opportunities you've uncovered. The business ideas should now be prioritized based upon the following:

· Probability of success
· Growth potential
· Ease of start-up
· Amount of personal satisfaction
· Degree of consistency with values, mission, and S.W.O.T. analysis

Any idea that conflicts with the results of your S.W.O.T. analysis or mission statement should either be disregarded or moved to the bottom of the list. If you find that most of the ideas generated by your analysis do conflict with your values, mission, or S.W.O.T. analysis, you need to re-evaluate your purpose for wanting to go into business and make sure that all of the important pieces are present.

Once the ideas have been prioritized, take the first three ideas on the list and begin a more thorough analysis of those ideas. This can be done by continuing with market research in the library and talking to business owners who are already in similar businesses. Learn as much as you can about start-up costs, marketing strategies, tricks of the trade, and other important elements of that business.

If after more detailed review you find that the three options chosen hold no promise, then it is appropriate to move down the list to the next set of ideas (3 to a set) and explore these in more detail. If you've been honest and diligent in developing your mission statement and in performing your S.W.O.T. analysis of yourself and if you've carefully surveyed your environment for business opportunities, you will at some point find a match.

With your freshly generated idea now burning inside your heart and mind, run with it until you're out of breath. You'll need to begin writing your business plan and seeking the appropriate counseling. Although this analysis does not discuss the specifics of writing business plans and identifying financial resources, there are a number of well-written publications that discuss these topics in great detail.

## *Executing, Executing, Executing*

This step needs no explanation!

## Walter W. Hill, Jr., and Eillen E. Dorsey
## ECS Technologies
## Baltimore, Maryland

From the front window of the ECS offices, the bright new headquarters of the National Association for the Advancement of Colored People (NAACP) can be seen clearly. The city of Baltimore, with its African-American mayor - Kurt Schmoke - and its sizeable African-American population, has become a mecca for minority-based organizations who want to relocate to an area that is economically attractive and yet sensitive to the issues that confront the African-American community.

So it was fitting that ECS sat there, a hub of activity, under the shadow of the nation's oldest civil rights organizations. As I waited in the small, but nicely furnished offices of ECS for Walter Hill, Jr., one of the company's two founders, I wondered how it was possible for he and his partner, Eillen, to generate so much business from such a small office with only a handful of employees? As I soon learned, this dynamic duo had a knack for taking very little and turning it into something sizeable and valuable, through courage, creativity, and hard work. This ability to leverage meager resources into long-term gain served both people well as they cut their business teeth in corporate America and prepared themselves to move into the entrepreneurial ranks.

## *Learning from Corporate Experience*

Walter, better known as Billy to his family and friends, decided after college that he wanted to work for the largest private employer in the state of Maryland - Westinghouse Electric Corporation. Although he was overqualified for the position, he accepted a job as a buyer. Billy did not find the job to be especially difficult. As a result, he was able to get quick promotions and additional responsibility at a young age. For his first three years, his role was an entry level buyer. Later, he was promoted to a contract specialist position and excelled at this role for two years before he was moved to the next level as a senior subcontract specialist.

Having obtained this level by the time he was twenty-six years old, Billy had set a new precedent and had surpassed the majority of his peers. Even though Hill had shown that he had the skills, business savvy, and boldness to be successful at Westinghouse, there were still many people who were in positions of power who just weren't ready for a twenty-six year old hot shot manager who happened to be black.

Eillen, Billy's partner, was a salesperson for a company that distributed electronic components, was facing similar issues, and was poised to make the conversion from employee to employer at the same time Hill was. No stranger to hard work and perseverance, Eillen was raised in Harford County, Maryland, the youngest of eight children. Her parents, Walter and Louvina Blackston, although members of a generation of black Americans that was harshly oppressed legally and systematically, taught their eight children that if they dreamed long and hard enough and if they were committed to their dream, they could defeat racism and ignorance and turn their dreams into reality. This message rung loud and clear in Eillen's mind as she matured into a young woman and began making her mark in the business world. As she and Hill began to forge their business alliance, Eillen's business experience in the electronic components business proved invaluable in allowing ECS to get off to a strong start. Eillen fondly recalls the genius of ECS:

> Walter and I developed a personal friendship during the early 1970s. During this period, we were both encouraged by the number of minority firms that were sprouting up in the Baltimore-Washington corridor to take advantage of the lucrative contracting opportunities with the Federal Government. To our chagrin, we later learned that some of these firms were only "fronts" for majority firms. Walter and I both felt that if we made the commitment to go into business that we would become a "true" minority firm and dedicate ourselves to providing high-quality products at competitive prices.

Billy's commitment to starting a business peaked at about the same time that Eillen's did. Although still an employee of Westinghouse, Billy recalls with a mischievous grin:

> I guess I was consciously planning my exit because I realized that every corporation producing machinery of any type had to buy some electrical components to complete the manufacturing of the product. I knew that many of these businesses were interested in doing business with minority firms and felt that an opportunity existed for Eillen and me to help meet this need.

Hill quit with the promise from his boss that if he failed he could always get his old job back. He would later say, "I realized what was being procured out there and figured let the best salesman win."

## The Birth of ECS

Although ECS Technologies has made the strategic transition

from electrical components distributor to computer systems integrator, the company's original charter was to sell electronic components to major manufacturers of electronic-based products from stereo systems to intricate department of defense radar systems. While a buyer at Westinghouse, Billy had made the extra effort to develop his potential client base. Eillen also went to great measures to solidify her customer base prior to her departure from Technico, and between the two of them, they wisely built the backlog of their business before opening the doors of ECS. Billy adds:

> Eillen was working for a similar company which was "fronting" a minority company and she had grown tired of that company. The managers asked Eillen if she were interested in buying the company. She called me because we had an excellent business relationship and had become friends. We decided not to buy that company, but to start our own. We got our first order in June and didn't open our doors until July. We had started networking way before that time.

In 1979, with orders from Westinghouse, Bendix, and Boeing, the company started out at a brisk pace. Hill thinks it was easier for his company initially because the business they chose to start was familiar to them. Both he and his partner had experience in purchasing. They kept in close contact with their clients and built a strong foundation upon which future business opportunities could be developed.

## Growth

ECS opened their one office suite in Towson, Maryland. Very quickly they realized they needed more space and added on three additional suites until they decided to move to a new location. They needed docking facilities and relocated to a larger office with docking space. The company thinks that the new location was exceptional because it put them in closer contact with some of their largest customers.

When Billy and Eillen first started out, they had white accountants and white lawyers. Now that they are doing well, they have black accountants and black lawyers who understand the plight of minorities. Billy feels that minority professionals can usually add more value to situations because of their sensitivity to the challenges facing minority business people.

Buoyed by their earlier marketing successes, Billy and Eillen did something that is rarely accomplished in any new venture - they made a profit the first month! The year remained profitable for them as they paid themselves $15,000 a piece and ended up spending only $500/month for the small office space they occupied. Because both of their spouses worked full-time jobs, Billy and his partner were able to divert more of the company's funds into new marketing efforts, hiring additional employees and acquiring more office and warehouse space.

## Living for the City

Hill's humble beginnings would have provided little warning of his future success. Born into a lower middle-class family in south Baltimore, he emerged from an environment that had little material wealth, but actively encouraged hard work. Billy, however, was never content with having little and always wanted more. "I wanted; that's what drove me," he says.

Hill's parents were proud people. His father worked for the Federal Government for most of his career, and his mom was a custodian in the Baltimore City Public Schools. Billy has appreciated the importance of working ever since his elementary school days. Ironically, it even appeared that work might prevent him from attending college, but when he presented this option to his father, it was sternly rebuked. As Hill later added, "My father told me okay, don't go to college, but don't ever ask me for anything else in life. I applied to college right away."

At his father's urging, Billy attended the University of Maryland at College Park. Although extremely bright, he had a difficult time academically while in college. Despite the difficulties, Hill continued with his studies and ultimately graduated from the University of Maryland in 1973. While still at Westinghouse, Hill earned his Master's of Business Administration from Morgan State University in 1976 before he started the business. He liked going to a black university and feels he not only obtained good business contacts, but a great education as well.

Both Billy and Eillen maintain close ties with the contacts they generated during their matriculation at colleges in Maryland. Eillen attended Catonsville and Essex Community Colleges, and Billy studied at the University of Maryland, and Morgan State University. The team amassed a network of cohorts that reaches from the marble halls of corporate America to the gray corridors of the local municipal governments. They both stress the importance of leveraging relationships in building one's business.

## *No Mistakes*

Eillen and Billy both echo a common complaint made by black businesspeople across America, i.e., black businesspeople are not allowed to make mistakes. One mistake with the wrong company and the wrong buyer at the wrong time could ruin a company's chances for generating any further business at that account. That same mistake could ruin your chances for contracts within that entire city or geographical area. One way to rectify this situation is to have more minority buyers. People like to buy from people they know and can relate to. Billy feels there aren't many black buyers currently and is emphatic about the importance of having more minority buyers in the major corporations. Billy adds:

If there were more minority buyers in corporate America, there would be a much greater probability that minority businesses would get their fair share of the pie. Black buyers can relate to black businesspeople and I believe there is a sincere desire to help one another. Black businesspeople have to first get in the company, then give them a good price, deliver on time, and minimize errors. You can't afford to make mistakes. It's not acceptable. White contractors mess up, but we don't have that luxury.

## *Financing*

Due to the nature of their business, Hill and his partner required very little up front capitalization to get their distributor business off of the ground. Both Hill and his partner initially contributed $5,000 to ECS's capitalization. The additional funds came from a $35,000 loan they secured by using the equity in both their homes as collateral. The fact that they had already won a contract also helped with the acquisition of the loan. This situation was quite a rarity for a small start-up minority business.

In 1982, responding to additional cash requirements caused by increased business, ECS went out to secure additional financing. Because each of the partners had enough personal collateral, the banks were a lot more flexible than they would have been and ended up giving them a $200,000 line of credit.

Despite these early successes, Billy is quick to point out that his company has had its share of financial difficulties. Overconfident by the company's early successes, Billy and Eillen began to aggressively expand their sales force in anticipation of aggressive sales growth. Unfortunately, about the time they made these expenditures, they experienced a dramatic drop in orders and business activity in general. Although this was a difficult time, it taught Billy and his partner one important lesson:

One of the things you need to do is borrow money when you don't need it. If you establish these financial channels before you actually need them, then the money will be available to you when you do need cash. It's a classic lesson I learned. I know that blacks have difficulty getting loans and the one thing that would help is if they had black friends at the bank. We need to be able to effectively network if we are to get a decent business loan. Unfortunately, blacks don't want to be loan officers. They want to be vice-presidents instead. The result is that we don't have many friends in those key financial positions.

## Difficulties

Hill concedes that his business has not been that tough on him, but occasionally he looks at his corporate friends, who still work nine-to-five days, who still go on nice, regularly scheduled vacations, who work regular hours with an almost guaranteed paycheck and wishes he were back there. Many of these people, he suggests, take these benefits for granted. He often reminds his peers:

I've got to be the accountant, check with the lawyer, be customer service, and work overtime - no time off, no vacation. My partner and I split up the responsibilities though and she usually does what she likes and I do what I like. Luckily, our skill sets complement one another. If I had to do it again though, I would.

## Representing Minorities

Even with the difficulties, Hill concedes he would never quit. It is clear that Billy gets a "high" from the work that he does. He approaches his business responsibilities with a missionary zeal:

I represent black Americans and there just aren't many of us out there working in our own businesses and succeeding. I have to be there for them, be a role model. Besides, the challenge is important to me as well.

Eillen shares Billy's zest for the business and the new direction in which ECS is moving. During 1992, ECS began a strategic initiative to diversify its business even more by building new business units. The company is aggressively building its technical and marketing staff and is well positioned to capitalize on the fast growing areas of LAN/WAN design and implementation, UNIX support services, telecommunications, systems integration, and other computer services. With an air of quiet confidence, Eillen Dorsey, the president of ECS, summarizes the firm's strategy for the future:

> We will always give the customer the best possible service that we can - consistently. While we strive to grow, we are also taking measures to ensure that the growth is controlled. As we leverage ourselves through various teaming arrangements with other firms, we will work diligently to keep communication lines open between our business partners and our employees. The life blood of our business is our employees, and we must constantly remind them that they have a major impact on the success of our business. They must always strive to conduct themselves professionally and commit themselves to excellence.

Excellence is what got ECS to this point and excellence is what will take them to the next level of success.

## Jim McLean
## Four Seas and Seven Winds Travel Agency
## Baltimore, Maryland

On a warm summer afternoon in Baltimore, Maryland, Jim McLean rushes from office to office in his modern downtown headquarters. The slim, youthful-looking CEO of one of the largest African-American owned travel agencies is engaged in the challenging task of concurrently running his company and his wife's campaign bid to become the next president of Baltimore's City

Council. Having addressed a multitude of issues and questions from his employees and having sent the campaign organization out to yet another day's canvassing, Jim eventually settles down in his well-decorated, but small office to discuss his business, his dreams, and himself.

Somehow the office seems overly modest for a man of Jim's wealth and stature. As he settles back in his chair and gazes out the window into the downtown inner harbor area, he reveals almost in a trancelike state, "You know, America is spelled B-u-s-i-n-e-s-s."

## America is Spelled B-u-s-i-n-e-s-s

Jim McLean's capacity for hard work was bred in him as a young boy growing up in Durham, North Carolina. Before he reached the age of three, his father died leaving him in the competent hands of his grandmother. Jim's grandmother, although just a plain woman to most, was a special person to Jim. She was a plain old Methodist woman who made a living ironing and cleaning for other people.

Although she never caught the entrepreneurial bug, luckily, Jim did. Since the age of seven, Jim has been hard at work, either shining shoes or selling newspapers. No stranger to education, he graduated from Loyola College in Baltimore, Maryland, with a degree in administration and accounting and actually stumbled into the business world by accident. Jim says:

> I always knew America was spelled B-u-s-i-n-e-s-s. If you live in America and don't see that's what it's all about, then you're stupid. Anyone that isn't in business for himself is un-American.

## Early Business Ethic

Jim learned at a very young age that if you have more than one person doing the same thing at the same time you could make money. As a young entrepreneur, Jim often collected soda bottles by paying other kids one cent per bottle when he could get two cents per bottle at the general store. That way he could get the little kids who couldn't cross the street to sell him their bottles and he'd end up making a one cent profit on each bottle. Jim's thoughts were always the same:

I just always thought that the more people you had doing something the more productive you were. I remember getting a prize in elementary school for saying this. No one person outthinks two, no two outthinks three, and no three outthinks four. I feel the same way about working.

## Loyola College

Jim came to Baltimore in 1953 to attend Morgan State University and discovered that he had won a small scholarship to North Carolina A&T State University. Since A&T offered money, Jim decided to attend A&T for one semester. Unfortunately, the money quickly ran out and he was forced to return to Baltimore to attend Loyola College. From Loyola, Jim went into the military and was stationed at Fort Holabird, headquarters for Army Intelligence. He was transferred to the Air Force with the help of a local congressman.

## Too Smart and Not Educated Enough

Jim was the first college graduate in his family. He recalls:

My grandmother said that someone should finish college in our family, and I thought that was the least I could do for her. I sometimes think that the less college you have in business, the more successful you are anyway. The sophistication of business is the reason to go to college - but I don't think it's absolutely necessary to be successful. Eight of the ten most successful businessmen in this city haven't been inside a college - well, maybe just to get an award.

## *Career Beginnings*

After the military, Jim accepted a job at the local post office in the cost analysis area. He later joined the Federal Government, and was responsible for the government payroll that covered all federal employees in the Philadelphia region, which included Pennsylvania, Baltimore, West Virginia, Virginia, and New Jersey. When Jim's division transferred to Atlanta, he decided to work for Seagram's, in the Sales and Marketing Department. During Jim's twelve years at Seagram's he was promoted to various positions including National Branch Manager with National Accounts. Later, Seagram's transferred him to New York, and there he spent twelve years.

It was during his tenure at Seagram's that Jim's wife asked him why he wouldn't go into business. The question was a logical one too. Jim had been in the record business and had been successful at opening a chain of record shops, which he later sold. Jim also remembered telling his wife that once you're in business for yourself, you'll always want to be in business for yourself. Jim theorizes that regardless of who you work for, you have a clock to punch. You have the physical clock you punch as a blue collar worker, the clock that says you'll make the quotas; and then when you work for yourself - the twenty-four hour clock.

## *Twenty-Four Hour Clock*

Jim's life-style is quite compatible with the twenty-four hour clock because it relieves him of the pressure of deciding what to do with his time:

When you work for someone else, you've got to worry about when you're going to play golf because you've got all this extra time on your hands. If you work in your business, you'll want to put that energy into something else. You can build more locations, you can build more profits, you can hire more people, etc.

Jim believes that a lot of people have hobbies and reach a plateau in their lives where they don't want to do anything else and retirement becomes their choice. Jim commented that a man might play golf 12 hours a week because he doesn't want to work 12 hours a week. He may feel like that's a personal satisfaction and that's great. However, when you want to accomplish something, you can't be two places at the same time. As a small business person, that's a luxury you can't afford:

I'd been in business a long time, so I said to myself, 'I'll retire. Jim won't work for a while.' I sold the business (record business) to Record Racks, and decided that I was not going to work until I'd spent every penny of that money. I always wanted to have enough money so that if I chose to take off for a few years, I wouldn't have to worry about how to make ends meet. We took off for five years, just took it easy, and traveled.

After his travels, Jim had $50,000 left. At this point, he and his wife began to think about investing some of the money into starting a business. They initially considered opening a dress shop, a service station, and even a travel agency. They eventually settled on starting a travel agency. Jim knew that in order for one to be successful, he had to go out there and learn the business from top to bottom. Jim and his wife decided that it made more sense for his wife to get some training in this business first. Therefore, he helped her get a part-time job at a travel agency.

After about one and one-half years at the firm, Jim's wife finally felt that she was ready to go it alone. At first, Jim had his doubts about her preparedness, but since he had promised her that he'd finance the venture, he went ahead and put the deal together. As it turned out Jim's wife became heavily involved in other projects and began losing interest in the day-to-day operations. It became apparent to Jim that he would need to play a more active role in the venture if it was to survive.

## The Loan

As the business started to expand, Jim began looking for additional funds to help fuel the growth. Jim remembered that he had set up a trust fund for his daughter a few years back and decided that these funds might be used for the business. To Jim's chagrin, the bank refused to let him remove the funds because the account was a trust account and could only be used by his daughter after she turned twenty one. The bank would allow Jim to take out a loan and use his daughter's trust as collateral. However, for every dollar that's used to start the business, Jim had to place an equal amount of shares in his daughter's trust account. This arrangement worked well. Jim said the advantage is he didn't have to pay taxes on the money and neither did his daughter as long as it went into a trust for her. He was able to use the money, didn't have to pay interest, and his daughter would get the returns if the company was successful. If not, she could fight him for the money at age 21.

After some accounting maneuvering, Jim took $15,000 from the trust account and used it to fund the company. By February of 1992, all of the corporate stock was purchased by Jim.

## First-Year Profits

Four Seasons and Seven Winds travel agency broke all kinds of records during its first year in business. Starting out in a little space in downtown Baltimore, they opened March 1 and did $780,000 in travel orders the first year. Jim figured that the average travel agency was only doing half a million, so comparatively speaking, his firm was doing outstandingly. With Jim's 40 part-time agents and the fact that they focused on the bus business, the next year his company really started booming. Helping to support Jim's success was the fact that it was a bicentennial year and Jim was involved with a bicentennial promotion for over two hundred schools.

That bicentennial year was also a time where automation in the travel industry was beginning to take hold. Jim was determined that his firm would take advantage of this new direction and requested that American Airlines and United Airlines tie him into their new reservation system in 1976. They responded with the stipulation that to automate him, his company would have to produce more than $100,000 of business per year with each of them. He ended up doing much more than that.

Jim's immediate client base consisted of members from the minority community. As the firm began to grow it also started going after more commercial accounts, such as IBM and Amoco Oil Company. Although these commercial accounts were still reluctant to let a minority firm service their headquarter locations, they were less reluctant to let Jim service most of their satellite offices.

Despite the resistance of many majority companies to do business with a minority travel agency, Jim's business has prospered beyond his expectations. Within a ten year time span, the business has grown from less than a million dollars in receipts to over $25 million. Jim suggests that the secret to successful growth in any service-oriented business is credibility and service:

> You must keep your word, Our company has a good reputation. When you do business with white companies (large companies), most of them think a small company can't handle the business. We were in business about three or four years and we picked up all of Black and Decker's travel. We'd say to a new company, 'You ever hear of Black & Decker? Well, we do business with them, over a million and a half worth.'

Until recently, Jim refused to pay himself a salary. Instead, he chose to plow back most of the firm's profits into the business. His conservative fiscal policy is one reason he was able to buy his current office building in the popular downtown area. He took what use to be an old storage warehouse and turned it into the corporate headquarters for his agency.

## Facing Prejudice Business Style

The first time Jim really needed outside capital was when he decided to go into the motor coach business. He opened a separate company and attempted to buy two or three motor coaches that were going for about $125,000 a piece. Initially, Jim went to a local bank (Mercantile Bank) to borrow $300,000. Jim felt he had a strong business case so he was surprised when they turned him down. The bank contended that the business return was too low. The loan officer felt that the commissions earned (9%) were too low and besides most small businesses like Jim's were susceptible to failure anyway. The guy was completely negative. Finally, having argued with this man for weeks, in disgust and anger, Jim gave up on the transaction and said, "The hell with it."

Jim shared the story of not getting another loan with a white contractor he knew. This time Jim was trying to buy a building (his corporate headquarters) in an up and coming area. The contractor suggested to Jim that he go to his bank, Central, which was a little bank uptown. Jim took his advice and called the loan officer that handled commercial real estate. That same afternoon the loan officer visited the building that Jim wanted to buy and concluded that if Jim put on a new roof and had a structural consultant check a crack that he detected in the wall, he would approve the loan for Jim to buy the building. Jim remarked, "This banker was astute enough to realize that the area in which I was buying was going to be big money one day and they (the bank) wanted to be a part of it."

Although he was happy to finally get the loan, he was still angry that his own bank, Mercantile, didn't want to do business with him.

In fact, he later transferred all of his money from Mercantile to Central. The president of the Mercantile Bank, who served on United Way's board with Jim, learned of his experience. After hearing the story, the president asked, "Why didn't you call me?"

Jim replied, "Why should I have to call you for $400,000 when I have a half a million dollars cash in your bank?"

He said, "You shouldn't," and got the point.

Jim believes that if banks are too prejudiced to make loans to minorities, then minorities should not do business with those banks. He later learned that Mercantile Bank was one of the most conservative and successful banks in the country and that their strict lending guidelines were applied to everyone and not just his business.

## What's Next?

Jim believes that his firm has reached its potential within the Baltimore market. The Baltimore market is not a major travel area, which explains why Jim has been aggressively expanding the business into other geographical areas. Currently, he is looking at an acquisition of another travel business, which would complement his current business. Jim is not completely devoted to the travel business though and continues to look at new business opportunities in other industries. As he puts it, "Everything is for sale, except my family, citizenship, and friends."

## The Secrets of Success

Although there have been ups and downs in Jim's business career, he feels good about his accomplishments. He states:

I'm the master of my own fate. As long as you use that thing on top of your shoulders, you will always be okay. Always assume the responsibility. Don't ever shift responsibility. Shift work, but not responsibility. When things happen and they go wrong or right, it's your responsibility. Don't blame. Be willing to accept the responsibility. The white community will learn you how to do. Not teach you, learn you. If you're disciplined enough to make the sacrifice and if you do it over and over again you'll be successful. You are director of your own fate. You can't believe that society is prejudiced against you, that's a given. Society is prejudiced. There are more bigots than liberals. Deal with the liberals. Go find them. What most of us fail to do is stay with it. When it starts working, we get away from basics. Plan your work and work your plan. Try to surround yourself with the best people to get it done. Black or white, friends or foe. It's who can get the job done.

Further, Jim adds that these times, like all times, are good times if you know what to do with them. He stresses that people who are serious should take advantage of every opportunity that comes their way. He reminds us that there were a lot of millionaires created during the Great Depression.

Jim still carries two business cards. One says President, and the other says Manager of a Corporate Division. There are people who have done business with him for years and still don't know that Jim owns the business. As long as they keep business coming his way, Jim probably won't mind that at all.

## Joyce Foreman
## Foreman Office Products
## Dallas, Texas

On the afternoon of November 22, 1963, President John F. Kennedy was brutally assassinated on the streets of downtown Dallas. Thirty years later, just the name Dallas brings back memories of my mother and father sitting in the living room of our home that fateful afternoon and crying, "They've killed the president, they've killed the president."

During a recent trip to Dallas, as I was tracing the route that President Kennedy's motorcade followed that day, I noticed that Foreman's Office Products was located very close to that infamous route. As I waited outside the front office of her store, I noticed a sleek, beige, Mercedes Benz roll to a stop in front of me. Out jumped Joyce Foreman, a young, slender black woman who looked like she was far too young to be the owner of such a business. Foreman Office Products is one of the few black-owned office products businesses in the city of Dallas. As she unlocked the door and entered the store, I was proud of what this young woman had accomplished, even though I hardly knew her.

## Beginnings

Joyce Foreman was born in Telma, Texas, but considers Dallas her home. A graduate of the Dallas Independent School District and Junior College, Joyce didn't finish her studies at the University of Texas at Dallas, citing frustrations at being a minority when there weren't many minorities. She felt that she stuck out like a sore thumb because she was one of the few African-Americans. At the time she attended college, Joyce was also working full-time, which added to her difficulties.

## Family

Growing up as an only child in a single-parent home, Joyce enjoyed a very close bond with her mother, a relationship that she feels gave her self-assurance. Her home provided a strong work ethic. Her mother told her never to give up and consequently, Joyce remained an honor roll student throughout her tenure at school. Families of black domestics are often perceived as poor, Joyce says, something that wasn't true in her family. Her mother worked two jobs to give her daughter all of the comforts she desired.

A naturally enterprising woman, Joyce's mother began her own business later in life, starting an organization to upgrade domestic workers, and they worked together to get the business going. Unfortunately, just at the time when the business received the necessary funding, Joyce's mother died and the dream was deferred.

## Purchasing Career

Joyce accepted her first job, as a file clerk at Zale Corporation, a Dallas-based corporation. After six weeks, she was promoted to the accounting department, doing bookkeeping. She was promoted again six months later to the position of assistant to the buyer in the jewelry division. As her reputation began to precede her, she was promoted to the construction division as a purchasing agent. She left the construction division and had several other jobs in the purchasing profession. Joyce stayed in the purchasing area, working for eight years for three different companies before deciding to venture out on her own.

## Career Turning Point

As the company started expanding, Joyce began to feel more insecure; particularly when a less qualified peer was promoted ahead of her. A power struggle ensued, she got frustrated, and decided to go into business for herself. After much consideration, and talking to friends and business colleagues, she decided to start a business in office products, of which she had some prior knowledge. While she put together a plan for her new business, she continued to work for Central and Southwest.

Joyce was familiar with office products (having purchased them), and she was also familiar with suppliers. Initially, she spent a long time talking with office product suppliers, doing research on what it would take to set up a company, and how to buy. She found that many of the companies were very receptive to her, some offering advice freely. It took about a year and a half for her to pull all of the things together. Even though Joyce had no experience writing a business plan, she pooled all of her resources, finished her business plan, and prepared to step out on her own.

## Loan Rejection

Joyce initially took her idea to the bank that she had done business with for years and requested a $50,000 loan. Joyce was familiar with the loan officer at the bank, but he was promoted and her loan application was assigned to a new college graduate. Needless to say, they were not willing to take a chance on a young black woman with big dreams. She also felt that the loan officer was prejudiced. Joyce left the bank feeling that if a banker likes you personally, the loan will go through. The bank listed the reason for rejection was her lack of a track record. Joyce doubted that was the real reason because when she applied for a small auto loan it was also rejected, even though she had enough collateral in the bank to cover the debt.

Later, in 1984, when the business became more successful, Joyce was angry to find certain banks "courting" her, asking her to move her funds to their bank. She feels that banks want to ride on a business's coattails only when it is successful and are often unwilling to take a chance on a young business that shows some promise.

## Start-up Costs

Frustrated and needing the loan money, Joyce called her real-estate agent and told her she wanted to sell her home. The agent advised her not to do this, but Joyce went ahead anyway and sold her home, shocking everyone who knew her. The proceeds from the house were used as start-up capital for Foreman Office Products. She admits at first this idea concerned her, but when she began to think of herself as a first generation black business owner she felt this was the least that she could do. She knew she had to be creative. If lending institutions aren't going to help you, she thought, then help yourself. You must have plans B,C,D, and E available and ready. She was disappointed that she could not get funding from a lending institution, but she also believed that even if they made a loan, it probably would not have been in the amount she actually needed anyway. She explains:

> The system is not set up for blacks to go into business and be successful. The system is set up for blacks to fail. Even if you do get a loan, most of the time you're undercapitalized anyway. That's why it takes minority businesses so long to grow, because they don't have the proper amount of working capital.

Later that year when Joyce went into business, she too was undercapitalized. She admits that she was scared to death. She had learned from her mother that if she did the best she could, somehow things would work out for her. As Joyce began trying to build her customer base, she realized a shortcoming that she had - she was not very sociable. Although she had excelled professionally in her jobs, she had not taken the opportunity to hone her social skills.

## *Undercapitalization*

Foreman Office Products started out as a sole proprietorship with only $25,000 cash. These same funds had to be used also to pay her living expenses. Financially, it was very difficult. First, Joyce rented a home and paid a high monthly rent, then she moved in with an aunt for a year and a half. Both options took a heavy toll on her emotionally and physically.

Unfortunately, the $25,000 she had invested didn't take her very far. Her start-up costs for bringing in the first order of supplies exceeded the available capital. Consequently, she was forced to use trade credit as a means of financing her products. After a while, Joyce leveraged the trade credit strategy into a science. Her suppliers would deliver twice a day. They'd ship it in, she'd fill the order, and the merchandise was out the door the same day. She turned the merchandise over very fast. It was a creative way to get started.

## Early Marketing Strategy

Joyce stays active within the purchasing community. She is an ex-member of the Purchasing Management Association of Dallas and had worked with other purchasing managers and took the opportunity to contact them to learn tips on effective marketing strategies to use. She learned that to be effective in attracting business she had to create a professional and inviting office environment. So, before she left her job to start the business, she secured office space in the same upscale building in which she was currently working.

With an idea of what she wanted to do and an office to work from, her original marketing plan was to go after minority businesses. It didn't work. She felt that it was one of the things she did wrong in the first year. Joyce says you can only sell minority businesses to companies who have programs and know what minority business means and understand them. If you just call XYZ company and say you're a minority business, they don't want to hear it.

After the first year, she realized that being a minority business was limiting and started selling to all businesses while targeting minority business where it made the most sense. She did telemarketing on her own, setting up appointments, saying who she was and her interest in doing business. She never mentioned that she was a minority business. Later, after she started attracting new accounts, she started hiring salespeople to assist with the marketing side of the business. Her theory is that her company sells business, and sells minority where it has to sell minority:

Minority business has a negative connotation, which is hard for minorities to understand. You can't sell minority because some companies may have used a minority business before and been disappointed because the firm may have made a mistake. In their warped thinking, if one minority firm makes a mistake then all minority firms cannot be trusted to do quality work.

Joyce is a businessperson first and a minority businessperson second. She only asks for a fair shake because she's aware that white firms make mistakes but they almost always get another chance. She only asks potential customers to give her the chance to fail, but she knows she'll succeed. People have to know that all businesses make mistakes. Yet, they refuse to let minorities make mistakes.

Joyce encourages all minority businesses to take the "rifle approach" to targeting business opportunities. Find out where you are most competitive and go for those opportunities. Second, Joyce explains, you have to find your niche in the market. She recently asked a client, "If we can go direct on orders of under $500, why aren't we directing some of those opportunities to minority businesses?" Joyce continues:

The amount of $500 means a lot to some minority businesses. State law says that on any bid under $10,000, you must call up three people on the phone. Are you assured that one of those three people is a minority business? The manufacturer is probably not going to fool with that $10,000 order. So the level of competition becomes greater for that MBE. For too long, we've gone out there and said, 'Give me some business.' We haven't been able to identify what we want. We need to ask for specifics and not let them identify what our specifics should be, leaving it totally up to them to define.

Joyce's niche is non-contract items. She explains why:

What they (customers) say to me is we sent you a bid; but what they don't say is that they also sent a copy to my suppliers as well. They don't know that I realize that every time they send me a bid my suppliers get a copy also. Obviously the manufacturers are not going to let me beat them out unless they have a commitment not to sell direct, and few manufacturers honor that commitment. They (manufacturers) get any business that they can. They'll sell to my customers too!

She admits she can't compete with those from whom she buys. So her selling technique is saying, "You sent me a bid. What other way do you purchase?" Joyce explains her point of view:

Any order under x amount of dollars, I'll pick up a telephone and call and say, 'Give me some of that business,' because I can't compete on that level and what they have historically done is knock us out because we can't compete against the people we buy from. Why send me a bid that I can't competitively bid on?

## Know Your Business

Historically, Joyce says, a person will see Joe Blow in a business making money and think that's great. Under the illusion that there is easy money to be made, they attempt to go into his business without finding out how the person is really making money. Joyce says it's key to know something about what you're going to sell and what you're going to do. Learning how to be in business, how to control your employees, how to deal with banks, and so forth is very difficult, she explains. You can't learn how to be in business and understand the nature of what you're doing at the same time. That's why she used the experiences from her prior jobs to prepare herself for getting her business off of the ground, and it worked well for her.

## A Central Location

Her start-up materials were expensive, and she felt that being a minority, she was watched very closely by suppliers initially because she feels they were concerned about her paying her bills on time. Many were put at ease once they saw her store and saw that she was right in the middle of the business district. She initially rented a place on the eleventh floor of a building. Her suppliers were a bit miffed, getting all her supplies to the eleventh floor caused problems, but the downtown address was important. Her particular commodity was to sell to major corporations and they (the corporations) can identify with a downtown address.

She fought for a street level walk-in location for a long time. People thought she wasn't ready for that kind of exposure. She talked to a building office manager about getting a street level walk-in location in the building. Joyce later was pleasantly surprised that the office manager was a white female who liked her and agreed to give her a fair chance. The two women negotiated a satisfactory deal. The overhead was extensive, but the identity of a street level downtown address means more than the overhead, says Joyce.

## The Door Is Always Open

Joyce's office door is always open. Some well-meaning business associates advised her not to leave her door open so that the public would not know that the owner of this business is a black female. Joyce rationalizes that if people see her only as a black and female, then she isn't interested in their business anyway. She believes that people come in to see her because she is available.

Joyce thinks of herself as an affirmative action baby. She went through the process of working for large corporations and learned how to do it "their way." She's a firm believer in doing it "their way." You can't make up the rules yourself, she says.

## Confident in the Future of Minority Business

Foreman is optimistic about the future of minority business in

America. In the last five years, she has seen a dramatic increase in minority entrepreneur's awareness and preparation, but believes that the structure of minority businesses has to change. If we start putting minorities to work, look at what happens to the development of the city as a whole, she says. Joyce believes we have to move quality minority vendors from level one to the next level where they can begin generating millions of dollars in business. We need to create businesses that will put more people to work. The more people we have working the broader our tax base becomes. Full employment provides members of the community with a heightened sense of security and well-being. People who feel secure are better positioned to address the other issues facing their community. If people are not working, they aren't going to get involved. Joyce thinks you have to be in a position to give back to the community, not necessarily working out of the minority community. This is her mission.

Joyce sees minority businesses that have been around for seven years and thinks they need to be pushed to another level. For the minority business owner just starting out, she sees a need for education. From the minority business standpoint, we've got to convince the business owners that they need education. She pushes education. She is convinced that her purchasing background helped her into another level, providing her with an education. She feels her background helped her to be successful.

## Lack of Business Experience Is No Sweat

The most important trait to success, according to Joyce, is attitude. She simply believes in being the best. Once she made the commitment to see her dream through, she stuck to it. She sees herself on one side as non-threatening, but on the other side, forceful, sometimes pushy.

If people know that you will work hard, says Joyce, they will tend to get on your bandwagon. You've got to maintain high morals and strong work ethics, she preaches to minority businesses. Joyce says she'll work seven days a week or all night. She doesn't care. She feels that Foreman Office Products is committed to excellence and will push until it gets its fair share. She demands quality from her workers and nothing less. Just because you're black doesn't mean you expect things that are substandard. That's a bunch of crap, she says. She wants people to see that she's doing good, quality work, and that her standards are high by anyone's standards.

### Don't Sell Minority, Sell Business

Don't sell minority, sell business, Joyce says. She just happens to be black and female. She refuses to go into a corporation and say that she wants her ten percent. She knows that it has to be earned. Joyce suggests that if you're going into an account for the first time, try to identify the problem and understand the customer's business first. She says you are not going to solve problems overnight that have been going on for years. The minority business problem, or solution, says Joyce, is the collective input from both sides. That's basically what works for Joyce Foreman. Joyce emphasizes that she is not pushing minorities for minorities sake, she's pushing quality minorities.

### Finding and Managing Your Staff

Joyce has ten people working for her. Women, she thinks, manage differently from men. She concludes that men like to carry the big stick. "Maybe it's a macho thing." Joyce does not use this approach. She prefers using the family approach, and the workers tend to support one another. However, the family approach doesn't always work, especially when men want to test her. When she speaks, she feels that everybody listens; what she says goes. Before hiring, she asks potential workers how they feel about working for a female. Most people say that it's no problem. She insists that all her people either fit in the fold or look for employment elsewhere. The bottom line is that Joyce demands excellent performance and respect.

Joyce is firm, but fair. When workers have failed to perform she lets them know that she expects excellence and that they've worked too hard to get put under. She also feels she's a very loving, caring person. Joyce has taken the added responsibility of nurturing her employees. She insists that they do their best. She knows that if the business folded tomorrow she could get a job and wants to ensure that they could also. She talks to her employees about being a minority business, telling them they are an example and that they aren't allowed to make mistakes. She believes the family management system has worked well for her. Joyce also recognizes that it doesn't work well for everybody.

## Being a Woman in Business

Many associate the family style of management with female managers. Unlike some female entrepreneurs, Joyce doesn't think you have to lose your femininity to be in business. While she is petite, she believes that her size can be an advantage. Although most view her as nonthreatening, when challenged, people look up to find themselves bleeding. She is single with no children and doesn't think she would have gotten where she is if she had been married. Joyce believes that typically women take the role of supporting their husbands rather than taking that step forward. If married, she wouldn't have been able to sell her home or spend adequate time developing Foreman Office Products. Joyce feels that understanding your constraints is key. She gets calls all the time from women interested in going into business and gives them the "Foreman Story." She had no commitments to tie her down.

Foreman also expects commitment from female employees. She believes female employees are more difficult to manage. "Women tend to be more nit picky," she explains. "Men don't have time."

## Building the Proper Support System

Most minority businesses are first generation, and a strong support system is critical for success. Although she had extended family support, they were unfamiliar with what she was trying to accomplish; therefore, their ability to support was limited. However, the support Joyce's family couldn't provide was adequately provided by other local minority business owners. Joyce's support group of local business owners meet regularly to discuss critical issues and problems. "It seems like our problems are the same," says Foreman.

Fortunately, the support that Joyce's group provides her will ultimately be provided by Joyce to the next generation of minority businesses. She explains:

> The process is going to be a lot easier for them because when my generation came through there was no one to talk to. At least the next crop of entrepreneurs will have a lot more potential role models to choose from.

## Start-Up Organization

When Joyce first started her business, she did everything herself. She had to because there was no one else. Her resources were so scarce that she had to deliver merchandise in her car. Being a minority business, you have to be willing to do grunt work because you are usually undercapitalized. Just for those occasions, she keeps a pair of jeans in her office should she have to assist in the warehouse. In the beginning, she was the marketing person, the salesperson, the telephone operator, and the delivery person. Jim Washington and Ken Carter were her confidantes and they offered support, telling her what to do, and where to go. She attended lots of seminars and workshops and believes that one never stops learning.

All successful businesses, explains Joyce, need to have clear and well-defined goals. This is especially true from a marketing viewpoint. The owner needs to understand where he's going to go to get his business, who you market to, and why you've chosen that particular market. She has two salespeople, far fewer than what she should have. She won't put people on the payroll that she can't afford. It goes back to being undercapitalized. She tries to keep things in perspective. She's trying not to grow too fast. If she hires five salespeople and they go out and get $5 million worth of business, it would be difficult. There's nothing worse, says Joyce, then having too much business. If for some reason you can't perform, you will probably never get a second chance.

## Growth Projection

Joyce sees Foreman Office Products growing by leaps and bounds. She has good reason to be confident. First of all, Joyce feels she's already proven herself and shown the value that her firm can bring to her customers. However, Joyce is uncertain how long she'll remain in the office products business. She has always believed that getting into the office products business was just a stepping stone to bigger and better opportunities. Now that she knows how to start and manage a business, it would be very easy for her to start branching into other businesses. Joyce is quick to admit that the office products business has been very good to her. But, if something better came along, she'd sell Foreman Office Products in a heartbeat.

She believes that once you're in the network, people bring the deals to you. If you're perceived as the "in" minority business, then they all will be talking to you. Even the banks will beat a path to your door to loan you money if you're a part of the deal stream. Joyce insists that she could easily obtain a loan now, but when you owe the banks, they own a part of you and Joyce is reluctant to this situation.

## Ten-Year Plan

During the last couple of years that Joyce has been in business, she has purposely grown the business slowly. Joyce has a "long-term greedy" mentality. She had no intention of getting rich in the first ten years because when you start out undercapitalized, the chances of you making big money in the short-term are slim. Usually it will take approximately ten years before things start to really cook. To remain within that ten-year plan, Joyce pays herself a small salary to cover living expenses:

> In the first ten years, you take care of the business. During the next ten years, the business will take care of you. After ten years, if I'm still getting up at 5:30 a.m., then I've failed. Right now I'm taking care of the business. If it was easy, everybody would be doing it. It's a hard job, worse than anything. You don't have one boss, you have many bosses, your customers.

She'd like her people to emulate her, leave their jobs at Foreman, and start their own businesses. Joyce hopes that her employees have learned some valuable skills while in her employ. She'd like to have an incubator for minority businesses. This would entail creating an environment with a building and a hand-picked group of minority businesses that she thinks would be successful:

> What sometimes happens with minority businesses is that you'll get guys leaving corporate America with very strong skills in certain areas but not always in critical areas like accounting, billing, invoicing, and things of that nature. Somehow these people need to learn these lessons quickly, and the incubator concept might prove helpful in situations like these.

## Getting In and Staying In

Joyce cautions all would-be entrepreneurs to first know why they want to go into business and to know something about the business they're getting into. She warns that it is extremely difficult to run your business effectively and learn it at the same time. There are business development centers around the country specializing in helping small businesses, and people should take the opportunity to use them instead of trying to learn everything on their own.

Those who choose to run their own businesses need to have strong organizational, social, and leadership skills. These skills must be applied at all times:

> Most deals are cut in places where you'd least expect them to be cut so you always have to be on your alert for opportunity. I recall a situation where I attended a meeting in Dallas on economic development within the city. The president of one of the local corporations was in attendance and was impressed by me for some reason. Even though I had been calling on this man's company for years with no success, he and I struck a deal that afternoon - on the spot.

Joyce Foreman's commitment to minority business development and survival is unwavering. In her opinion, it goes far beyond just the businesses themselves, but to the African-American community in general. African-American businesspeople provide role models for young people and gainful employment for some struggling adults. Joyce logically concludes that if there are more businesses created in the community, then there will be more people employed.

When people are transferred from the welfare rolls to the job rolls, an amazing thing happens. First, their self-esteem is restored and their self-hate and negative attitudes are diminished. Second, they begin to focus on other critical issues within their community.

As Joyce works her way to the front door of her store to receive her first customer of the day, she looks back at me and in an almost trance like state utters, "Clearly, there is a direct correlation between black economic empowerment and the level of social problems facing that community." This is a relationship she understands well.

# PART 4

# ANALYSIS OF AFRICAN-AMERICAN ENTREPRENEURS

**As** was mentioned earlier, my trips around the country interviewing entrepreneurs required me to keep records of my conversations. I tirelessly sifted through the experiences of each to identify the "secrets of success." Like Ponce de Leon searched for the fountain of youth, I searched for "turnkey solutions" to complex challenges, which, if adopted, would quickly lead one to wealth and fame. Well, I'm sorry to report that there are no "secrets of success." There is nothing known to man that guarantees success. As a matter of fact, the same strategies that may bring one man success may take another man down the path of failure and destruction.

However, it has been my experience that serious "would-be entrepreneurs" are not looking for an easy formula to follow or for someone to hold their hands and protect them from the cold realities of owning and managing businesses. Serious entrepreneurs are willing to take the risk on their own and want only to learn from the experiences of those who went before them so that they don't make the same mistakes. They have learned that to be successful, they must do what successful people do. The United Negro College Fund says, and which summarizes the desires of this special breed, "We're not looking for a hand out, just a hand."

For those entrepreneurs who are looking for a hand, I'm happy to report that although there may be no magical secrets of success, there are some common traits among African-American entrepreneurs that I observed from interviews, frank conversations at quiet moments, and just general observation that will definitely help you. Don't look at these traits as an all-or-nothing deal. Don't assume because you only possess a few of them or none at all, that you're unfit to become an entrepreneur. Absorb all of the information initially, review your situation carefully, extract the parts of this analysis that you find beneficial, and pass the rest on to someone else. For others, the information on traits of African-American entrepreneurs may help to fill some void in your understanding of how successful businesspeople create and manage thriving enterprises.

It is difficult to discern which characteristics of black entrepreneurs are unique only to this group and not to mainstream entrepreneurs as well. Obviously, there is a common set of traits associated with all successful entrepreneurs regardless of their race, creed, color, or religion. However, due to the unique circumstances that define the African-Americans experience, they have been forced to develop additional traits just to survive. I've tried diligently to only focus on these unique qualities. I'm afraid though, that no matter how hard I tried, there is still some degree of overlap. Regardless, blacks often must call upon unique strengths within themselves to fight for what is rightfully theirs in an environment that is increasingly hostile. It is these special qualities that I've attempted to capture in this book.

## *The First Hit Phenomenon (Significant Event)*

Early in my analysis, I began to uncover an interesting phenomenon. Almost without exception, all of the businesspeople in this study struggled during the early phases of their venture. Usually during this phase of the journey, the entrepreneurs were forced to make major sacrifices and faced major disappointments. In many situations, the minority entrepreneur worked diligently for years

**Exhibit 4-1. Investment/Return Curve**

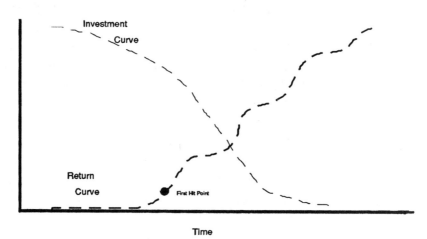

without ever reaping any significant benefits or rewards.

For those strong enough to persevere through those dark and uncertain periods, an interesting phenomenon usually occurred. These people would score their "first hit" ultimately. What do I mean by the "first hit?" I have characterized this as any event that was preceded by a difficult and tenuous period and culminates in a success of a significant magnitude. The "first hit" could be the awarding of the first contract from a client who's been marketed to for years. Or it could be the successful purchase of and the ultimate turnaround of a small struggling manufacturing company. In some instances it could be resolving an operations problem that's been negatively affecting customer satisfaction and operating efficiencies at your company. With the problem solved, you go on to produce high-quality products at a brisk production rate.

As shown in Exhibit 4-1, after the first hit, the entrepreneur usually finds that the second, third, and subsequent hits come along more frequently and often with much greater impact and potential for reward. Experiencing the "first hit" is like making a difficult shot at a critical point in a championship basketball game. Prior to taking the shot you may have been burdened with self-doubt and low confidence. However, after the shot, you become buoyed with confidence and anticipation of making even more difficult, but exciting shots.

The tragedy in this situation is that many aspiring entrepreneurs never hang around long enough to experience their "first hits." They usually get so disgusted and disillusioned with the seeming lack of progress, they give up on their dreams and settle for a life of mediocrity. They fail to understand that the process of achieving your goal requires that you pay some dues first and that you maintain your course (assuming it is the correct one) until you experience your "first hit." Beyond the "first hit," your return for paying your dues begins to multiply.

## *The Water Bucket Theory*

Understanding the first hit phenomenon is critical because it provides aspiring entrepreneurs with linear guidelines for maintaining perseverance and commitment to their business goal. The Water Bucket Theory takes the first hit theory one step further and attempts to explain the process of business formation from a two-or three-dimensional standpoint.

As shown in Exhibit 4-2, obtaining business success is analogous to pouring water into a bucket and eventually using that water to nourish the flowers you've planted. If we assume that the bucket remains stationary, the simple act of pouring water into the bucket will not suffice to provide water to the flowers. There is a certain amount of water that must be poured into the bucket before the static water level is high enough to overflow through the spout.

Every man and woman who wants to start and own a business has a unique bucket that to fill to some level before seeing benefits and rewards from their inputs, investments, or costs associated with making their business dream a reality. The costs or investments considered in this analysis include things such as time, capital, frustration, recreation time, disappointments, stress, opportunity cost, and others. The sum quantity of these costs helps fill each individual's bucket.

**Exhibit 4-2. The Water Bucket Theory**

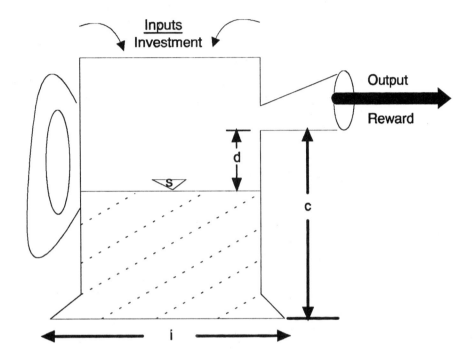

For the sake of this discussion, if we assume that intensity of purpose (I) and commitment (C) are the basic ingredients, then I times C equals the quantity of investment made. D represents the quantity that is still outstanding before the individual will begin seeing some pay back or reward. It is my assumption that the quantity of each person's investment is cumulative. This idea implies that if an entrepreneur starts filling his bucket and for one reason or another stops filling the bucket, the quantity in the bucket remains stagnant until the entrepreneur picks up where he left off and resumes work on making up the quantity D. There may be some losses in the content of the bucket depending on the goal being sought, but in general the contents of the bucket should remain stagnant for some time, as shown by Exhibit 4-3.

Although I submit that the opportunity buckets for each

individual are different, I also suggest that the size of the opportunity bucket of African-American businesspeople and other businesspeople of color are much larger than their white counterparts.

There are numerous reasons the bucket for businesspeople of color is much larger than that of whites but the two most apparent reasons are overt and institutional racism and oppression of the mind. Before aspiring African-American entrepreneurs even get a chance to present their ideas or business plans, they must first burn valuable resources justifying why they should even be listened to!

Beyond this first step things become even more difficult. Black entrepreneurs' access to capital is much more limited than whites; they have to work longer and harder to build a strong customer/client base; blacks normally don't travel in the social circles of their prospective customers, and therefore, must develop strategies for working their way into those circles; blacks have more people telling them that they can never be as successful as their white counterparts; family members of black businesspeople probably don't have any experience in the specific business area so black entrepreneurs are usually out there all alone; African-Americans are constantly bombarded with negative images of themselves and their community, and after being told enough times that blacks can't be successful in this country, the sub-conscious mind will actually begin to believe it.

In spite of the inequalities in bucket sizes outlined above, there is a silver lining to this seemingly dark cloud. Because blacks in business are required to fill a bigger bucket before they reap any rewards, the quantity invested is greater; therefore, over the long term, the output or reward also will be greater than many of their white counterparts. This assumes that black entrepreneurs will have the strength and fortitude to see the process to the very end. At times it may appear that justice doesn't prevail, but it really does. Sometimes, it just gets delayed. The biblical teaching that "you reap what you sow," is valid even in business.

## The Invisible, Sixth-Person Phenomenon

The third phenomenon identified in this study is the sixth-person

**Exhibit 4-3. Water Buckets Commensurate with Goals of Entrepreneurs**

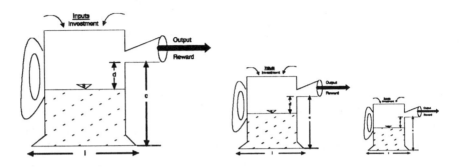

concept. I happen to adore the sport of basketball. Although I once played the sport seven days a week, I'm lucky now if I get to play once or twice per week. Anyway, one of the observations I've made over the years in watching thousands of basketball games on the streets and on television is the number of times that a mediocre team of players ends up kicking the butt of a team of so-called superstars.

For a long time, I couldn't understand how this could happen. I became enlightened one day when my friends (all over 35 years old) and I were challenged to a game by some "yo boys" (i.e., young, urban teenagers). As the game commenced, I observed that on our team, even though we were slower, weaker, and clearly not as physically gifted as our younger counterparts, we communicated well with each other, supported one another, and developed a strategy and stuck to it as a team. We encouraged each other when one of us made a mistake and praised each other when one of us made a good shot or showed a little more hustle than was expected.

The "yo boy" team, on the other hand, while loaded with unbelievable talent, was fraught with chaos and mayhem. First, it was clear that the boys didn't respect one another. They called each other names, refused to pass the ball to the open man, had no game strategy, took stupid shots, and refused to support one another. Well, you probably guessed it. We embarrassed them so terribly that they never came back to that court.

The reason a team of old, slow, overweight basketball players could defeat a team of young, quick, and talented players was due to the help of the invisible sixth person. The invisible sixth person is a energy source that is created whenever a group of people who work well together and care about one another come together as a unified group to achieve a common goal. Do not underestimate the power of the sixth person. It will often determine the success or failure of a particular engagement.

When attempting to build a strong team to go after a business, many people tend to only focus on where the person went to school, degrees earned, and work experiences to determine their fit in the group. Although these qualities are important it is probably more critical to ascertain the individual's ability to work within the group, their style of conducting business, and whether you like the person.

## Manage the Lows and the Rest Will Take Care of Itself

Vince Lombardi once said, "Success is not in ever falling, but in rising every time you fall." How true this statement is. History has shown that the process of achieving any worthy goal is a cyclical one - there will be temporary periods of successes and temporary periods of failure. Ordinary people can generally figure out how to manage the success intervals that occasionally come their way. However, it takes special individuals to be able to manage through the uncertainties of the failure intervals. This fact is especially true when there is a great amount at risk - house, job, family, independence, and perhaps sanity.

Successful African-American businesspeople have learned to anticipate the low periods and prepare themselves for managing through them. They understand that if they can make it through the tough times the good times, will be a piece of cake.

## The Three Tiers of Business Formation

When analyzing any event or object, it is usually helpful to evaluate it within the framework of a model. In studying black entrepreneurs, I've created a set of models that I've used to describe in some logical way the differences within the group. Like all businesses, enterprises owned and operated by blacks come packaged in many different ways. In positioning the businesses within the African-American community, I've identified three categories in which each business could be accurately placed: Tier #1 Businesses, Tier #2 Businesses, and Tier #3 Businesses.

## Tier #1 Businesses

Companies that generally fall into this category are very small businesses. Tier #1 usually includes most start-ups, small franchises, and the "mom and pop" operations. As a group, these firms tend to generate less than $500,000 per year in revenues and often cater to the basic needs of the community in which they're located. The owners of these businesses have a tendency to be very active and visible within their local communities but not as visible in the mainstream community.

If minority communities are to recapture control of local economies, most likely this effort will be spearheaded by the players at the Tier #1 level. Although it is possible for a Tier #1 business to migrate to a Tier #2 or even a Tier #3 business eventually, it appears that most Tier #1 businesses remain at Tier #1 for the duration of their existence unless it is sold to someone who has Tier #2 intentions.

## Tier #2 Businesses

Tier #2 businesses tend to generate significantly more revenue than Tier #1 businesses, producing somewhere between $500,000 and $15,000,000 per year. This level of business activity does not necessarily make its base physically within the minority community and typically operates somewhere on the periphery of the community. The products or services it produces are consumed both by the

**Exhibit 4-4. Types of Business Enterprises**

| Characteristics | Tier#1 Businesses | Tier #2 Businesses | Tier #3 Businesses |
|---|---|---|---|
| a) Revenue | -Sales less than $500,000/year. | -Sales between $500,000 and $15,000,000/year. | -Sales over $15,000,000 per year. |
| b) Typical businesses in this tier | -Corner grocer<br>-Gas stations<br>-Small restaurants<br>-Liquor stores<br>-Janitorial services<br>-Accounting /legal services<br>-Counsulting | -Transporation<br>-Fast foods<br>-Steel fabrication<br>-Plastics fabrication<br>-Low tech manufacturing | -Medium/high tech manufacturing<br>-Trucking<br>-Biotechnology<br>-Computer services<br>-Railroad car manufacturing<br>-High tech applications |
| c) Customer set | Minority community | Minority and majority communities | Predominantly majority community and Fortune 500 companies. |
| d) Recognition within the minority community | Strong | Strong | Weak |
| e) Recognition within the majority community | Weak | Medium | Strong |
| f) Requirements for success | -Good service<br>-Respect for customers<br>-Grass roots involvement within community<br>-Recession proof product (e.g., gas, food, clothes) | -Strong contacts within majority community<br>-Politically active<br>-Competitive product or service | -Strong contacts within the majority community<br>-Strong political ties<br>-Strong ties to financial community<br>-Competitive product or service |

black community and the mainstream community. Although these types of businesses are active in both environments, they are still recognizable within the black community. Well-managed Tier #2 businesses that survive the early years have a good chance of migrating to a Tier #3 business at some point.

### Tier #3 Businesses

The interesting fact about Tier #3 businesses is that there are "sub-levels" within this group of enterprises. Although this tier of businesses generates upwards of $15,000,000 per year, it also includes big deal makers like the deceased, Reginald Lewis, former CEO of Beatrice Foods. Last year Beatrice Foods had sales approaching the $2 billion mark. Typically, customers of the goods or services produced by this group of businesses are mainstream consumers, usually large corporations or the Federal Government. Unfortunately, the majority of these companies are not recognizable within the African-American community.

Consequently, the accomplishments of these firms (with the exception of companies like Johnson Publishing Company and other household names) go unrecognized by a large percentage of the community. Because of the types of businesses usually operating at this level, it is essential these companies maintain strong ties with the mainstream community, particularly the financial community.

It is rare for a new entrepreneur to immediately migrate to a Tier #3 type business. An entrepreneur starting out would usually come in at the Tier #1 or maybe a Tier #2 level and then build that business into a Tier #3 enterprise over time. However, I believe by the mid 1990s, we will see many young, black entrepreneurs taking over mainstream businesses and positioning them as Tier #2 or Tier #3 businesses.

These "would-be entrepreneurs" are the "best of the breed" and are recipients of some of the best on the job training programs in the world. Some have strategically embedded themselves in the Fortune 100 companies, in boutique consulting firms, and even at mid to senior levels within the Federal Government. They're like sponges, soaking up every bit of knowledge and technical expertise that they come into contact with, they patiently await the opportunity to "make their move." This special group of people is like water behind a dam. As time goes on the level rapidly scales the walls of the dam. When Wall Street opens back up (and it will) and society once again seeks to satisfy its insatiable appetite for new goods and services, these young professionals will spill over, like the water behind the dam and assume their positions as prominent business leaders. The 1990s will be the decade of Tier #3 businesses. Exhibit 4-4 summarizes the differences between these enterprises.

## Types of Minority Entrepreneurs

Similar to evaluating the types of businesses within the community, it is equally difficult to define the types of entrepreneurs present in today's environment. However, it is important to segment the various types of entrepreneurs within the community and attempt to define the various types in some way. Specific strategies then can be formulated to assist these groups in not just surviving, but excelling in their respective areas. Grouping of entrepreneurs also helps "would-be entrepreneurs" to evaluate themselves and maybe align themselves with one of the groups in order to formulate their entry strategy effectively.

Again, the use of a model to define the different characteristics of the various types of entrepreneurs is helpful. Exhibit 4-5 segments the types of African-American entrepreneurs into three distinct groups. Depending on the level of detail desired, the number of groups defined could have been much greater than three. However, within the scope of my analysis, the three groups within my model adequately define the subjects. The basis of this model assumes that the majority of the African-American entrepreneurs can be defined by one or a combination of the following types of entrepreneurs: Brown Bomber Entrepreneurs (BBE), Blood and Guts Entrepreneurs

(BGE), and the Daring Dashing Dan Entrepreneurs (DDDE).

It would be an erroneous assumption to assume that the three groups are separated by their degree of success, with the BBEs being the least successful and the DDDEs being the most successful. Although the term Brown Bomber Entrepreneurs may not sound as glamourous as the Dashing Dan types, there are many BBEs around who make more money and live far more fulfilling lives than most of us. Likewise, there are some DDDEs who tried to play ball in the big league and ended up worst than when they started. Keep in mind that each type of entrepreneur can be as successful or unsuccessful as he wants to be.

### Brown Bomber Entrepreneurs

Joe Louis (a.k.a., The Brown Bomber) was arguably the greatest heavyweight fighter in history. He came at a time when blacks had to fight to retain even the smallest amount of dignity and respect. In spite of these formidable challenges, Mr. Louis won the 1934 Golden Gloves championship in the light heavyweight division and three years later took the heavyweight title from James Braddock, becoming the second African-American to hold the world championship. He later successfully defended his title 25 times in twelve years, knocking out six world champions.

My father knew Joe Louis and often told me of how honest and kind, but somewhat naive, Mr. Lewis was. Of all the millions he earned as a fighter, much of it was stolen by crooked managers and fast women. Yet, Mr. Lewis continued to love and have faith in people and was always humble in his personal and business dealings.

Like Joe Louis, the Brown Bomber Entrepreneurs are honest, worldly people who maintain strong respect for individuals. In their minds, their greatest assets are their trust and their word. Typically, the members of this group tend to be male with little or no formal college training. Although they usually are able to generate and

**Exhibit 4-5. Traits of Successful African-American Entrepreneurs**

| Characteristics | "Brown Bomber" | "Blood and Guts" | "Daring Dashing Dan" |
|---|---|---|---|
| a) Age | All ages | All ages | Young |
| b) Sex | Majority male | Male and female | Majority male |
| c) Educational level | Up to 12 years | More than 12 years | More than 16 years with Ivy League exposure |
| d) Business vision | Make ends meet | -Make ends meet<br>-Build empire on his/her own | Build empire using his brain, but other people's money and sweat |
| e) Strengths | -Honesty<br>-Respect for individuals<br>-Humble<br>-Worldly<br>-Excellent people skills | -Diligent<br>-Worldly<br>-Attention to details<br>-Tactical strategist<br>-Multi-talented<br>-Capable of multi-tasking | -Leadership skills<br>-"Slickster"<br>-Team coalition builder<br>-Brave vision<br>-Skilled at delegating<br>-Wall Street connected<br>-Embraces new and young talent<br>-Strategic thinker<br>-Superb decision maker |
| f) Weaknesses | -Naive<br>-Short-sighted<br>-Refuses to think strategically<br>-Runs business day by day<br>-Suspicious of young, well-educated talent<br>-Puts out fires | -Weak delegator<br>-Suspicious of young, well-educated talent<br>-Afraid of failure<br>-Weak strategic thinker<br>-Impulsive decision maker<br>-Distrustful of those around him | -Operates close to being ruthless<br>-Impatient<br>-Fails to pay close attention to details<br>-Blinded by ambition<br>-"River boat gambler" |

**Exhibit 4-5. (continued)**

| Characteristics | "Brown Bomber" | "Blood and Guts" | "Daring Dashing Dan" |
|---|---|---|---|
| g) Reason for going into business | Necessity | -Dream <br> -Right opportunity | -Lifetime dream <br> -Dissatisfaction with corporate old boy system |
| h) Work background | Frequently moved from job to job | -Fortune 500 training <br> -Multi-functional experiences | -Experience working with Fortune 500 companies <br> -Recipient of executive/ management training program |

maintain loyalty in their customer base, they often are short sighted and refuse to view their businesses strategically. They prefer to make short-term dicisions and often are suspicious of the young, well-educated talent available to them within and outside of the community.

### Blood and Guts Entrepreneurs

Blood and Guts Entrepreneurs come in all ages and both sexes. This group is characterized by its members' strong desire to "make it on their own." They like to show the world how tough they are. These folks take pride in the fact that no matter what the world throws at them, they can take it. Women entrepreneurs are prominent within this group primarily because of their belief that they must be twice as good as men in order to get the same breaks and recognition that men of lesser skills receive (which is probably true).

Their vision of the business is that its primary purpose is to satisfy the needs of today. Members of this group could be considered potential "empire builders." They're often open to building an empire, but only if it's done with their blood, sweat, and tears.

Successful Blood and Guts Entrepreneurs pay great attention to detail, usually at great cost, and excel at being strong tactical thinkers. However, like the Brown Bomber group, this group tends to be suspicious of young, well-educated talent and tends to be distrustful of those around them. "No one can do a job better than them," is their motto. Therefore, they end up doing most of the jobs instead of delegating to others.

### Daring Dashing Dan Entrepreneurs

The 1990s will reveal a cadre of young, swash-buckling, Daring Dashing Dan Entrepreneurs (DDDEs). This group of young, well-educated, aggressive, risk-prone entrepreneurs will consummate deals that may even surpass the Beatrice deal in terms of size and complexity. Individuals who fall under this group are basically "empire builders." But they're not normal empire builders. These are people who want to build an empire with their brains, but with other people's sweat and capital.

As shown in Exhibit 4-5, people in this group will perform well in the new world order of competition because they tend to be strong leaders with brave, bold visions and the "heart" to go with it. They are strong, strategic thinkers and consequently will embrace new young talent if they see how such people will help them achieve their goals. In this fast-paced environment, DDDEs finds themselves not having the time to learn the details of the operation, which requires heavy reliance on the management team. This group of entrepreneurs goes through wide swings in their performance. When they hit, they hit big. However, when they fall, they typically have a long and painful fall. Occasionally, the fall ends up being fatal.

## Traits of Successful African-American Entrepreneurs

As mentioned earlier, with such a diverse group of businesspeople, it is difficult to paint a picture of the characteristics of the super successful, minority entrepreneur. However, there are some traits that appear to be present to varying degrees. Those identified traits include:

Trait  #1: Spiritual Fortitude
Trait  #2: When In Doubt, Do Something!
Trait  #3: The Amoeba Effect
Trait  #4: Leveraging the Buffalo Soldier Legacy
Trait  #5: Managing the Ride
Trait  #6: Intensity of Purpose
Trait  #7: Ghetto Cunning
Trait  #8: Feeling at Home on the Nile
Trait  #9: The "X" Factor Is a Big Factor
Trait #10: Learning from the Conversion of Saul to Paul
Trait #11: Resisting the "Herd Instinct"
Trait #12: Living by "The Pain Don't Hurt" Point of View
Trait #13: Long-Term Greedy Versus Short-Term Greedy
Trait #14: Experiencing a Gut-Wrenching Event
Trait #15: The "Natural High" from Making Money
Trait #16: Being Comfortable with Being Uncomfortable
Trait #17: Correlating Exactitude with Chaos and Bringing Vision into Focus
Trait #18: Believing that Competitiveness Usually Defeats Sexism, Racism, and Classism
Trait #19: Perpetual Dream Chasers
Trait #20: Ascending the Incremental Energy Levels of Success

### *Trait # 1: Spiritual Fortitude*

Most African-American entrepreneurs readily admit that they've seen and experienced the power of God in their lives. It has probably been the most successful means of helping them withstand the forces of injustice and oppression and they appreciate how this same power will guide them to even higher levels of achievement.

It is my observation that African-American businesspeople, due to their volatile and uncertain position in American society, possess a greater appreciation of the frailties of human existence and have been more successful than their white counterparts in putting the relationship of God and man into its proper perspective. African-American entrepreneurs appreciate that the reason black people have been able to survive more than two hundred years of terror, torture, oppression, violence, poverty, and hatred was because of the power of our Father in heaven. It is no accident that the civil rights struggle in this country was for all intents and purposes, orchestrated from the pulpits and boardrooms of our churches. His presence and power, whose manifestation has allowed us to endure, struggle, fight, and hope, also has helped blacks survive.

The survival of the African-American community cannot become limited to only our pursuit of dignity and justice. Although the fight for justice has not been concluded, it has now moved to different and sometimes unfamiliar battlegrounds. On the battleground of economic empowerment, we're fighting a formidable opponent, but God is there and guess what? He's still in charge. He is guiding the hearts and minds of our businesspeople, just as He did our brothers and sisters during our quest for basic respect and human dignity.

Successful African-American entrepreneurs seem to welcome this spiritual ally with open arms and great anticipation. They know that this power, if used effectively, can help them chart their course clear into the next century. As any intelligent businessperson will do, these businesspeople use all of the resources at their disposal, including spiritual resources, to help them achieve their business objectives and to keep their success (or failure) in the proper perspective.

### Trait #2: When In Doubt, Do Something!

Whatever city you come from, daily life for people living in the projects is a tough and brutal one. Between the violence, drugs, police brutality, and self-hate, it is amazing that anyone is able to survive the environment yet alone become productive members of society. I remember my days in a project community in South Baltimore called, Cherry Hill. Contrary to popular belief, I never was much of a "yo boy." I took school seriously and concentrated much of my time on preparing for college and playing sports.

During the fall semester, when I played football, my home boys always helped me celebrate after a victory. This one Friday in particular, we were especially happy because I had just won a big game and really wanted to celebrate. We wanted to locate a party to meet some girls and have some fun. It just so happened there was a party in an adjacent low income community called, Westport.

Westport was like Cherry Hill in many ways. It was a low-income area that was predominantly populated by African-Americans. There were some whites living in the area, but their numbers seemed to dwindle daily. Like Cherry Hill, Westport had a number of Federal Project developments in which low-income people lived. The community faced the same social problems that most urban centers faced, but had difficulty solving most of them. One thing was certain. There existed an old rivalry between the young men of both communities, which often bordered on lunacy. The two groups despised one another. So it was for many years.

It was my misfortune that the only party happening that night was in Westport. Determined to have a good time, all four of my buddies jumped into my friend Donnie's car and sped away to find the party. After arriving within the boundaries of Westport, it soon became apparent to us that we were very drunk and very lost. Due to the poor design of the Westport area, there is only one way in and only one way out. The streets are arranged in a haphazard fashion with many of them being dead endings without warning or logic. As we weaved our way through the maze of streets and alleys, we finally arrived at a street that appeared to be the correct one. As we made a right turn onto the street, we all began to breathe a sigh of relief as we thought we had finally arrived at the party.

A few seconds later, to our dismay, we not only learned that this was not the correct street, but that the street abruptly came to a dead end. Donnie cursed as he yanked the transmission into reverse to back out of the street. Unbeknown to us, while we were weaving our way through the neighborhood, one of the local gangs recognized us as Cherry Hill kids and had organized a mob to teach us a lesson about trespassing on their "turf." This mob was waiting for us at the entrance to the street. Donnie, still unaware of what was unfolding, backed his car to the entrance of the street before coming to a halt due to a truck blocking the exit.

As the mob began to surround the car with bats waving and knives ("shanks") glistening under the dim light of the lamp post, the four of us sat there terrified, contemplating our fate. I don't know what my buddies were thinking, but thoughts were racing through my mind as I searched to find a quick solution to our deadly dilemma. I don't know why, but I immediately thought about some advice that my father had given me after a football game in which I showed a great deal of indecision. My father said, "Son, when in doubt, do something!" What he meant was that there are often times in our lives when we're temporarily confused and uncertain about which choices to make. Most people in this situation usually choose not to make a decision because they're concerned they'll make the wrong one. My father's view was that in those times you need to make a quick decision - even if it is not the best one.

With my fathers words ringing in my mind, I began to cry, pray, kick, curse, yell, and punch, all at the same time. My buddies must have had the same thought because they started doing the same thing. To make a long story short, by the grace of God, we made it out of Westport alive that night with just a few cuts and bruises. It was a long time before I ever set foot back there again.

If you are serious about becoming a successful entrepreneur, as sure as you're born, you will be faced with situations in which you are confused and uncertain about what your next step should be. You will sometimes travel down uncharted avenues that may dead end at anytime. The difference between those who are successful and those who meet their demise is that when in doubt, successful businesspeople do something. They refuse to allow the changes and vicissitudes of the situation to paralyze them into a state of indecision. They quickly analyze the facts, review their options, and make decisions. They have enough confidence in themselves to believe that most of the time they will make wise decisions.

## Trait #3: The Amoeba Effect

While a student at the University of Pennsylvania, my wife, Carolyn, a pre-med major, was extremely fascinated with biology. She was especially fond of the lab sessions in which she studied the world of microorganisms under the amplifying eye of the microscope and then presented her findings to her classmates.

Of all the millions of organisms known to man, none aroused her curiosity more than the amoeba. The amoeba is a tiny, one-cell organism that can be seen only under a microscope. Amoebas vary in size from about .001 inches to .01 inches across. Some amoebas live in water and moist soil. Others live in the bodies of animals and human beings.

Only one cell makes up the amoeba's whole body. The cell is a shapeless mass of protoplasm, the living, jelly-like material found in the cells of all living things. A thin, elastic membrane surrounds the protoplasm and holds it together. Water and gases pass in and out of the amoeba through the membrane.

In order for the amoeba to move from one point to another, it must change its body shape. The protoplasm pushes out the elastic membrane to form a fingerlike pseudopod (false foot) and seemingly without much effort, the protoplasm flows into the pseudopod. For every step that it takes in any direction, it must first form a pseudopod and the protoplasm then must flow into that new member.

The successful entrepreneurs reviewed in this study reminded me of those amoebas. Often very fluid, these businesspeople do not allow themselves to be categorized into a specific area that will ultimately minimize their ability to compete and move into new areas. In a way, these people are shapeless, continuously molding themselves into various shapes and forms to accommodate very dynamic and often volatile business environments.

When successful businesspeople recognize opportunities, they marshal all of their resources and direct them in that direction, much like the amoeba squeezes its protoplasm into its newly created pseudopod. They then move as unified entities in the direction of the new opportunities. Generally, the entrepreneur makes this transformation without much thought, and the transfiguration is usually transparent to those around him.

### Trait #4: Leveraging the Buffalo Soldier Legacy

One of my favorite comedians is Richard Pryor. During the '60s and '70s, he was one of the hottest entertainers around. I believe I must have all of his albums, including the one in which he talks about the differences between black folks and white folks. I recall in one dialogue he was joking about the way black folks can "buffalo" situations in order to get what they want. Although Richard may have only been poking fun at our community, I think that he stumbled onto a characteristic that is rampant throughout the community - especially among African-American entrepreneurs.

This characteristic, which I've termed the "Buffalo Soldier Legacy," was epitomized by the group from which this characteristic derived its name - the Buffalo Soldiers of the American 19th century army. Our businesspeople who are stubborn, strong, brave, and relentless epitomize these characteristics and follow in the legacy of their earlier ancestors. Because an analogy can be drawn between the African-American businessperson of today and the rough riders of the last century, it seemed appropriate to draw the comparison.

Let's briefly step back through history. At the end of the Civil War, the United States government created several black volunteer Army units. The two black cavalry regiments were the Ninth and the Tenth Calvary. By 1871, the majority of these soldiers were stationed at various posts in Texas and the Indian Territory. The Indians gave these soldiers the name "Buffalo Soldiers" partly because of their dark skin and curly hair and partly because of their great strength and the superior fierceness of their fighting. Although these soldiers fought with great valor, they were often treated worst than the horses and other livestock owned by the United States Army. Punishment for the least infraction was severe; food was often rotten; respect was non-existent; and death was forever near. In spite of these conditions, the desertion rate of the Buffalo Soldier was often the lowest in the Army.

With few exceptions, the entrepreneurs profiled in this book display the traits characteristic of our military forefathers, i.e., bravery, tenacity, the unwillingness to accept defeat, and the beliefs that their equitable sharing of this country's resources is just and right, and that capitalism is good and that it works.

The experiences of today's black entrepreneurs are quite similar to our Buffalo Soldiers of yesterday and their reaction to overwhelming adversities is also comparable. Although the weapons and battlegrounds are drastically different, the battle is a familiar one. Like their ancestors, the entrepreneurs depicted in this study remain proud, confident, and mentally tough despite persistently demoralizing conditions. Their challenge, which they readily accept, is to make the system work for the African-American community as well as it works for everyone else.

### Trait #5: Managing the Ride

Business is like life - one big roller coaster ride. Sometimes you're up and sometimes you're down. Those who are wise quickly realize that these changes are a part of the process and are not unique to them individually. Some people have the mistaken belief that to be successful you only need to be able to manage the tough times, and the good times will take care of everything else. This is just not the case. Successful black businesspeople understand that you must also manage the good times as effectively. You must know when to spend or when to save. It is understood that additional resources generated during good times need to be leveraged for the upcoming roller coaster ride.

### Trait #6: Intensity of Purpose

When discussing this trait, one of the entrepreneurs was reminded of a young man with whom he worked at IBM who had an impact on most people who got to know him. He was a personable young man, highly educated and warm, yet very intense. He always seemed to have a serious look on his face and had a brisk walk that made it difficult for normal people to keep up with him. When he went through IBM's Marketing School, unlike many of his class-mates, he refused to cheat on the exams and laboratory exercises and often had to work by himself late at night to ensure his understanding of the principles and guidelines being taught.

When in the branch, this young man seemed to have little time for chit-chat and always took his work seriously. Indeed, this fellow was intense. People often commented that he was on a "mission." As it turns out, while all this was going on, this young account marketing representative was actually making plans to leave IBM to start his own business! Each day, he was driven by his vision of starting his business and nothing else mattered.

Successful black businesspeople possess an intensity of purpose just like this young IBM Account Marketing Representative. Once they commit to a dream or vision, they have the ability to focus all of their energies on realizing that vision. They let nothing stand in their way. Even when they're uncertain about how to go about achieving whatever it is they're after, they're intense enough to become unconcerned about making the "wrong" decision.

Just making a decision becomes a good decision because it often opens up other opportunities at the same time. Intense people understand that time is short and that you must squeeze all that you can into that time. Their intensity of purpose serves as a generator for added enthusiasm and as a compass for plotting the next steps.

### Trait #7: Ghetto Cunning

Some of us who were born and raised in the ghetto often expend great amounts of energy trying to forget it. In our attempt to forget, we sometimes try to change the way we dress, the way we talk, the crowd of people with whom we associate, and most importantly, the way we think. In our haste to change ourselves to become more "acceptable" to our mainstream counterparts, we often give up certain elements of our ghetto experience that would serve us well in our professions, our businesses, and our lives.

Some successful blacks who were raised in the ghetto or "on the streets" have learned to leverage the lessons they learned growing up in the slums and apply them within the business world. These people possess what has been romantically called "street smarts."

For example, in the ghetto, you learn early on (or you don't survive) that if someone doesn't like you, that person will eventually come after you. To protect yourself, you never turn your back on that person or let him catch you in a position where you're vulnerable. You keep the person at bay until you can figure a way to get him. Even when a truce is called, you remain alert for that person whenever he's in striking distance.

Black entrepreneurs realize that these same principles of survival apply in the business world. There is a toughness that being raised in the ghetto provided some of the entrepreneurs and they're not ashamed of it. On the contrary, they leverage it to their advantage.

### Trait #8: Feeling at Home on the Nile

The Nile River is the longest river in the world. It flows for 4,145 miles (6,671 kilometers) through northeast Africa. The Nile rises near the equator and flows into the Mediterranean Sea. The Nile irrigates about 6 million acres of land in what is now known as Egypt and about 2.4 million acres in Sudan. Majestically embedded in the Nile Valley, the river runs from what use to be the ancient nation of Kimit, northward to the Mediterranean Sea, in what was once called Upper Egypt. Unlike the sometimes erratic Euphrates River, the level of the Nile River rose and declined with such predictable regularity that the Nubians of the area developed calendars, agricultural strategies, and construction projects based on the river's movements.

Each year the Nile flooded, nurturing the crops that lined its boundaries. The monsoon rains dumped enormous amounts of water causing the river to swell and feed the major tributary, the Blue Nile. The now aggrandized river rumbled northward before eventually merging with the White Nile. The predictable flooding of the Nile River led to the development of irrigation technologies thousands of years before being used by Europeans. The process of irrigation along the Nile promoted a significant agricultural surplus and a spirit of collective discipline. The need to develop additional irrigation projects up and down the Nile promoted communal links along the river and helped unite the region known as the Nile Valley.

Successful African-American entrepreneurs are familiar with this irrigation effect. They understand that the flow of resources runs in both directions. There is some degree of "irrigation" from the majority community. This irrigation may have come in the form of a partner, business advisor, friendly banker, elected government official, concerned corporate purchaser, or just a friend with ties to the local business community. Conversely, these entrepreneurs understand that they must supply nourishment to their communities so that the community remains vibrant and so that the seeds of entrepreneurship and business formation are fertilized in the minds of coming generations. This nourishment may take the form of adopting local schools, conducting workshops or seminars on entrepreneurship, providing scholarship funding to needy students, or just using their influence to affect relevant local policies to their communities.

Clearly, any attempt to start and grow a minority-owned business using only the resources found within the boundaries of the minority community is doomed for failure. Yes, it sounds good to say that all of the resources necessary to grow a business reside within the African-American community, but reality tells us different. The fact of the matter is that all "sub-economies" are usually mutually dependent on one another and on the aggregate economy as a whole. Therefore, one sub-economy cannot prosper without developing irrigation channels to the others. This is especially true given the fact that the world is moving from a local economy to a global one. Dr. Sybil Mobley, Dean of Florida A&M's Graduate School of Business Administration, while speaking at Dartmouth College's Tuck School of Business Administration, recently said that the fact that Americans don't hesitate to buy Japanese, Taiwanese and other products produced by foreign countries indicates the existence of a world economy that has no allegiance to any country or any group.

The business leaders who contributed to this book understand the impact of a global economy and make extensive uses of resources within and outside of the minority community. For the most part, they view themselves as astute businesspeople first and as minority businesspeople second. A few didn't view themselves as minority businesspeople at all! Just businesspeople. Typically, when it was determined that additional resources were required, these people made every attempt to identify sources within the community. However, if the particular resource was scarce, they had no difficulty seeking the appropriate resources elsewhere.

Whether the irrigation is taking place from within the minority community or external to it, the flow of resources will dwindle unless the proper channels are developed and kept open. Just like our ancestors of ancient Egypt (Kimit) built channels to tap into the rich and fertile Nile River, the participants in the Dartmouth study consistently work at building the proper channels to tie into the information and financial resources found in the mainstream and within the community. They tend to belong to "strategic" civic and professional organizations. They understand the importance of supporting the appropriate politicians of both parties. By serving on the boards of specific corporations and non-profit organizations, they tap into resources that would normally not be available to them.

This "irrigation effect" that I speak of takes place not only in business settings, but also can take place in social settings. Basically, people do business with people that they know and like. As odd as it may seem, it is difficult to develop a long-term business relationship with a client with little social contact. Therefore, most businesspeople use social functions to learn more about prospective business associates. These functions could include golf outings, baseball games, dinner parties, political functions, and fund raisers.

The challenge that minority businesspeople face concerning irrigation through social channels is that whites tend to socialize with whites and blacks tend to socialize with blacks. Consequently, minority contact with potential white business associates through social channels tends to be limited. However, as awkward as it may have been, successful minority businesspeople develop social irrigation channels effectively and feverishly work to keep existing channels open while working on opening new channels to yet untapped resources.

### Trait #9: The "X" Factor Is a Big Factor

One of the most interesting observations made during this study was an issue that's been around a long time and one that most of us are familiar with. After careful thought, I decided to call this observation the "X"-factor because it specifically reminded me of some of the painful issues that Malcolm X dealt with during the early years of the civil rights movement. Keeping with my belief that the destiny of all African-Americans is indelibly linked to all people of color in the struggle, past and present, I've chosen to define this observation relative to Malcolm X.

To appreciate this analogy, one must first understand Malcolm and what he stood for. By some accounts, Malcolm had to be the most misunderstood African-American leader during the turbulent civil rights movement. Malcolm spent the majority of his public career in dedicated service to Elijah Muhammad, the then fiery, controversial leader of the Nation of Islam. With the support of the Nation of Islam behind him, Malcolm almost single-handedly moved the message of Elijah Muhammad from the temples where the Muslims worshipped across the nation's air waves and onto the university lecture circuit.

Malcolm's message, and it's delivery, prior to his break with the Nation of Islam, alienated him from a large segment of the black community and from most of the white community. Black leaders of the nonviolent movement, lead by Dr. King, viewed Malcolm as a serious threat to the civil rights movement. Concurrently, white Americans were fearful because early in his career Malcolm preached that white people were a race of devils whose sole purpose was to torment African-Americans. As would be expected, the majority of white Americans saw Malcolm as an apostle of violence and hate.

Malcolm's message changed drastically after his break with Elijah Muhammad and his subsequent visits to Africa and Mecca. Inspired by his experiences in Africa, Malcolm would later say with great dignity and humility:

> Because of the spiritual rebirth which I was blessed to undergo as a result of my pilgrimage to the Holy City of Mecca, I no longer subscribe to sweeping indictments of one race. In the future, I intend to be careful not to sentence anyone who has not been proved guilty. You may be shocked by these words coming from me, but I have always been a man who tries to face facts, and to accept the reality of life as new experiences and knowledge unfold it.

The core of Malcolm's message changed from espousing a separate black nation to his advocating that blacks gain control of the institutions, politics, and economics of their community. Unfortunately, at the time of his death, he was still to some degree confusing to some members of the black community and remained a "wild man" and a segregationist in the eyes of many white Americans.

Data from this study reveal that African-American businesspeople often find themselves wedged between the confusion of the black community and the fear and hostility of the white community. The black community is confused because although they'd like to support the minority businesses in their community, they feel that shoddy service and disrespect for its minority customers is the trademark of most black-owned businesses. The belief that anything produced by black people is inferior has become so prevalent that even some blacks themselves are convinced that it is true.

Concurrently, the white community, which in general has very little contact with the minority community, espouses similar beliefs, in most cases unjustifiably. Many whites have only limited exposure to African-Americans, usually within the formal structure in a work environment. For others, their only contact is through television and the movies. All too often though, the white-dominated media choose to sensationalize the failures of black businesses instead of magnifying the many successes. The unsophisticated among them often write off minority businesses as "fronts" for majority businesses. They're quick to attack the special programs designed to booster minority enterprises (the same way the government designed special programs to booster the aerospace companies during the Eisenhower years) as merely "give aways" that will ultimately amount to nothing.

The unfair assessment of black businesses by both the black and white communities places the African-American entrepreneur in an awkward position. Like Malcolm, many possess a sincere desire to build and strengthen the black community through various enterprise initiatives. This desire is partially responsible for them opting to go into business instead of pursuing the leisurely corporate existence. Yet they face a community that seems baffled at times and often divided about how it should deal with its own businesspeople. Although the white community doesn't fear minority entrepreneurs as it did Malcolm, it nevertheless doesn't understand them. This lack of understanding forces the minority businessperson to expend additional resources to address these misconceptions instead of using these same resources to produce jobs and wealth.

African-American entrepreneurs recognize the predicament that they're in and are beginning to put strategies in place to neutralize these concerns. Forums to bring together the minority consumer with the minority businessperson have become common in most cities. Most large corporations have specific units in place to help bridge the gap between the white corporate structure and minority businesses.

### Trait #10: Understanding the Conversion of Saul to Paul

One of the most powerful set of passages in the holy Bible is the

Epistle to the Romans. Written by Paul, this book covers justification by faith, spiritual counsel, God's plan for Jew and Gentile, and what we must do to gain the road to salvation. It's hard to believe that this inspirational book was written by Paul since he was one of the most vicious persecutors of Christians in his community.

Although Paul was a Roman citizen, he was a Jew of the tribe of Benjamin. As a typical Jewish boy, brought up in Tarsus, the capital of Cilicia, he learned the trade of tent making. In his youth, his devout parents sent him to Jerusalem, where he studied under the renowned Jewish scholar Gamaliel. Thus, Paul became a Pharisee, devoted to the strict observance of the law as a means of salvation. Unfortunately, as a Pharisee, Paul became an arch-persecutor of the Christian community. Paul was part of the group who stoned Stephen. He often breathed murderous threats against the disciples of the Lord, later obtaining special permission authorizing him to arrest anyone he found who followed the new way that was Christianity.

However, God was not finished with Paul. One day, while he was on the road and nearing Damascus, a light suddenly flashed from the sky all around him. He fell to the ground and heard a voice saying, "Saul, Saul, (he was Saul before Paul) why do you persecute Me?"

"Tell me, Lord, who are You?" asked Saul.

The voice answered, "I am Jesus, who you are persecuting. But get up and go into the city, and you will be told what you are to do."

Meanwhile, the men who were traveling with him stood speechless. They heard the voice, but could see no one. The Lord made Saul blind for three days, at the end of which, a man named Ananias healed his blindness and Saul, who became Paul, soon began proclaiming Jesus publicly in the synagogues.

Successful black businesspeople have an uncanny ability to change what on the surface appears to be bad and unchangeable into something that is worthwhile and rewarding. These businesspeople usually found themselves in dire situations at some point during their business careers. In some cases, they couldn't find the financing to maintain and expand their businesses, or like in the case of Earl Chavis, put trust in a business partner who turned out to be dishonest.

No matter what the ordeal, talented minority businesspeople tend to have the foresight to take what appears to be a hopeless situation and convert it into a promising and exciting opportunity.

### Trait #11: Resist the "Herd Instinct"

I interviewed a businessperson from New England who talked about how so many people possess the "herd instinct." These people, he said, are constantly on the move, but end up nowhere. His perspective reminded me of the sheep farm just down the road from where I live.

Each morning as I drive by, I fondly watch the sheep marching out to the corners of the meadow to feed. Usually, there is one sheep out front leading the herd while the others, apparently oblivious to their surroundings, blindly follow the herd out to pasture. I suspect there is a group of leaders within the herd who take turns leading the sheep to eat in the mornings and then leading them back to shelter at dusk. Without exception, each morning that I drive by, the sheep herd seems to carry itself as if it is one big monolithic unit versus hundreds of individual animals. This phenomenon has been termed the "herd instinct".

Successful African-American businesspeople have made it a habit to resist the "herd instinct." True leaders chart their own courses. Charting their own course has become the trademark of Ron and Cynthia Thompson. The Thompsons own what I believe to be the only railroad car manufacturing company owned and managed by African-Americans. Although it would have been safer for the Thompsons to pursue more traditional small businesses, they chose instead to study the market, understand their strengths, and weaknesses and chart their own course.

### Trait #12: Living by "The Pain Don't Hurt" Point of View

Sparky Anderson, former manager of the Detroit Tigers, had a knack for making some of the most profound statements in baseball. I recall reading a comment he made to one his players who was nursing an injury he had received during the previous season. The player, while going through spring training, was obviously in a great deal of pain. Sparky, in his infinite wisdom, tried to encourage the young player to continue playing despite his injury by saying to the player, "C'mon you can do better than that. You know the pain don't hurt."

In a way, this is very true in the lives of successful black entrepreneurs. When they commit themselves to their business goal without holding back, even with the many disappointments, failures, and uncertainties, they refuse to let the "pain" stop them. They continue to work their plan and plan their work as if "the pain don't hurt."

### Trait #13: Long-Term Greedy Versus Short-Term Greedy

Eliott Powell, a friend and former president of SDGG Holding Company, often stated that minority businesspeople need to become long-term greedy instead of short-term greedy. Although the word greed usually conjures up negative images in the minds of most people, it is one of the most essential elements for survival in the business world. Greed, properly applied, serves to keep the struggling entrepreneur motivated and somewhat frightened. A healthy dose of fear acts to keep the adrenaline flowing and also sharpens the senses. Those entrepreneurs who get in trouble because of greed do so because they allow it to cloud their judgment and coerce them into making short-term decisions that produce short-term gains; and end up causing them to fall short of their long term-goals.

It has often been said that the race is won, not by the swiftest, but by the runner who is steady and who perseveres to the end. Those African-American entrepreneurs who survive have learned to pace themselves in terms of reaping the rewards from their labors. They possess a quiet confidence about them that echoes out every so often that if they continue to do the right things at the right time and if they never give up, they will eventually win. Not only will they win but the rewards that are commensurate with the degree of effort, patience, and commitment invested will be theirs ultimately. These people have learned that being "short-term greedy" may feel good but the euphoria generated by these temporary gains normally dissipates soon thereafter. Successful African-American entrepreneurs have adopted a "long-term greedy" strategy and its paying handsome dividends for them.

## Trait #14: Experienced a Gut-Wrenching Event

As is true with most projects in life, getting started is usually the most challenging hurdle to overcome. For most, the reason it's so hard to get started is because doing it requires us to expand our "comfort zone." All of us like to operate in our own little "comfort zones." There are certain places that we're use to, certain groups of people we're comfortable with, and specific tasks that we're confident and comfortable in doing. We fail to realize that the tasks we become accustomed to doing on a routine basis begin to dictate for us the dimensions of our comfort zone. Unless we force ourselves to venture outside that comfort zone or to expand it, we will never grow, expand our skill base, or try new things.

The transition from an employee to an employer requires a major leap outside of our comfort zones, and the catalyst for such a leap is generally a gut-wrenching event in the life of the converted entrepreneur. A gut-wrenching event is any occurrence in your life that causes you such pain, anxiety, fear, and apprehension that you are forced to make a decision that under normal conditions, you are unlikely to make. Some examples of gut-wrenching experiences that I've heard are:

1) I was fired from my job and have no visible way of paying my bills or feeding my family.
2) Someone I knew who had far less talent than me started a successful company and has since become a millionaire.

3) My father died, left me the business, and made me promise to run it and not sell it.

4) My company had a lucrative early retirement program and "suggested" that I participate in it.

Of course, what may be a gut-wrenching experience for one person may mean nothing to another person. However, you will know when you've experienced a gut wrenching event.

The beauty of gut-wrenching events is that if they're accepted in the proper way, they can be used to your advantage as events to stimulate you to redefine your comfort zones. Those black entrepreneurs who ultimately accepted the entrepreneur challenge generally experienced one of these events before venturing out. To their credit, instead of letting it demoralize them, they used it to stimulate and to motivate them to make their dream a reality.

### Trait #15: The "Natural High" from Making Money

Successful black entrepreneurs enjoy making money. Although money is not always the primary motivator for these people, making it is fun and exciting. Often it is the "process" of making money that provides them the most satisfaction or "high" versus the end result of putting the cash in the bank.

### Trait #16: Being Comfortable with Being Uncomfortable

The transition from being an employee to becoming an employer is full of twists, turns, and surprises. This usually results in entrepreneurs being thrust into unfamiliar situations; nevertheless, entrepreneurs must still perform. Times such as these require black entrepreneurs to appear comfortable, even though in actuality they in fact are extremely uncomfortable.

### Trait #17: Correlating Exactitude with Chaos and Bringing Vision into Focus

At the University of Pennsylvania's 250th anniversary, the dean of the engineering school, Dr. Joseph Bordogna, a friend and mentor, was asked to describe the role that engineers play in society. His response was to say that "engineers are people who can consistently and effectively correlate exactitude with chaos and bring vision into focus." Like their engineering counterpart, successful African-American entrepreneurs possess the ability to translate their vision of an idea, product, or business, and bring it into focus. They are good at turning the dream into reality. While attempting to translate the dream into something real and concrete, they often find themselves in a chaotic situation that requires some degree of exactitude before progress can be made. These people have a keen ability to absorb the chaos and in turn structure and set direction so that the venture is able to develop and mature.

### Trait #18: Believing that Competitiveness Usually Defeats Racism, Sexism, and Classism

To accelerate the closure of WWII, the United States government released a horrible weapon on the world that created such an inferno that even Dante probably could not have imagined. This terrible weapon was the atomic bomb. When released over the blue skies of Japan, the bomb rained death and destruction, on the Japanese people in two of Japan's major industrial cities. Japan was bombarded into submission and with much of its industrial infrastructure destroyed, surrendered to the Allied forces, and thus the final chapter of WWII was closed.

As expected, it took the Japanese people a couple of decades to rebuild their country and their technological/industrial complex. Although Japan was able to produce and sell some products during the transition, the products that made it to the market were usually rejected and ridiculed as being inferior and not up to United States standards. I suspect there also existed a certain amount of animosity, racism, and mistrust by Americans toward the Japanese people.

Undeterred, Japan never gave up its quest to rebuild its infrastructure and continued to look for help from the West through people such as Dr. Deming, who worked feverishly and assisted them in modeling their industrial complex after that of the United States. Persistence eventually paid off for Japan and despite an obliterated infrastructure, and America's blatant racism against people of color, Japan rebuilt its economy and developed into one of the premier manufacturing forces on the face of the earth.

Successful African-American businesspeople have learned from the Japanese experience and understand that regardless of race, sex, ethnic origin, social/economic position, or scarcity of resources, if they can produce competitive goods and provide value add services at competitive prices, customers will buy the product or services, regardless of skin color. In most situations, competitiveness is the great race equalizer in business.

## Trait #19: Perpetual Dream Chasers

"Dreaming is an act of pure imagination, attesting in all men a creative power, which, if it were available in waking, would make every man a Dante or Shakespeare."

H.F. Hedge

During the late 1960s, Robert Kennedy, well on his way to becoming a successful politician and national leader at an unusually young age, explained, "Some men see things as they are and say why. I think of things that are not yet and ask, Why not?"

In this short, but insightful comment, Bobby defined the differences between people who chase dreams and people who don't.

Black business leaders who enjoy various levels of success always focus on events that are not yet and not only ask why not, but take it one step further and implement strategies to make the dream a reality. Ron and Cynthia Thompson of General Railroad Equipment & Services, Inc., conjured up the dream of owning and operating one of the few, if not the only, black-owned railroad equipment and services company in America. They didn't have any role models in this area to guide them through the rigors and difficulties of conquering such a herculean task. Unlike the franchise route, the road for Ron and Cynthia was uncharted and uncertain. Yet, they continued undaunted because they were chasing a dream.

The dream chasers are an interesting group of people. First they never have just one dream, but instead have a steady progression of dreams. Each successive dream appears to get much bolder and more encompassing than the prior one. It is not unusual to find a much larger, loftier dream unknowingly dissected into smaller dreams that work in harmony to achieve the bigger dreams. This often happens without the successful businessperson even being aware that this is taking place.

This progression of dreams that seems to define successful black businesspeople usually starts at some point during their childhood and remains a part of their lives until they die. Although most experience this phenomenon at a young age, it is unlikely that they are born with this trait or that it can be taught. In general, it appears that the trait is assimilated into black entrepreneurs through two channels: personal experiences and the proper types and amount of exposures. Successful businesspeople take seriously the issue of exposure because they realize that the dream-chasing virus is extremely contagious. Consequently, they try to surround themselves with other dream chasers.

Whether through personal experiences or exposure, these dream chasers learn early on that it is not the object of the dream that brings them joy, but is the "rush" they experience just knowing that the object of their dream is achievable and clearly within their grasp. Getting closer and closer to the object of their dreams is more exciting than the actual achievement of the dream itself. That is why dream chasers conjure up new dreams every time an old dream is realized.

The process of moving closer to making a dream reality is in itself magical. During the process, the dream chaser is injected with high doses of energy, excitement, creativity, and serenity that often spills over into other aspects of the dreamer's life. Thus, these dream chasers tend to be a pleasant and charismatic lot that act as magnets to other people and whom other people enjoy being around.

### Trait #20: *Ascending the Incremental Energy Levels of Success*

Delbert and Lula Mullens of Wesley Industries in Flint, Michigan, learned years ago how to leverage the incremental energy levels of success. For years, they struggled to build a painting and foundry business to support the manufacturing requirements of the major auto manufacturers. Although it took them years to achieve the dynamic and growing enterprise they now own and manage, they quietly and confidently achieved and accepted the smaller levels of success during the process of achieving the aggregate success component. Like most successful business leaders, Del and Lu get stronger and more determined as they ascend more levels.

**Exhibit 4-6. Success Levels to Goal Attainment**

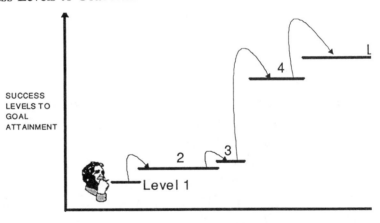

What are the incremental energy levels of success? As shown Exhibit 4-6, success, or the achievement of one's dreams, does not come in one big chunk. Successful businesspeople understand that to achieve ultimate success the individual must make his way from one success level to the next. After some specific period of time, if the entrepreneur's plan is sound and his commitment unwavering, the successful businessperson will go through a series of "level jumps" as he slowly makes his way to his objective.

Although all successful African-American businesspeople set a steady course of ascending these energy levels, they also understand that the duration of each level may vary and that the incremental jump to each successive level can be either very small or very large. However, he is committed to making the jumps regardless of the distance and duration of each successive level.


## Willie Artis
## Genessee Packaging
## Flint, Michigan


"The most important thing that a minority business can do is persevere. Perseverance is critical to success."

Willie Artis

Political and business deals are cut everyday in the nation's capitol. Men and women in designer suits frantically make their way throughout the many hotels initiating and closing business deals. It was no surprise that Willie seemed to fit right in with all the hustle and bustle that surrounded him in the lobby of one of Washington D.C.'s most elegant hotels. As we sat down to discuss Willie' ascent from his humble beginnings in Memphis to his successful manufacturing business in Flint, Michigan, his calm demeanor and soft voice quickly put me at ease. His relentless smile was only a precursor to an important meeting he was hosting that evening. Due to his proven track record, he had been invited to Washington by some local businesspeople to discuss a joint venture. How convenient. Having deals find you versus you chasing them is just one of the fringe benefits of owning and managing a successful business enterprise.

Although Willie looked comfortable in the successful CEO role, his advent into the business world was anything but comfortable. Early in his career, Willie accepted a job with a large manufacturing company. Because of his experience, he was given a significant role in managing the operations. It didn't take long before the owner of the parent company decided to expand his operation by spinning off a new subsidiary. The uniqueness of this new subsidiary is that he wanted it to be a "minority" company so that he could take advantage of all state and federal minority set-asides. There was only one problem. He didn't have any minority participation and needed to find a few minority players. Because Willie was already working for the parent company, he was a perfect candidate to become a silent partner of the new enterprise.

Although Willie did not perform any day-to-day functions for the new firm and continued to carry out his duties at the parent company, his participation in the venture legitimized the firm's claim of minority status. Consequently, by taking advantage of minority programs, the subsidiary was able to increase its annual revenues quickly from $250,000 to $4,000,000.

It didn't take long before Willie realized what had taken place. After confronting the owner about the improper company, Willie promptly resigned from the company. He began looking for a way that he could seek revenge on the greedy businesspeople who took advantage of programs that were specifically geared toward building the commerce base within the minority communities. After careful and deliberate thought, Willie concluded that the best way to punish this company was to go out and compete against it. Why not? He knew the business inside and out.

He knew that particular company's strengths and weaknesses and knew where the exposure points resided. But wait a minute! He had never started a business from the ground up. Yes, he knew the corrugated cardboard manufacturing business, but what about capitalization, marketing, financial analysis, and all of the other functional skills necessary to be successful in business.

To his surprise, Willie received his most ardent encouragement from an unlikely source. A General Motors buyer with whom Willie and his associates had done business was the first person to suggest that Willie leave the company and venture out on his own. Not only did this man make the initial suggestion that Willie start his company, he even went as far as to help them obtain financing, set up the proper business controls, and accompany them to strategic business meetings. Later, he proved to be instrumental in helping the new company obtain its first three contracts from General Motors. It became evident that this man believed in Willie and his partner and sincerely wanted to see them succeed. As is usually the case with new entrepreneurs, Willie was marching into unfamiliar territory and his friend in General Motors helped him to bridge the experience gap during the early days.

What Willie supplied was constantly changing. When he first started the company, he and his partner initially started in the contract packaging business. Nine months into the first project, they decided to try their hand in the corrugated paper business. Moving into the paper industry was a natural progression for these men because of their previous experiences with their past employers. At the time, neither thought they would ever get back into that business again. However, fate stepped in and revealed an opportunity they could not refuse. As Willie recalls it:

In the city of Flint, there was a corrugated business that was supposedly owned by an American-Indian. However, in reality it was a front minority business that was really owned by five non-minority businessmen. Again, these people thought that they could take advantage of minority set-aside dollars, but the company was clearly doomed for failure. My partner knew one of the owners and happened to meet him in the lobby of one of the local hotels and suggested to him that if he and his partner ever decide to sell, we would be interested. My partner was only joking but the man took him very seriously. My partner and I joked about this little episode and didn't think much more about it. However, we learned shortly thereafter that the owners of this company were serious about selling their business. They kept coming back at us with different proposals, and it became difficult not to accept their offer. At this point in time, they were doing about $250,000 of business per year and employed ten people. We were able to purchase the business for $65,000 and agreed to pick up the $80,000 debt. This business now generates over $4,500,000 in sales per year and is more profitable than the packaging company! I know that this is an unusual story, but it is certainly true.

If Willie were to be judged on his finesse at finding and consummating deals, one would think that he was a seasoned entrepreneur with strong and deep entrepreneurial roots. This assumption couldn't be further from the truth. Willie was born in Memphis, Tennessee, the youngest of five children. Although his parents were loving and patient, they didn't have much money and everyone in the family was forced to work and help make ends meet. Most work that his family could garner was working for someone else and consequently no one in his family ever seriously considered creating a business of their own. Even Willie never had any particular desire to go into business.

After high school, he went to work and attended college at night. He never was one to change jobs frequently and consequently ended up having only four different employers (including his present business) in his life.

In 1956, to obtain his first work experience in the corrugated business, Willie had to tell some untruths. On his initial job interview, when the employer asked him had he had any experience in the corrugated business, he replied yes, although he had none. Somehow Willie convinced the employer that he knew what he was talking about and was ultimately hired.

That was his first experience in this industry. For most of his working life, he has been in the corrugated business and really learned his trade while working for a corrugated manufacturing company in Chicago. Between all of this job experience, he did manage to attend college for a few years, but didn't seriously consider becoming an employer until 1975.

## *The Seeds of Discontent*

By the start of 1975, Willie had gained enough experience that he felt confident of his ability to start and run his own business. After finding himself a partner who was outside of the parent company that he had been working for, he decided to start a wood pallet business. This was to be his first attempt at starting his own business. Unfortunately for Willie, it became apparent that he and his new partner had great difficulty working together. While Willie's partner thought solely in terms of minority set-asides, Willie had a much more grandiose view of the company and made it very clear that he wanted to be able to successfully compete on all fronts - minority and non-minority. Willie had a more practical view on the proper use of minority programs:

> I do believe in minority set-asides as a start. Then after you've participated in these set-asides for a while, if that's what you want to do, you should then move out and participate in the other 90 percent of the business. You then become a normal businessperson with no minority stigmas attached to you whatsoever. Genessee competes with everyone and not just other minority companies. We have our own affirmative action program, which is unusual for a minority company.

After two years of trying desperately to make the partnership work, Willie and his partner went their separate ways. It didn't take long before Willie was able to identify another business partner with whom to go into business. Fortunately for Willie, this time, the two men were quite compatible and thus, this man became Willie's partner for his current business, Genessee Packaging, Inc.

## *Genessee Today*

Genessee's present organization is broken into two distinct

business units. One is the Corrugated Division, which produces corrugated paper containers for many different products for different industries. The other is the Packaging and Light Assembly Division. This division obtains numerous sub-components of a product (some of which are sent to them by GM, but the majority of them are purchased by Genessee) and assembles those components in-house to produce the final component. The end product is then sent to the customer and in most cases is used in the assembly of automobiles and other pieces of equipment. This second unit also re-packages automotive parts along with the assembling of final automotive parts.

They are currently tied into the GM Just-In-Time (JIT) inventory system which helps to minimize inventory expenses for GM and keeps Genessee well connected with GM's business flow opportunities. The accelerator used in some of GM's newer vehicles were assembled by Genessee. This accelerator has about eleven different component parts. Willie shipped out about 8,000 of these parts per day. Another product that Willie assembles is the MacPherson Strut Suspension System that's used on the Buick LeSabre, which is produced in Flint, Michigan. Genessee also assembles many of the oil filters that are produced by AC Spark Plug, which are used in automobiles and heavy equipment. With sales surpassing the $18 million per year mark, the bulk of the business is coming from the packaging side of the business.

## Staffing and Financing

When discussing the staffing of his company, Willie is quick to point out that in the early days of his company, the key positions were staffed by non-minorities. At that time, there was not a sizeable minority population to chose from nor was it easy to find the skills that he needed in the minority community. Consequently, several non-minorities got into key positions.

In 1979, Willie and his partner went to one of the local banks in Flint for additional financing. This bank agreed to loan them

$250,000, which was just enough money to drive them out of business. The GM buyer who was assisting them at the time tried in vain to convince the bank that this was not enough money to capitalize a business like theirs and that it was important that they be able to finance their inventories, payroll, and receivables. Even the SBA tried to reason with the bank to increase their level of financing, but it was all for naught. The bank refused to approve additional funds, and so Genessee reluctantly accepted the deal and the loan was guaranteed by the SBA.

Undaunted, at the suggestion of their CPA, Genessee decided to go across the street to another bank and apply for a business loan. The new loan officer understood the issues that faced this new business and tried to defend their case before the loan committee but his decision was overturned. This episode was terribly upsetting to the team that Willie had put together. As expected, the $250,000 did not provide the company with enough capitalization to support the business throughout the year and consequently forced Willie to revisit the last bank with which he had tried to do business. This time, however, the loan officer submitted a written proposal instead of a verbal one, as was used the first time. As fate would have it, the loan was approved! According to Willie:

> The loan was approved the second time around because of someone's name. My last name is Artis, and it just so happened that there was a very prominent family in Flint whose last name was Artis. I am not a part of that family, but one of the bank directors thought I was. The director looked at the application, saw the name Artis, and stated that he knew this family, it's a good family and that he thought that the committee should approve the loan. Just like that, the bank approved the loan for $750,000, without any guarantee from the SBA. They paid off the first loan and provided us a $500,000 line of credit. Since that time Genessee has had a fantastic relationship with that bank.

This experience epitomizes the hardships that minorities face when dealing with most financial institutions. Unless you know someone inside who will support you and that person is a part of the decision-making process, your chances of getting loans approved are significantly diminished.

## The Equity Piece

The equity participation in the initial funding was quite low by recent comparisons. The first bank wanted Willie and his partner to both put up $5,000. Willie strongly believes that if a business has a known business leader running the company with an established track record, 100 percent financing from a reputable bank can be obtained. With his present business status, right now, every acquisition that requires outside financing is financed 100 percent. For example, there is a $400,000 machine that they just obtained that will be shipped and installed into his plant at no significant cost to his company. He recently opened up a new plant in Milwaukee, Wisconsin, which again will require very little up front capital from Genessee. Clearly, the right businesspeople know of his accomplishments and view doing business with him to be a low-risk venture.

## Succeeding as Stated by Artis

### Profit Motivation

Whatever business you get into pursue it with one thought in mind - make money! Everything that you do must be profitable. You must think in terms of profits. If you have any philanthropic motives, put them on the back burner until you're able to enhance the corporation's profitability. If you pursue all of your business dealings with the idea of generating profits, all the other things - goodwill, job creation, support for the community and other niceties - will fall into place.

Genessee presently has 300 people working within the organization. The only other company, other than hospitals and banks, that employs more people than Genessee in Flint is General Motors.

## Business and Marriage

Business can sometimes play havoc with an owner's marriage. Willie warns young entrepreneurs:

Your thinking will change as you work to make your venture successful. You're often away from home, and you can't expect to spend normal working hours with your business and still succeed. Unforeseen problems occur all of the time, sometimes causing havoc with the business. The process of going from an employee to an employer is a difficult one that is just as difficult for a spouse.

The growth that takes place changes one's social habits. Willie found himself mingling with non-minorities on a more frequent basis and making more social commitments. Unfortunately, his spouse had not shared in this growth and consequently stress soon developed within the marriage, resulting in divorce.

## Business Conduct

Never, never, never, flaunt your wealth, once you've obtained it. Often minorities will hurry out to buy fine cars, diamonds, and furs as soon as the first profits come rolling in. This is the worst thing that a minority businessperson can do - particularly if she does a lot of business with buyers from the large corporations. When at work, Willie is rarely seen wearing jewelry or any other eye-catching accessories. He adds:

People need to remember that in most cases when you're trying to establish a customer base with corporations, you'll be dealing with the little guy (buyer) in the little cubicle. This person will most likely be a white male who may have three or four kids at home and a house in the suburbs that he's struggling to maintain. The worst thing that a minority person could do is to flaunt their wealth in the face of the buyer. You can bet the buyer knows that you're either a millionaire now or that you'll be one some day in the future. You never talk about that. If you need to flaunt your wealth, do it somewhere else, but never where you do business. Many minority businesses fail because they failed to follow this simple principle.

## Dealing with Competition

"I kill competition regardless of whether it's a minority or non-minority company."

Willie Artis

Willie is very clear on how he handles competition. It doesn't matter what race, creed, or color his competition is. He treats them the same. He goes for blood and often gets it. Competition is also beaten by playing the niche game. Creating a niche is very important and once it's created you take steps to keep other people out. Many companies will try to come in and steal your customers. Willie becomes very political when he needs to be and always tries to become the sole supplier for most of this customers, sometimes quite successfully. His determination to remain competitive is revealed by the fact that at one point he was leasing the same facility that his former employer also leased. Additionally, it was the same building that was used for the "fronted" minority company.

Genessee is also protected from downturns in the automotive industry. Willie has wisely diversified his customer base and has included many non-automotive industries in his client portfolio. This diversification has also served to help keep his competition on the defensive and less able to absorb any of his market share. Willie is a firm believer that you kill competition before it takes hold. This should be done regardless of the competition's ethnic origin.

## Establishing a Solid Customer Base

In the long run, a business, whether it's minority or non-minority owned, establishes a lasting customer base by leveraging its own reputation. Willie has followed this strategy by taking his profits aggressively and plowing them back into his business to buy new equipment, hiring young, bright engineers to implement the latest in technology, recruiting good people to help make the business strong, and providing some form of competitive edge. Basically, Genessee implements the same intelligent business strategies that all well-run businesses do. When potential customers hear of Willie's success and his format for conducting business, they often seek to establish business relationships with him! It is not suggested, however, that a new business sit back and wait for business to come its way. But it does illustrate again some of the perks of being a successful and established businessperson.

As wonderful as this all sounds, it was pretty tough for Willie to develop a strong customer base in the early days of the company. Although he was fortunate to get off to a good start, having won three major GM contracts, to begin really generating business, he had to go from door to door, selling himself and his company. He states emphatically that this is not always an easy thing to do. Establishing business relationships with non-minorities is sometimes difficult because of the cultural differences between the two groups. These differences sometimes cause suspicion, uneasiness, and distrust. However, no matter how difficult, the minority business person must stay in the buyers' and non-minorities' faces. He must pursue continuous social contact with potential customers so that the comfort level is enhanced.

As for which levels of the purchasing hierarchy new entrepreneurs should focus on, well, it depends. Although Willie spends significant time wooing the upper purchasing executives, he does not neglect the many front-line buyers in the little cubicles. The cubicle with the little guy is where the action really is. Recently, executives of some of the larger companies have mandated that their companies increase the percentage of goods and services that are purchased from minority businesses. While Willie sees nothing wrong with taking advantage of these opportunities, he adamantly refuses to use his minority status as a marketing tool. He says:

> I don't want anyone to be forced into doing business with me. I never sell minority. I never talk about it, and I never mention it. I don't wave the flag. The first thing that I do is sell myself. Then I move ahead and sell Genessee.

Willie reasons that except for corporate minority purchasing goals, why should this buyer want to buy from a business solely because it is minority owned? Why would he buy from someone whom, on a normal basis, he has no business or social contact with? Concurrently, if he has racist tendencies, how is that handled? Willie, in his usual style, attacks these issues head on. He continues:

> After making an appointment to see this buyer, the first thing he says to me when I walk in was that he didn't need any minority dollars and that his quota for minority purchases was already met. He kept using the word minority in everything that he said. He never stopped using the word. This was enough to drive me through the roof. However you can't let this type of reaction affect you. Although I never did business with this particular buyer, he did refer me to another buyer who held more promise for me. This guy would talk about golf, his grandmother, everything else except the business that I came to discuss. In spite of this disappointing first encounter, I never stopped coming to see him. I went to see other buyers at this company, but I never stopped visiting this particular buyer.

Every Friday, I would see this man for lunch. It became a standing appointment. In many cases, I would take him and his girlfriend out to dinner and we'd talk some more. Well, it took me nine months to get a contract from this man. The contract was only worth $1,100, but it was my first contract from this company and I was very appreciative of it. I was just as happy to receive this purchase order as I would have been had it been for one million dollars. I later framed that purchase order and placed it on my office wall. I look at it everyday. It tends to keep me humble. That $1,100 has now grown to over several million dollars of business.

Perseverance and staying power are of the utmost importance. Buyers will turn you off, say things to try to turn you away, and will try to beat you down. Most feel that if you want the business bad enough that you'll stay around. This is exactly what Willie Artis plans to do.

## Jim Miller
## AB&W Company
## Boston, Massachusetts

The voices inside of the board room seemed to get louder and angrier as the meeting of the board of directors of AB&W continued. Here was AB&W, seemingly converted from an old Penn-Jersey store or Pep-Boys retail shop, nestled within the concrete confines of a lower-income urban conclave called Roxbury. Actually, the front of the building gives the impression that the factory is actually very small. However once inside, the size of the structure seems to expand the further you move away from the front entrance. Beyond the offices in the rear are many different types of metal bending equipment, drills, presses, and so forth. Metal shavings are everywhere and the smell of freshly oiled machines dominates the aroma of the building.

As Jim Miller, the CEO of AB&W, emerges from the board meeting, he looks concerned, but in control. The other board members are smiling and chattering among themselves. Jim thanks them for attending the meeting and mentions to them that he appreciated their input and that he would be in contact with all of them concerning the issues that they discussed. As the men filed out the front doors and jumped into their Mercedes and BMWs, the concerned look on Jim's face remained. Clearly something in the meeting had captured his attention, and I wondered how he found his way into this business and why he chose this location right in the middle of the city?

## AB&W - Background

Like most of urban America during the middle to late 1960s, Boston was shaken by a cascading series of civil unrest from its urban minority community. As with most of the unrest during that period, much of the people's frustration with the system was that it did not provide people of color economic justice. Able and willing African-American men were shut out of many of the blue-collar jobs and were prevented from becoming working members of the critical trade unions.

It was in this atmosphere that United Carr, a division of TRW at the time, attempted to assist the minority community in rebuilding its own local economies and creating employment for its citizens. Jim Miller's boss at the time, Dick McGinnis, was a member of the United Carr executive management group that developed this concept and who had shown some commitment to making it all work. McGinnis hand picked Jim to come into AB&W and assist the fledgling firm with succeeding in the metal bending and metal fabricating business.

Initially, United Carr chose two black employees from TRW, Jesse Vailes and Jim Miller, to take charge of the company. The company wanted to start something that would grow and prosper, in contrast to the racial unrest that was going on in the country. To help AB&W get started, United Carr donated all of the equipment and a portion of the initial working capital. The company also gave AB&W their first contract which was worth over $100,000.

With the full support of United Carr, AB&W grew from a two-man operation to a full-fledged corporation enjoying consistent, steady growth. In 1976, although the company had achieved some modest success, it still was not a minority-owned operation. They (TRW) felt that if the black community was to embrace this venture, the company needed to be minority owned and operated. To entice both Vailes and Miller to buy the company, the two were given additional financial support and substantial salary increases. Eventually, AB&W became minority owned, although TRW still owned the voting rights and still maintained some control by remaining on the board of directors.

Due to his excellent performance at TRW, Jim's boss asked him to be on AB&W's board of directors in 1981. Jim accepted and later became AB&W's new president. His first step was to find African-Americans to replace most of the white board of directors. Jim went to major companies in the Boston area and found the highest-ranking blacks that he could find. He knew beyond a shadow of a doubt that in order for him to achieve the lofty goals to which he aspired, he would need the best talent around. Never having run a company before, what made Jim think he could manage it and make it grow?

## Beginning

Jim grew up in Darby, Pennsylvania, a small town 20 miles outside of Philadelphia. Like many kids from his neighborhood, he came from a broken home and grew up with his one sister and two brothers under the guidance of his mother. Although Jim was an extremely bright boy who did well in school, he never had any aspirations to attend college or to continue his education in any way. With no strong ambition driving him, Jim chose to drive a trash truck after graduation from high school instead of attending college.

Fortunately for Jim, before he started his new job hauling trash, his aunt from Boston, who happened to be visiting, learned of his decision not to attend college and became quite angry. She convinced Jim to come visit her in Boston, which he did. Little did he know that her plan was to get him to Boston and make him stay there to attend college. With his aunt's support, Jim attended college preparatory school at night and later enrolled at Northeastern University to major in accounting.

## Preparing for the Future

While Jim was still in college, he married. Only nineteen years old, with a new wife and mounting college expenses, Jim accepted his first job as a clerk at Cable Raincoat Company. While working and going to school, it took Jim over eight years to earn his degree, but earn it he did.

Jim proceeded to move rapidly through the TRW organization and assumed positions of increased responsibility. One of his accounting positions required him to supervise indirectly seventy people in accounts payable. Later, he also got involved in purchasing. In 1978, he was working as an administrative manager at TRW, dealing with lease negotiations for commercial tenants and working as a personnel coordinator. One lesson he learned was to report every piece of information that affected his group to his manager. His manager was a very detail-oriented man and wanted to have all of the details of all situations promptly communicated to him.

Jim's performance in his various roles within TRW caught the attention of some key executives there and resulted in his being asked to help build the AB&W Company.

## Business Difficulties

Since Jim has been running AB&W, the company has faced

some cash flow difficulties, but none so severe that it's necessitated filing for bankruptcy. Usually when the business runs short on cash, they have enough friends and ideas to be able to manage their way through it. Jim firmly believes that in spite of a few successes, the company has missed some major opportunities simply because it is a minority firm. He says:

> People told us, 'We just don't trust you because you are a minority. You'll have to prove yourself because we were burned once by a minority business and don't want to get burned again.' The tragedy here is that these were minorities themselves who felt this way.

AB&W has never applied for 8(a) status with the Small Business Administration, but may file for it soon. Jim's reluctant to do business with the Federal Government because of the time and resources necessary to earn business. But, if they decide to pursue federal contracts, then the 8(a) certification will become even more critical.

## Secrets of Success

AB&W is a debt-free corporation and Jim feels this is the major reason it has been successful at surviving difficult business conditions and severe cash flow crunches. TRW did an outstanding job at setting them up and structuring the corporation so that it could weather difficult times. To be successful, Jim suggests that the owner stay very close to the business instead of injecting multiple layers of management between him and the production environment. Jim adds that luck or divine intervention doesn't hurt.

## Advice to Entrepreneurs

Jim contends that wise businesspeople must always look for

ways to minimize their exposure. This could be financial, marketing, or other modes of exposure. Having strong people in the financial and marketing areas is essential. As far as family is concerned, if they bring nothing to the table, then leave them home. Many businesses have failed because owners allow family members to get in the way of making sound business decisions. Bring in other people who have a critical skill. Share the risk.

Lastly, Jim warns that preparation is key. You must do a good job when you are given the opportunity to meet a contract. When it comes to minority businesses, the public is very unforgiving. There is little room for error and hardly any goodwill toward minority businesses. Train your people and allow them to participate in off-site training as much as possible. Invest in good people, and they will reward you with a vengeance.

## Jerome Sanders
## Eliot Powell
## Robert (Bob) Wallace
## The SDGG Holding Company, Inc.
## Summit, New Jersey

The noise coming from his three sons horse playing in the back seat of the car could not stop Bob Wallace from thinking about the exciting business opportunity he had just uncovered while attending Dartmouth's annual Minority Business Executive Program (MBEP). For the last five years, he had been attending MBEP, hoping that eventually he would locate a medium-sized manufacturing company that the owner was ready and willing to sell. He and his buddy from his DuPont days, Jerome Sanders, had planned for such an acquisition for a long time. When Bob called Jerry from New Hampshire to share with him the good news, Jerry insisted that Bob stop by his home in New Jersey to explain the details of the deal. After a long six-hour drive, as Bob and his family finally rolled their old, green Volvo into Jerry's driveway, Bob's wife, Carolyn, kept wondering aloud, "Is this the deal? Is this the deal?" Bob shrugged his shoulders and replied, "I hope so, honey."

It was no coincidence that this meeting took place on Labor Day, 1987. Jerry was hosting a picnic at his home and had invited another friend, Kevin Brown, to attend so that the three of them could discuss business opportunities. Kevin was a classmate of Jerry's at the Wharton Business School and was also interested in creating wealth through business formation. Jerry would later admit that he purposely invited Kevin and Bob to his home so that they could size each other up as potential business partners. The three planned to spend much of the afternoon discussing their entrepreneurial interest and how the three of them might work closely together to pursue acquiring a business. Another twist of fate revealed - unbeknownst to all attendees, a friend and classmate of Bob's from the Tuck School at Dartmouth College, Eliot Powell, lived within a few blocks of Jerry's home. Feeling Eliot would be interested in discussing possible business ventures, Bob also invited Eliot to the picnic. Shortly after Eliot arrived, it became apparent that he had his sights on starting a business and had developed strong financial connections during his tenure on Wall Street. The four eager and excited young men discussed their entrepreneurial dreams far into the night under the watchful eye of the moon. This chance encounter was the beginning of SDGG Holding Company.

## The Dream

As the four dreamers shared their entrepreneurial visions, they all agreed that the key to developing wealth and success was through equity ownership in a company. Although no specific business or industry was identified, the group believed they could use their educational background, creativity, energy, work experience, and minority ownership in the company as leverage to acquire, build, and manage a portfolio of businesses.

Indeed, their shared view was that the business should be based on the collective strength of the individuals. Bob and Jerry had undergraduate engineering degrees and each had worked in the Engineering Services Division at DuPont. Having received their MBAs, Bob went to work for IBM in its marketing and systems engineering division while Jerry chose the consulting life and took up residence at Cresap, McCormick and Paget in New York. Kevin's background was in marketing and Eliot's background was in finance. After earning his MBA from Tuck, Eliot chose the high finance route and cut his financial teeth at Goldman Sachs on Wall Street during the "go-go" 1980s.

## But Which Business?

Besides the metal fabricating business that Bob had so excitedly rushed to Jerry's home to discuss, another business that seemed equally promising, based on the discussion that night, was contract manufacturing and contract packaging. Given the high concentration of pharmaceutical and personal products companies in New Jersey and the contacts of the individuals on the team, it was felt that this would be a promising area to exploit. Over the course of the next two to three months, Jerry, Eliot, and Bob kept in contact and slowly developed an interest in pursuing contract manufacturing and packaging deals in New Jersey and elsewhere.

## The Biotechnology Option

As the team quickly wrapped itself into the deal loop, they identified an available pharmaceutical freeze-drying facility just outside of Chicago. This particular plant was owned by Zenith Laboratories, a generic pharmaceutical manufacturer. SDGG realized that this was an opportunity that could not be passed up. The facility was under-utilized, running far below its known capacity. While only producing approximately $1 million of generic pharmaceutical per year, the facility was capable of handling a far greater capacity. Further research revealed that there was a limited national capacity of qualified freeze-drying facilities for pharmaceuticals, thus supply was far out of line with demand. In contacting several biotechnology firms in both the Boston and San Francisco areas, it was discovered that this type of facility was often required by biotechnology firms that could not afford the time or expense necessary to build and maintain this type of facility for experimental products. These companies often require short-run, freeze-drying capacity under FDA approved specifications. In fact, the team's market research indicated that there was only one other contract manufacturer in the country who provided freeze-drying services, and this vendor was operating at capacity all year round and was booked solid for the next couple of years.

The team felt confident that they had stumbled upon a lucrative business opportunity. As they quickly learned from talking with experts, attending biotechnology conferences, and conducting extensive industry research, most biotechnology products have shelf lives of less than 90 days, and the advanced planning required for this primary freeze-drying vendor was at least 90 days or more, leaving little or no alternative for many of the bio-tech companies to preserve their products. They realized that the freeze-drying facility in Rosemont, Illinois could easily be converted to a contract manufacturing company servicing the biotechnology industry.

Excited about their new "diamond in the rough" opportunity, the team set out to explore financing options to finance the proposed acquisition. Because Bob was still in Baltimore, he focused on identifying sources in the Baltimore-Washington area. Jerry and Eliot, who had worked in New York for many years, pushed on the contacts that they had made in the consulting and investment banking businesses. To their surprise, many of these contacts showed a strong interest in working with SDGG, and thus they were able to quickly secure soft commitments to finance the acquisition of the facility and develop their contract manufacturing business. Little did they know the challenge that awaited them.

The next two to three months were fast paced and grueling. The team spent a large amount of time developing a business plan and negotiating with the company to purchase the freeze-drying plant and other strategic facilities. Bob spent hundreds of dollars commuting back and forth between Baltimore and New York on the train. Concurrent to negotiating this deal, some of the owners of SDGG were still employed so the team had to be careful about how it communicated information about the deal to one another. To keep their identities a secret and to inject some fun into what was rapidly becoming an intense engagement, the three team members (Kevin Brown left to pursue other opportunities) adopted code names. Jerry's code name became "N-man" because of the network he had developed over the years. Eliot's code name became "Storm" because of the intensity he displayed when transacting business. Bob's code name became "Neutron" because of his disdain for unions and the missionary zeal he displayed in his attempts to "neutralize" unproductive workers.

## Reducing the Exposure

Although the freeze-drying deal was showing some promise, the team wanted to minimize its exposure so it decided to look at other business opportunities should the freeze-drying facility not work out. In April of 1989, Jerry and Eliot had scheduled a meeting with the president and CFO of Zenith Laboratories to discuss the acquisition. Zenith was a troubled company nearly in bankruptcy. This sale would have provided a means for Zenith to raise capital for its primary business - generic pharmaceuticals. Two days prior to their meeting with the officers of the company, they learned of the officer's dismissal by the board members and their replacement by an interim consultant. As a consequence of this series of events, the acquisition of the freeze-drying facility in Rosemont was no longer feasible.

With operating expenses increasing and no steady revenue being generated, SDGG was confronted with the dilemma of having to divide its time between pursuing acquisitions, which tend to have long payoff horizons, and diversifying into other businesses that could generate a quick cash injection for the firm, but which would require little start-up capital. After the team again reviewed its strengths and weaknesses, it decided to diversify into the auto/ equipment leasing and consulting businesses. The new organization looked as shown in Exhibit 4-7.

**Exhibit 4-7. SDGG Holding Company, Inc.**

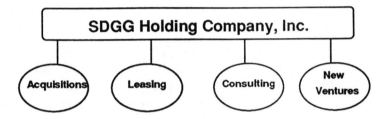

Diversifying into these two businesses was a natural fit for the team. First of all, one of Eliot's and Bob's classmates at the Tuck School of Business had recently purchased a tractor manufacturing company in Wisconsin. This company made tractors for specific commercial applications and special Department of Defense uses. To assist his clients in financing their purchases of these tractors, their classmate wanted to provide a leasing option to his customers. They agreed that SDGG would start a leasing company (Atlantis Leasing) and that Atlantis would provide the leasing arm for the financing of tractors. The consulting division of SDGG sprouted its roots after the advent of the Atlantis Leasing Company. Consulting came easy to the team because Jerry had many years of consulting experience and generated an extensive network in which solid consulting leads could be developed. The little cash generated from these two ventures would help prolong the life of the SDGG Holding Company.

## *Lawyers, Accountants, and Financial Sources*

Now that the three divisions - acquisitions, leasing, and

consulting - had been set up and the Zenith business plan had been prepared, SDGG spent a substantial amount of time searching for accounting, legal, and financial assistance to complete the rounding out of their team. Because the majority of the activity up to that point revolved around the New York City area, Jerry and Eliot focused on identifying legal and accounting consultants in the city. They interviewed all six of the big six accounting firms looking for assistance in developing the business plan, financial contacts, and references. Each of the firms had a small business group dedicated to assisting start-up companies like SDGG. Although the accounting firms understand the huge risk they assume when they bet on start-up firms, they also appreciate the tremendous returns they can achieve if they bet on the right company. The only way they can realize the benefit is by finding these companies while they're still in their embryonic stages. After numerous meetings with some high-ranking officials at Ernst & Whiney (now Ernst & Young) accounting firm, SDGG chose this firm to handle all of their accounting and financial work. As the two companies became more comfortable with one another, Ernst & Young would go on to play a major role in SDGG's pursuit and evaluation of other acquisition candidates.

In addition to searching for accounting support, a search was performed throughout greater New York for qualified legal firms to assist SDGG in managing the legal aspects of its business. Although at first a qualified minority firm was sought out, the search was broadened to include all firms that could provide appropriate acquisition services at competitive prices. Having interviewed over a dozen firms, Cleary, Gottlieb, Steen and Hamilton was selected. To the group's chagrin, very few minority firms were qualified to handle the type of work that SDGG was interested in pursuing. In fact, the only minority firm that came close to meeting SDGG's requirements were the law offices of Lewis and Clark, headed by Reg Lewis. Unfortunately for SDGG, Lewis and Clark had their hands full working through the Beatrice acquisition which has since become the largest black business in America.

Although cost was a major consideration in choosing a law firm, it turned out that Gottlieb was not the cheapest legal firm available.

In fact, it was the most expensive of those interviewed by SDGG. However, their abilities and insight into the merger and acquisition process was the strongest. This criterion, along with their established presence in the Wall Street deal flow, was the basis for their selection by SDGG management. The exposure that SDGG ultimately received to senior partners of the firm would help the struggling company weather the many stormy issues that would soon appear.

## Financial Sources

Another key aspect of selecting Cleary Gottlieb was their connection in to the financial community. Cleary provided inroads to Drexel, Burnham and Lambert, the Wall Street firm that was doing substantial junk bond financing in the mid to late '80s. Drexel was a source of equity dollars badly needed by SDGG. For the size and quality of transactions that SDGG was interested in pursuing, smaller companies like MESBICS were incapable of providing adequate financial resources.

## Additional Searches

Throughout the rest of the year, Jerry, Bob, and Eliot looked for other companies to buy. The spectrum was broad and the company's intensive research included evaluating a small precision glass company in Connecticut, capable of financially supporting only one of the three owners. The largest acquisition candidate was a food wholesaler and distributor based on the east coast that did $500 million dollars in annual sales. While this acquisition looked promising initially, the deal collapsed when the family who owned the business, changed their minds and decided not to sell. Undaunted, SDGG continued to evaluate deals across the country. They analyzed trucking companies, oil companies, and a variety of other opportunities. However, near the end of 1988, the team grew frustrated and fatigued for not having successfully located the type of company that would adequately provide the vehicle for the growth envisioned by the three. Would this be the end of the line?

## NEW YEAR'S, 1989

After committing themselves to seeing the process through the end, the team agreed to conduct a planning session during the first weekend of the new year. Jerry and Eliot joined Bob at his home in Baltimore for a weekend to discuss the successes and failures of the past year, revisit their goals, and try to map out a plan for SDGG to achieve its goals in 1989. The trio also chose to meet in Baltimore so that they could continue negotiations on the $500 million food distribution business. This deal failed to close due to "seller remorse."

Contract manufacturing still held an allure for the three. As a result of the intensive weekend discussion, they decided to focus on building or creating a primary assembly or sub-assembly company that focused on high-quality manufacturing and had substantial growth capacities. They did not expect to find such a business in the near future. Instead, the strategy was to build the business from the ground up.

Coincidentally, one week later, the team heard of a small finishing and assembly company available in Newark, New Jersey. This unknown company turned out to be a perfect acquisition candidate. It was a very profitable family business owned and managed by two brothers who had operated the company for over thirty years. This multimillion dollar company consistently generated $2 million in income for the two brothers along with healthy net incomes to service any debt and support projected growth. In addition, the brothers were able to take out of the company at least $350,000 in "life-style expenses." Clearly, the company had sufficient cash flow to support a leveraged acquisition.

In spite of the strong financials, there were inherent problems with the transaction. First, a high percentage of the business in the company came from one customer, IBM. This firm was the primary vendor for furnishing the computer covers for many of IBM's systems. This, however, represented 75% of their business. Additionally, the profitability of the company made it difficult to negotiate a price in terms favorable to the buyer. Additionally, the company's financial statements were merely compiled, not audited.

The company's CPA had only one client, the two brothers, their real estate holdings, their personal finances and the assembly company. The business had been run for many years as a family enterprise and the challenge for SDGG was to try and identify the true corporate profits and convince the lending community of the veracity of those profits. For a $12 million acquisition price, $2 million dollars would be taken back by the brothers, in the form of purchase money financing, $5 million dollars would be provided in the form of Mezzanine financing from Drexel, and $5 million dollars would come from senior debt bank financing. SDGG was to provide limited hard equity into the transaction, but would devote three full-time employees to the success of the company. In essence, this was a sweat equity deal. At this point in time, the three partners were getting very little sleep and were quite fatigued from the process. However, as each day drew to a close, they felt themselves moving closer and closer to owning this assembly company. Unfortunately, there were unseen events occurring that were out of their control, but would serve to close the door on the transaction.

During 1989, several events occurred that reduced the likelihood of this deal being completed. First of all, IBM had a poor operating year and sales were down. This company depended on IBM and suffered along with it. The positive aspect of buying a company in an off year is the downward pressure or the purchase price. The negative side was trying to demonstrate that the company had sufficient cash flow to sustain this transaction price of $12 million dollars.

Concurrently, Drexel had substantial problems following the Dennis Levin case, the Milken insider trading probes, and the weakening of the economy. The so-called credit crunch was in its early stages, and the ability to finance a transaction, as had been routinely done only a few years earlier, was now very difficult. This was no more evident than in the due diligence process when the company's compiled financial statements were inadequate to provide lenders and Drexel the comfort that sufficient cash flow was there to support the proposed transaction. In addition, the two brothers were uncomfortable in divulging factual information on the company to alleviate lenders' concerns, for fear that they would have to re-file former tax returns and pay penalties (and potentially face legal charges). One at a time, the wheels came off and it became more difficult for SDGG to reasonably expect to acquire the company in a short period of time. The deal died a slow, painful death.

Perhaps, most telling for SDGG was that the efforts of the officers were being funded solely from personal savings. SDGG had been counseled many times to find an avuncular source of financing that would allow them to continue pursuing their goal over an extended period of time. At the time, the urgency of getting a company acquired and under management seemed more important than finding the financial resources to sustain their efforts over a longer period of time. By the start of 1990, although the leasing and consulting divisions were throwing off some cash, it was not enough to sustain the cash drain that the acquisition efforts had created. At this juncture, the team decided to maintain SDGG as a going concern, but also to pursue revenue generation individually until a satisfactory deal could be identified.

## Let's Do It Again

Staring out the window of Eliot's new Chicago office, Eliot and Jerry ponder the lessons learned from this experience. First of all, in spite of the difficulties, both executives have resolved that a lot of things were done right. SDGG went out and found the right resources, and accounting, legal, and financial help, and established a company that had the right kind of goals, - goals that were well received in the market place. SDGG kept costs low by leasing the necessary equipment where possible, working out of their homes and in confined office space, "borrowing" supplies from previous employers, using their cars as the major mode of transportation, and taking advantage of free consulting services from their enormous network of friends and associates. This strategy allowed them to operate for more than two full years on an erratic income stream.

Conversely, it's simple to find the mistakes that were made. The primary mistake was having poor capitalization of the company. As a corollary to having limited funds, SDGG had to put all of its hopes into the acquisition of one company and hope for the best. Near the end, the firm was left with very few options. Jerry and Eliot echo each other's comments when they admonish anyone who is seeking to do a similar type of transaction to put their funding in place before spending time chasing deals. By having the funding already committed, the buyer can often use this situation as leverage in negotiating more attractive pricing, terms, and conditions.

**Part 5**

# WHERE DO WE GO FROM HERE?
# A STRATEGIC ANALYSIS

"We will either find a way or make one."
Hannibal

**As** the minority community contemplates where should it go from here in order to achieve economic justice in America, the image of Hannibal and his army's attempt to conquer Rome quickly comes to focus. Hannibal, who lived about two hundred years before the birth of Christ, rose from a North African city called Carthage. Historians often acknowledge that he was one of the greatest generals in the history of the world. His exceptional military strategy and leadership qualities are still taught in today's exclusive military academies.

During Hannibal's lifetime, the Roman Empire ruthlessly dominated that part of the world, which did not endear the Romans to Hannibal or his countrymen. Instead of focusing on the size and power of the Roman Empire - with its large, well-trained armies and exclusive dominance of the seas - Hannibal set out to conquer the Roman empire by outsmarting the Romans. Unaffected by Rome's seeming invincibility, Hannibal set out to instead conquer Rome! With about 65,000 troops, 7,000 horses and a herd of elephants, Hannibal brilliantly planned his attack on Rome by first crossing the Pyrenees, France, and then the Alps Mountains, before descending down on the Roman Empire. Although Hannibal lost most of his men, horses, and elephants during his passage through the Alps and although his army was severely outnumbered by the well-equipped Roman army, his army repeatedly outmaneuvered and outsmarted the Romans as they attempted to stop Hannibal's march on Rome. The Romans eventually did turn Hannibal back but only after paying an extremely high cost.

## *Where Do We Go from Here?*

Like Hannibal, the minority community must not focus on the size and enormity of the economic empowerment problems facing it. It must instead look for new ways and strategies to outmaneuver and outsmart the forces in the American society that seek to keep the community in a powerless position. This chapter attempts to construct a strategy to be used as a guideline in creating tactical responses to this economic dilemma.

When this research began a few years ago, it was determined that the success or failure of this project would depend upon the degree to which the following objectives were met:

1) To bring the issue of economic empowerment of the African-American community to the forefront of all of the other issues that confront our community today and to keep it there.

2) To underscore the critical role that African-American entrepreneurs play in completing the power structure of the community, thus broadening and deepening the power base of all African-Americans.

3) To stimulate the latent entrepreneurial spirit in some of us and motivate these "would-be" entrepreneurs to engage in the business development process, thus accelerating the formation and growth of businesses within the black community.

Achieving these objectives should not leave you with a feeling of "gloom and doom" concerning the fate of our community. Although I do believe the problem we face is a serious one, I have never doubted the minority community's resolve and determination in solving the problem. Being an engineer by training, I've always been one to look at a problem logically, dissect the critical pieces of it, and then develop a set of alternatives that would provide viable solutions for the problem. Consequently, as a fitting conclusion to this work, I've included a strategic analysis of our community's economic position and some tactical and strategic suggestions that will allow us to capitalize on our strengths while acknowledging our weaknesses.

## Strategic Analysis

Before a strategic plan can be developed to help guide the African-American community to economic maturity during the 1990s and beyond, we first must understand and evaluate the community's strengths, weaknesses, opportunities, and threats. As mentioned before, the strengths are those features of the community that are assets and could be leveraged to produce positive events that benefit the community as a whole. The weaknesses are those features that are non-leveraged and serve to make the community more vulnerable to internal and external threats. Based on the community's identified strengths and weaknesses, numerous opportunities can be generated.

Opportunities are those potential events that capitalize on the community's strengths while minimizing its weaknesses and that serve to thrust the community toward its ultimate goals. The threats are those existing or potential events that seek to prevent the opportunities from being realized. If the threats can be either prevented or reduced, then the opportunities have a better chance of becoming reality. Exhibit 5-1 outlines the strengths and weaknesses of the African-American community as perceived by the author.

Based on strengths and weaknesses as shown in Exhibit 5-1 and a review of external factors that affect the community, Exhibit 5-2 lists both the opportunities that can be realized along with the threats that could easily derail any progress in pursuing these opportunities.

With a clear understanding of the black community's strengths and its current weaknesses, Exhibit 5-2 outlines some opportunities that capitalize on our strengths but takes into consideration its weaknesses. However, success is never guaranteed because there are always threats lurking on the periphery that serve to impede or destroy any attempt to capitalize on the opportunities. Based on this analysis, it is suggested that the African-American community's strategy for the 1990s and beyond be conducted as follows.

W.E. Deming, one of the founding fathers of statistical process control and statistical quality control, once said, "A shared and commonly accepted philosophy of excellence helps provide constancy of purpose."

It is indeed constancy of purpose that will allow African-Americans to rid themselves of economic lethargy and dependency and assume their rightful positions as leaders of commerce and business. The philosophy and strategy that follows summarizes the author's views on what the African-American community must do to achieve economic empowerment and maintain a "constancy of purpose."

## African-American's Economic Statement of Purpose

-Provide services and products that are competitively priced, of superior quality and value, and best fill the needs of consumers within the black community, the overall American society, and ultimately the world.

-Achieve that purpose through the rapid formation of business enterprises within the black community initially and later within the overall community. Provide a working environment where the best and brightest young talent are allowed to hone their business skills and assume prominent business leadership roles.

-Through the successful pursuit of this commitment, expect the goods and services produced by members of the community to be second to none and to achieve leadership share and profit positions, and as a result of this commitment, black businesses and the black community will grow and prosper.

-Become expert professionals in the fields of law, medicine, business, commerce, education, science, and the trades. Recognize the value of the proper education and training in developing young people to assume leadership roles in local and national economies.

**Exhibit 5-1. Strengths and Weaknesses of the African-American Community**

| STRENGTHS | WEAKNESSES |
|---|---|
| Strong and persevering people. | Pervasive "mental block" concerning success and business development. |
| Make up the largest minority group in America. | Failure of the system to educate and prepare our young people properly. Lack of training in technologies. |
| Significant buying power (~$220 billion/yr.) | Continue to operate outside the "old boy" financial network. |
| Cultural diversity within our own culture. | Serious breakdown of values within the family unit. |
| Changing workforce demographics will make blacks, other non-whites, and women the dominant groups in the new workforce by the year 2000. | Lack of clear and directed focus by young blacks. |
| Recipients of a proud and rich history dating back to ancient civilization. | Failure to control or participate in the local economies within the black community. |
| Over-representation in the areas of professional sports and entertainers. Collectively, this group represents a potentially significant source of investment capital. | Owns only 3% of the U.S. business firms and generates less than 1% of total business receipts. |
| Growing and more astute African-American middle class. | Blacks make up a small percentage of the overall American population. |
| Blacks maintain pockets of political strength throughout the country, mostly in the major urban centers. | Overall, the black community finds itself in a weak economic position. |
| Blacks maintain strong leading edge educational institutions to train and prepare our young people, which will help move the community forward. | High black-on-black crime in major cities. Potential for proliferation of weak family structure due to rampant teen pregancies and fatherless homes. |

**Exhibit 5-2. Opportunities and Threats**

| OPPORTUNITIES | THREATS |
|---|---|
| Actively participate in emerging technologies. | Escalating racism and accelerating political swing to the right. |
| Leverage black political gains to help strengthen the urban areas. | Weakened economy over the long term. |
| Regain control of the economic base within the black community. | Deterioration of the family structure. |
| Develop mentor program between the African-American entrepreneurs and promising young talent within the community. | A lost generation of young blacks due to crime, drugs, violence, poverty, television, and indifference. |
| Teach entrepreneurship to our young people at a very young age. Emphasize the private enterprise option to young professionals. | Failure of our community to engage in the enterprise formation opportunities that abound. |
| Actively engage in the economic mainstream of society. Promote joint ventures between black-owned companies and white mainstream businesses. | Loss of desire to compete and to win. |

-Work effectively together to achieve common objectives; work individually and as a group to produce superior business results.

–Value others' differences. It is these differences that produce a diverse and powerful community. Members of the community assumes ownership of their individual and collective destinies and are committed to total excellence. The community recognizes that in order for it to grow, each individual must experience personal growth and be valued as an individual.

Overall, the above statements of purpose underscores the point that the economic philosophy of black nationalism is simply for the black community to take control of its own economies. Furthermore, if blacks fail to gain at least this control, their power base will be eroded further, leading to the ultimate annihilation of the community.

## The Purpose

To accumulate wealth within the community by first meeting the consumers' needs as well as that of the residents and the aggregate community better than anyone else.

## The Mission

· Control the businesses in our local communities!
· Accumulate wealth!
· Engage in business opportunities nationally and internationally!

## Strategies

The overall strategy should entail diverting sources of capital that exist within and outside of the African-American community in lucrative business ventures that regain control of our local economies. This will thrust us into leadership positions in the national and international business arena.

To support this strategy and to deliver the stated mission and move toward our new vision, strategic choices will have to be made that channel our energies, enthusiasm, and initiatives. By concentrating on these areas of strategic focus and working effectively together across all disciplines, sustainable economic momentum will be achieved. The suggested implementation strategies are as follows:

1) Leverage the Black-Based Political Muscle
2) Aggressively Engage in New and Emerging Technologies
3) Regain Control of Local Economies
4) Develop Mentor Programs for Potential Young, Black Entrepreneurs
5) Teach Entrepreneurship to Our Children
6) Actively Engage in National and International Mainstream

7) Gain Ownership of Strategically Positioned Mainstream Businesses

8) Engage in Joint Ventures with Mainstream Companies

9) Create and Leverage Business Network Among Minority Professional Athletes, Entertainers, and Aspiring Minority Entrepreneurs

10) Leverage the Power and Influence of the Black Clergy

11) Promote Sports Transmutation

12) Create Business Incubator Sites Within Strategic Locations

13) Ensure That the "Talented 10 Percent" (of African-Americans) Assume Their Destiny

14) Encourage One Another to Look Between and Beyond the Bars and Not at Them

15) Develop Joint Ventures with Other Minority Companies

16) Increase Buying and Selling Among Minority Companies

17) Keep Your Head to the Sky

## Strategy #1 - Leverage the Black-Based Political Muscle

When Maynard Jackson was mayor of Atlanta, Georgia, the state was in the process of expanding its local airport. Initially, of all the money being spent to rebuild the airport, very little was going to minority firms. Using the weight of his office, Mayor Jackson postponed the completion of that multi-million dollar complex until minority businesses were provided an opportunity to participate. Mr. Jackson had leveraged his political muscle to fortify the position of minority businesses.

Minority political leaders need to learn from Mayor Jackson and become more aggressive in championing the cause of minority enterprises. Keep in mind that leveraging a community's political strength is not new to the American scene. The European immigrants; the Irish, the Italians, the Jews, and others always used your newly won political muscle to help build up the small and burgeoning businesses within their communities. With the recent attempts by the right wing elements of our society to "circumvent" our hard fought business gains, it has become increasingly difficult to legislate fairness into the business arena for minority businesses, but new and creative ways must be found to accomplish this objective.

## Strategy #2 - Aggressively Engage in New and Emerging Technologies

Typically, all new products or industries move through a "life cycle" from the time of their inception to their replacement with new or substitute products or industries. This life cycle typically experiences three major phases as shown in Exhibit 5-3.

1) Development Phase
2) Growth Phase
3) Maturation Phase

**Exhibit 5-3. Product or Company Life Cycle**

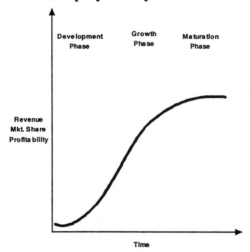

To take full advantage of this industry, you must first enter it as it moves into its growth phase or point of momentum. In this phase, you as an investor or player will experience explosive growth in a relatively short period of time. The maturation phase is the point at which the industry has shaken out; there remain a few competitors and the aggregate market size has peaked. In general, it would be unwise to enter a market or industry that has moved into the maturation phase.

There are, however, some industries that have moved into the maturation phase and still provide some opportunities for sharp and creative entrepreneurs. These industries are what I call your "bread and butter" industries. These are industries that will continue to grow and thrive as long as there are people. These industries include food, clothing, and pharmaceuticals. Although the annual growth of such markets may not be very aggressive, they will typically experience positive growth over the long term, thus making them prime acquisition candidates.

One of the biggest mistakes we can make is to blindly embrace old and mature technologies and industries at the expense of participating in new and exciting ones. The bread and butter industries should be used as "anchor" industries to generate cash while we leverage these companies to capitalize on new markets. Some examples of these new industries/technologies might include:

- Systems Integration
- Cellular Communications
- Total Quality Management
- Microgravity Research
- Small Satellite Technologies
- Space Transportation
- Space Communications
- Space Materials Processing
- Telecommunications
- Energy and Environmental Products
- Materials Recycling
- Automation and Advanced Manufacturing
- Satellite Imagery
- Robotics Systems Design

Along with the above technologies, the National Center for Advanced Technologies has also identified the following technologies as critical to America's competitiveness and survival:

- Rocket Propulsion
- Advanced Sensors
- Ultra-Reliable Electronic Systems
- Air-Breathing Propulsion
- Advanced Composites
- Artificial Intelligence
- Optical Information Processing
- Computational Science
- Software Development
- Superconductivity
- Advanced Metallic Structures

By penetrating these new technologies, or the industries that will support their development, we can position ourselves for future opportunities and growth.

## *Strategy #3 - Regain Control of Local Economies*

With all due respect to the Asian and Jewish communities, there is no way that the local grocery, pharmacy, cleaners, and convenience food stores should be owned and operated by anyone but members of that community. If these other groups are physically members of the local community and participate in it there is no problem. When these people only serve to suck resources away from the African-American community and concurrently show disrespect to our people, then they must go.

The beauty in these small, community-based "bread and butter" businesses is that you don't need a college education in order to own and operate them. Anyone with some basic smarts, energy, and drive can open a store and make it work. This must be the first action point in our strategy. The African-American community must regain its local economy and then use this economic base to leverage into opportunities outside of the local economy. Regaining our local businesses not only provides some economic muscle, but also serves to rebuild our confidence and help our people reverse the negative mind set about our ability to perform in business.

## *Strategy #4 - Develop Mentor Programs for Potential Young, Black Entrepreneurs*

The community's greatest asset is its young people. In spite of all the negative press that our young people receive, I'm still convinced that there exists a critical mass of young black men and women who are hard working, trustworthy, talented, and energetic enough to become the next generation of business leaders. Unfortunately, they will never be allowed to blossom unless they're given the opportunity to polish their skills in a real business environment.

I look to those members of the entrepreneurial ranks to identify this talent, commit resources to them, and make it their mission to nurture them until they're ready to venture out on their own. Those business leaders may have sons or daughters to fill this role. Using your son or daughter is great, but entrepreneurs need to reach beyond familial boundaries to capture others who may not have the good fortune of having mothers and fathers in business.

## *Strategy #5 - Teach Entrepreneurship to Our Children*

Given the resources that they have, and the problems they face, our public school systems do an excellent job of educating our young people. However, one area of weakness is that the system is not teaching our children about being entrepreneurs. As a child, I remember my teachers and parents admonishing me to go to school, get a good education, and find a nice job in some large corporation that would "take care" of me. At that time the big fatherly companies were Bethlehem Steel, Westinghouse, IBM, Procter & Gamble, and a few more. Not once did anyone explore with me the option of getting into business for myself.

If the cycle of economic dependence is ever to be reversed, we must stop encouraging our children to depend on large corporations for security and instead motivate them to develop enterprises of their own. This training must start as early as possible, preferably in the elementary schools. The emphasis, however, must remain throughout their formal training cycle. This includes teaching the rudiments of business formation in our high schools and community colleges.

It is unfair to place this burden solely on the shoulders of the school system. Parents have the ultimate responsibility to foster this type of thinking and growth among their own offspring as well. Not being in business is no excuse for not exposing your children to the entrepreneurship option. There are many ways in which parents can expose children to this option. Strategies that include putting them in contact with existing entrepreneurs, pointing out the importance of controlling your own destiny, and encouraging them to start child-oriented businesses such as grass cutting, selling lemonade, selling papers, or shoveling snow, are easy to do. Use these experiences to highlight the nuances of actual business ownership. Teach them to take pride in whatever they create.

As a general rule, we need to de-emphasize the corporate option and emphasize the entrepreneurial option.

## Strategy #6 - Actively "Engage" in the National and International Economic Mainstream

When I went through IBM's marketing school, one of the things that I learned was that in order to drive the business and meet my quota, I had to "engage" the competition actively and ultimately create opportunities. The act of engaging simply means to become a part of the process - to become a player. As shown in Exhibit 5-4, engaging allows you to direct enough opportunities into the pipeline such that you have sufficient qualified opportunities that emerge from the other end, having gone through numerous personal filters.

Even with the various levels of filtering that go on as the opportunities are sifted through the process, it is reasonable to assume that the more you engage, the more qualified opportunities you'll be able to identify.

It is not being suggested that you engage in a reckless manner, but instead to use S.W.O.T. and value analysis to screen options and employ limited resources efficiently. But, by all means, remember these three lessons: Engage! Engage! Engage!

**Exhibit 5-4. The Act of Engaging**

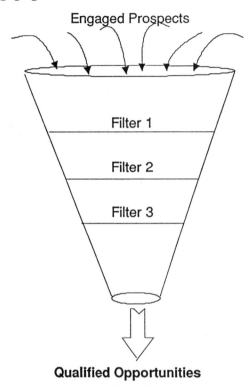

Strategy #7 - Gain Ownership of Strategically Positioned Mainstream Businesses
*Strategy #7 - Gain Ownership of Strategically Positioned Mainstream Businesses*

The 1990s will provide some unique business opportunities for those who dare to take charge. With Europe and Japan's manufacturing complexes being either totally destroyed or severely damaged after World War II, the world turned to the United States to produce the products necessary to rebuild these foreign, decimated economies. America's entrepreneurs rose to the challenge and responded by starting a flurry of businesses to respond to this national and international demand. On average, these companies started after WWII are about thirty to forty years old, and the original owners are ready to retire. Those who have children interested in the businesses will likely pass the businesses on to them. However, those who don't have children or who have children uninterested in the businesses will be looking to cash out, and that's where we need to position ourselves to assume these established, viable businesses.

In certain instances, even if these businesses are in mature industries, a few changes here and there by an imaginative marketing and technology-driven management team could squeeze a few more years and profits out of the business. Caution needs to be exercised, though, when evaluating which of these enterprises is worth acquiring.

## Strategy #8 - Engage in Joint Ventures with Mainstream Companies

To the credit of our legislative body, in some instances mainstream firms are encouraged to initiate joint ventures with minority firms. The idea behind this strategy was to provide some knowledge transfer between an established mainstream company and an emerging minority firm. The partnership would also serve to get that minority entrepreneur through doors that would normally not be open to him.

The joint venture strategy is a potentially powerful one. With mainstream companies economically encouraged to assure the success of the minority firm, both organizations grow and benefit. Once the minority firm learns more details of the business and is given an opportunity to exercise what's learned, the next time around the firm can go out and pursue similar opportunities on its own.

## Strategy #9 - Create and Leverage Business Networks Among Minority Professional Athletes, Entertainers, and Minority Entrepreneurs

Although there hasn't been much analysis on this topic, I would bet that in general, the people who generate the highest level of income within the African-American community are professional entertainers and athletes. Bill Cosby, Oprah Winfrey, and Eddie Murphy have the distinction of being three of the highest paid entertainers in the industry today. Michael Jordan, Bo Jackson, and Earvin "Magic" Johnson are three of the most marketable and visible professional athletes on the circuit. Just the income earned from endorsements usually far exceeds the millions they earn from playing ball. Michael Jackson makes millions simply by allowing his name to be attached to a line of sneakers. Ironically, the new sneakers failed but Michael still made his millions.

One only needs to take a closer look at the incomes of African-American entertainers to understand the enormous dollar potential that this special group of people control. Consider the 1992 earnings estimates that Forbes magazine compiled. They ranked the incomes of the top 40 highest paid entertainers in the industry today. The results of this analysis shown in Exhibit 5-5 may surprise you.

Once again, although African-Americans make up only 12 percent of the American population, 20 percent of the top 40 entertainers in America are black. The combined income of these eight performers is estimated to be close to one-half billion dollars ($418 million). This represents significant capital possibilities for the funding of business enterprises.

The income earned by African-American professional athletes is

**Exhibit 5-5. Highest Paid African-American Entertainers**

| Entertainer | Forbes Ranking | Est. Total Income From 1990 and 1991 ($Millions) |
| --- | --- | --- |
| William H. Cosby, Jr. | 2 | 113 |
| Oprah Winfrey | 3 | 80 |
| Michael Jackson | 5 | 60 |
| Janet Jackson | 13 | 43 |
| Eddie Murphy | 15 | 42 |
| M.C. Hammer | 19 | 33 |
| Arsenio Hall | 35 | 23 |

Source: *Forbes* Magazine

equally impressive. A review of the incomes of the professional football, basketball, and boxing athletes as shown in Exhibit 5-6 will underscore this point. According to the NFL Players Association, in 1988 the average salary was $229,000. The minimum salary was $50,000. The NBA salaries are a little more impressive with the average salary in 1989 being $500,000 and the minimum being $100,000. The superstars in the league, however, tend to earn significantly more.

Boxing is another sport that is overwhelmingly dominated by African-Americans. Although there are far fewer noteworthy boxers than basketball players, the salaries earned by the top boxers are even more impressive, as shown in Exhibit 5-7. There is no question that the African-American professional athlete and entertainer generates significant income that could be a viable source of funding for business ventures.

Although the earnings picture for African-American athletes sky-rocketed in the 1980s, the earnings picture for this group looks even more astounding for the 1990s. *Forbes* magazine's annual list of the 40 top-paid athletes for 1992, Exhibit 5-8, reveals that the top two highest paid athletes are African-Americans whose combined income exceeds $60 million. Another interesting fact pointed out in the *Forbes* study was that a boxer has earned the top salary at the beginning of each decade since 1940, when Joe Lewis earned $250,000, a large sum for that time period. Exhibit 5-8 is a ranking of black athletes pulled from the top 40 list, showing total income earned in 1992. As you can see this group continues to reap more than its fair share of earnings.

Although not as wealthy as the professional athletes but just as promising, is a large group of well-educated, highly professional, highly motivated, young business people who are rich on ideas and creativity but low on cash. There are even some black entrepreneurs who are running stable and promising businesses but need only a major cash infusion to catapult their business from a tier 2 business to a tier 3 one. If we can successfully marry the "deep pockets," market appeal, popularity, and charisma of our professional athletes and entertainers with the education, training, and drive of our young businesspeople, our community's ability to build large and profitable corporations could be significantly enhanced. A vehicle needs to be put in place to "connect" the two groups.

**Exhibit 5-6. Highest Paid African-American NBA Players**

| NBA Player | NBA Team | 1989 Salary (Millions) |
|---|---|---|
| Kareem Abdul Jabbar | Lakers | 3.0 |
| Patrick Ewing | Knicks | 2.8 |
| Magic Johnson | Lakers | 2.5 |
| Michael Jordan | Bulls | 2.2 |
| RalphSampson | Worriors | 1.9 |
| Akeem Olajuwon | Rockets | 1.8 |
| Alex English | Nuggets | 1.7 |
| Charles Barkley | 76ers | 1.5 |
| Moses Malone | Hawks | 1.5 |
| Danny Manning | Clippers | 1.5 |
| Robert Parrish | Celtics | 1.5 |
| Dominique Wilkins | Hawks | 1.5 |
| Joe Barry Carroll | Nets | 1.4 |
| Terry Cummings | Bucks | 1.3 |

Source: Forbes Magazine

## Strategy #10 - Leverage the Power of the Black Clergy

Ever since I've known Walter Thomas, he has impressed me as a spiritual, God-fearing man. Even when we were children growing up in the projects, there was always something about him that made me believe he would one day be a great worker for God and somehow play an important part in fulfilling God's will on earth. He was much older than me, but I often observed how he usually refrained from the abusive language, the violent outbursts, and drunkenness usually

**Exhibit 5-7. Top African-American Boxers**

| Professional Boxer | Boxing Income (1988) ($Millions) |
|---|---|
| Mike Tyson | 22.1 |
| Michael Spinks | 13.5 |
| Sugar Ray Leonard | 11.7 |
| Larry Holmes | 2.8 |
| Thomas Hearns | 1.5 |
| Marlon Starling | .78 |
| Evander Holyfield | .78 |
| Tony Tubbs | .67 |
| Michael Nunn | .60 |

Source: Sports Magazine

associated with the young males in my old neighborhood.

After I went away to college, I lost track of Walter for a couple years until one day I happened to pick up a magazine in my doctor's office and came across an article about my friend Walter and the new, progressive church of which he had just become pastor. The article went on to pontificate about how he had taken over the church, increased the membership by 400 percent, introduced various programs to feed the hungry, protect the weak, clothe the naked, and provide housing for the homeless. He had indeed become somewhat of a celebrity in the city at a very young age.

When I returned home, I made it a point to visit Walter at his new church - and what a church it was. Housed in a glorious cathedral, his congregation was energetic, young, educated, and proud of its blackness. It was amazing for me to see how easily he moved his audience with his silver tongue and strongly-articulated thoughts.

**Exhibit 5-8. 1992 Top Earning African-American Athletes**

| 1992 Ranking (Top 40 in USA) | Athlete | Sport | Total Income (Millions) |
|---|---|---|---|
| 1 | Michael Jordan | Basketball | 35.9 |
| 2 | Evander Holyfield | Boxing | 28.0 |
| 11 | Larry Holmes | Boxing | 8.2 |
| 19 | George Foreman | Boxing | 7.0 |
| 22 | David Robinson | Basketball | 6.7 |
| 23 | Magic Johnson | Basketball | 6.5 |
| 31 | Dwight Gooden | Baseball | 5.4 |
| 34 | Patrick Ewing | Basketball | 5.0 |
| 38 | Barry Bonds | Baseball | 4.8 |
| 40 | Cecil Fielder | Baseball | 4.6 |
| **Total Income ($Millions)** | | | **112.1** |

Source: Forbes Magazine

Then it hit me. What would happen if after Walter finished talking about God he then talked about economic empowerment and business formation within the African-American community? With the influence and respect that this one man had with hundreds of people, he could easily transform the community's dormant entrepreneurial complacency into a bustling hub of commerce. What if all of the Walters across this country, who are blessed with the same influence as he, started preaching economic empowerment and black entrepreneurship to their respective congregations? What if all of the young people in those churches could hear the news and respond to it? What a difference that would make in the number of people within the community who engage in viable business opportunities!

We, as a community, need to leverage this special relationship that our men of God have with their communities. Although this special relationship is what helped blacks through the early days of racism, I submit that this same relationship can be leveraged to aid in our climb to achieve economic parity through rapid and successful business formation within our community.

## *Strategy #11 - Promote Sports Transmutation*

According to the 1990 census, there are 29,986,060 blacks living in this country (more if you believe the census undercounts poor black folks). This fact implies that blacks make up 12.1 percent of the American population. Based on this group's percent of the population it would be logical to assume that blacks should make up approximately 12.1 percent of the players in professional sports. Although the more equipment intensive sports such as tennis, hockey, swimming, gymnastics, and others have very little minority participation, less cost-intensive sports like football, basketball, baseball, track and field, and boxing are often dominated by minority athletes.

Recently, it has been estimated that blacks alone make up over 60 percent of all football players in the National Football League and over 90 percent of the players in the National Basketball Association. In the area of boxing, there has not been a serious non-black contender since the days of Rocky Marciano - even that was questionable. Clearly, in the more visible sports, blacks are over-represented among these ranks.

Why do black men make up such a large proportion of these professional athletes? Are black men, as some would have us believe, "natural" athletes and outperform their white counterparts because of their innate physical superiority? I doubt it. Is it because white owners and coaches prefer the dark gladiators over the white ones, to carry out the owner's bidding on the fields and ultimately earn the franchise millions of dollars? There may be some truth in this hypothesis, albeit a small amount. I submit that the reason black men dominate these sports is because they are the best players, not because they are naturally better but because they work at it the hardest.

The time our young men invest in playing sports from early childhood to adulthood is staggering. Many begin the training and indoctrination process before they reach the age of one.

For those of you still not convinced of this phenomenon, conduct the following test. If you have sons, how many times do well-meaning friends and family members tell your sons, "You're going to be a great football player one day or a boxer or a basketball player." Or you'll hear, "Look at the legs on that boy. He'll make a good tightend or lineman." Consequently, the boys grow up trying to fulfill this expectation and end up spending all of their spare time playing and practicing sports. Over time, the young man begins to equate his esteem and respect from peers as a function of his sports prowess. It becomes his badge of acceptability. Why do you think that so many young men engage in death threatening arguments over a game of basketball? Because too many equate how well they can play basketball with how much of a man they are or use it as a measure of their respectability. How frightening all of this is.

Sports transmutation suggests that the African-American community needs to re-direct some of the resources and energy that it channels into creating super athletes into avenues that will create super businessmen and businesswomen. Sports transmutation means the community should begin de-emphasizing the sports option and emphasizing more the entrepreneurial and business options. It means instead of always telling a young black male that he'll be a great football or basketball player, tell him instead that one day he'll be a great doctor, lawyer, inventor, or entrepreneur. Sports transmutation means that we encourage the young men to engage intellectually with their white peers on every front and teach these young men to believe they can excel in these areas as well as in sports.

Sports transmutation does not mean a young black male is denied the chance to participate in sports. Sports within the proper overall development strategy can be a powerful vehicle for teaching young people important lessons in life and for preparing them for the responsibilities of adulthood. Sports transmutation does suggest that the same qualities that help create a super athlete (endurance, leadership, mental and physical fortitude, etc.) are the exact same qualities that help build successful businesspeople. The only difference is the target end point. The African-American community needs to reassess its end point for its young males and begin redirecting them.

## Strategy #12 - Create Business Incubator Sites Within Strategic Locations

As a young pre-med student, one of the projects my wife, Carolyn, had to complete was to design, build, and operate an incubator system for young chicken eggs. This was a very demanding project because in order for the eggs to hatch into young healthy chickens, a number of critical environmental factors had to be created and monitored over some period of time. The temperature, pressure, humidity, air flow, and other critical factors had to be monitored and occasionally adjusted to maintain the proper incubating environment for producing healthy little chicks. If the environment was especially fertile, the little chicks would have a good probability of maturing into healthy, young adult chickens.

This same incubator concept that is taught in science classrooms could also be applied to small, fledgling minority businesses in our communities. This concept, although tried before, is seldom implemented correctly. For this strategy to work it requires that we:

1) Identify the appropriate businesses to participate in the programs. The businesses should be owned/managed by conscientious business-people who have the commitment and skills necessary to be successful.

2) Create successful businesses quickly. The public must see visible signs that the program is working. Success feeds on success. Consequently, early successes will motivate the other incubator businesses to strive for the same degree of accomplishment.

3) Choose candidates that are either in growth industries (e.g., systems integration, client/server systems development, telecommu-

nications) or are in businesses that may not be high-growth areas but satisfy a long-term need within the community (e.g., food, fuel, auto repair).

4) Create a capital fund before the incubator is started to fund the chosen businesses as necessary. Contributors might include the local government, local corporations, private donors, and insurance companies. Make sure that the financial commitment has been made before advancing the concept too far.

5) Use the local graduate schools of business administration to provide free consulting services to the incubator businesses. Work out a deal with the business school administrators where the students can earn credits based on the work that they complete for the small businesses. Where appropriate, invite certain students or the school to become equity partners in some of the ventures. Obtaining the buy-in of talented young people or the local college will provide a readily available source of funds and talent throughout the venture's existence.

6) Effectively leverage the "WIFME" (What's In It For ME?) concept. To win the full support of the local government, the incubator group must be successful at showing the government how it will benefit by supporting the incubator projects in their jurisdictions. Usually, the benefits will be blatantly obvious - boost for local economy, reduction in welfare roles, reduction in local unemployment, rejuvenation of sub-economies within the minority community, and reduction of the load on the social programs. Once the government buys into the concept, the next step is to gain their commitment to donate one of the vacant buildings (usually there will be plenty around) to be used to house the incubator businesses. The municipality will likely be amenable to some form of tax reduction for the businesses participating in the incubator program.

One successful entrepreneur who has been successfully applying the incubator concept throughout the Virginia, Washington, D.C., and Maryland region, is C. Michael Gooden. Mr. Gooden, president of Integrated Systems Analysts, Inc., in Arlington, VA, is founder of one of the most successful systems integration firms. Yet, he has found time to mentor dozens of minority businesses in the Federal Government marketplace. Mr. Gooden's assistance to these small-fledgling firms includes advice on obtaining financing, guidance in developing business plans, help in setting up finance and accounting systems, assistance in understanding federal acquisition regulations, marketing, building strategic alliances, and the awarding of subcontracts.

Mike Gooden is unwavering in his belief that minority business is a critical link to mobilizing talent from within the minority communities. Mobilizing this talent to productive ends allows the minority community to fully contribute to America's economic well-being. Remember, the incubator concept can work as long as all of the pieces are in place.

## Strategy #13 - Ensure That the "Talented 10 Percent" Assume Their Destiny

In 1908 W.E.B. DuBois suggested in his work titled, *Philadelphia Negro,* that within the black community there existed a group of achievers who were capable of providing the creative leadership necessary to lead the community in solving its many problems. I believe the same holds true as it pertains to business leadership within the African-American community.

I have never been able to convince myself that everyone has what it takes to start, develop, and manage a thriving business enterprise. On the contrary, it has been my observation that most people, regardless of race, ethnic, or religious persuasion, do not have what it takes to become successful in business. However, there exists a group within our midst who possesses the skills necessary and who are destined to do great things.

The challenge remains: How do we get this talented 10 percent to recognize their talents and concurrently motivate them to resist wasting these talents working for someone else and making them rich when they should be enriching themselves and their communities? W.E.B. DuBois sounded the charge when he said:

Above all, the better classes of the Negroes should recognize their duty toward the masses. They should not forget that the spirit of the twentieth century is to be the turning of the high toward the lowly, the bending of Humanity to all that is human, the recognition that in the slums of modern society lie the answers to most of our puzzling problems of organization and life, and that only as we solve those problems is our culture assured and our progress certain.

## Strategy #14 - Encourage One Another to Look Between and Beyond the Bars and Not at Them

My childhood friend Jimmy was not a bad kid; he just did bad things. Jimmy, who was intellectually keen and street-wise always seemed to find himself in the middle of any trouble that erupted in the neighborhood. Whether it was gang fights, snatched purses, breaking into the freight trains that passed through our neighborhood, or burglarizing the local stores, you could bet that Jimmy was somehow involved. Unfortunately, because of Jimmy's propensity for injecting himself into the midst of controversy, he spent a great deal of time behind bars - locked in prison.

On one of my many visits to the penitentiary to see Jimmy, I found him in a very depressed mood, more depressed than normal. As we talked and I brought him up to date on all the latest gossip from the neighborhood, his eyes remained cast on the cement floor of the prison visiting room. No matter what I said his eyes continued to search the four corners of the floor as if he was waiting for a hole to open up and he could then flee the cold and treacherous environment that had become his life. Finally, after trying everything I knew to cheer him up, I asked him, "Jimmy, what the hell is wrong with you, man? I've been pouring my heart out to you for the last thirty minutes and all you've done is blankly stare at the floor of this damn room. What's wrong?"

Jimmy slowly raised his head from his hands and with tears

streaming down his bearded cheeks his eyes met mine and I understood instantly what was happening. Jimmy confided in me, "Rob, this place, these bars are driving me crazy. During the day, I do nothing but fight my cell mate because he has on numerous occasions tried to rape me. I can't sleep at night because I'm afraid he'll either slit my throat or succeed in taking my manhood. Every morning that I wake up, I see these bars and when I lay down at night, I see these bars. Maybe this is the best I'll ever do. Maybe I should just give in and let him rape me. At least I'll be able to get some sleep and not worry about getting sliced to pieces in my bed at night."

Unable to find the right words to encourage and soothe him, I responded, "Jimmy, you've got to stop looking at these bars and try looking between and beyond them." Without knowing it, at that moment, I had given Jimmy enough encouragement to keep fighting, to survive the prison experience, and ultimately to turn his life around.

How many of us are like Jimmy and have bars that define our lives for us? These bars, if stared at too long, prevent us from reaching our potential and from going on to achieve great things. Our bars are anything that we use as an excuse for why we can't achieve and why we can't be great. Some of the bars that people use are:

1) Race
2) Economic Status
3) Sex
4) Physical Handicap
5) Education
6) Social Status
7) Physical Appearance
8) Weight
9) Speech or Accent

What are your bars? Can you add to this list? The point here is that all of us need to encourage one another to accept the hand that life has dealt us and formulate a strategy that leverages the hand that we've been dealt into a winning hand. Anyone can make this contribution. By caring, communicating, and taking ownership of someone else's lack of confidence, we can help aspiring black entrepreneurs to not look at the bars created by the mere fact of their ethnicity, but instead look between and beyond those bars to the destiny that is truly theirs.

## *Strategy #15 - Develop Joint Ventures with Other Minority Companies*

It often appears that minority companies have a more difficult time entering joint ventures with other **minority** firms than they do with majority firms. Some minority entrepreneurs who could be categorized as Brown Bombers or Blood and Guts businesspeople are distrustful of people outside of their respective companies and frequently fail to take advantage of larger opportunities.

Despite these fears, minority businesses have to begin identifying and leveraging joint venture opportunities among themselves. I wonder how much business has found its way back into the mainstream business channels because a minority firm did not have the resources to adequately do the job. This situation is even more tragic when you consider that the firm competing may have had 80 percent or more of the necessary skills and resources to complete the engagement, but was rejected because it didn't have the remaining 20 percent.

In developing potential joint venture partners, older, larger, more established minority firms should look not just to joint venture with other large firms. There are many smaller, younger, firms that have very talented young people working in them who could benefit greatly from the experience of an older firm and still provide some value to the partnership. An arrangement like this would also allow the more established firm to shape and mold an emerging minority firm into the larger firm's image and provide the groundwork for a long and profitable business relationship between the two firms. Remember, 1 percent of a big deal is a lot greater than 100 percent of a little deal. Think about it.

## *Strategy #16 - Increase Buying and Selling Among Minority Businesses*

Earlier in this book, I discussed the importance and impact of Africa-Americans buying from and supporting African-American businesses. However, the buck doesn't stop there. The corollary to this theory is that African-American businesses must buy from other minority businesses as much as possible! The impact of the community realizing this strategy is phenomenal. Let's conduct a little exercise here to illustrate my point. Assume the following:

1) African-American businesses currently generate approximately $20 billion in revenue each year (close enough).
2) On average, black firms spend 30 percent of their revenue stream on expense items such as rent, automobiles, energy, office supplies, travel, printing, accounting and legal ex penses, and so forth.
3) African-American businesses mirror the African-American community and only 16 of every 100 dollars spent by the community is given to African-American businesses.

Given the above assumptions, the total dollars available for black businesses is:

$$(\$20,000,000,000) \times 30\% = \$6,000,000,000$$

The amount of money that is currently being spent by black firms with other black firms is:

$$(\$6,000,000,000) \times 16\% = \$960,000,000$$

Therefore, the amount of funds available to be spent with black firms that is currently being spent with mainstream firms is the following:

$6,000,000,000
$ -960,000,000
$5,040,000,000

Whatever way you want to split the hairs, the result is the same. By just doing more business with ourselves, the black community can increase the annual receipts of its businesses by more than 25 percent (conservatively speaking). If we don't buy from ourselves, then who will? If not now, when?

## Strategy #17 - Keep Your Head to the Sky

The African-Americans' objective of realizing economic justice in the United States for the next decade and beyond will be a tumultuous and difficult one to achieve. Not only does the community have some internal challenges that it needs to face but it also faces some formidable challenges from forces external to the community. It is unlikely that those who are already in control of America's economic engine will willingly relinquish even a portion of such power without a struggle.

Someone recently said, "Those in power do not concede power to the powerless unless the powerless first demand it and secondly show a determination to fight for it." Inevitably, there will be some casualties as a result of this struggle. Some talented, aspiring black entrepreneurs will never get their chance, and some black-owned businesses won't survive long enough to assume their rightful place in the journals of industry and commerce. However, if this is the price to pay for achieving economic justice for blacks and other minorities, then let the struggle begin. African-Americans must continue to demand and fight for economic justice and achieve economic empowerment or the community's long-term survival will at best be questionable.

Despite these challenges and the difficulties that face the community, African-Americans and other people of color must remain optimistic about the ultimate outcome of this fight. "Keep your head to the sky" means that you ultimately believe in the final morality of the universe and in the power of maintaining the moral high ground. This phrase, made famous by the music group Earth, Wind and Fire, conveys the thought that if you keep trying and never give up, ultimately you'll succeed. It means that no matter how dark and pessimistic the community's economic condition may seem, one must maintain faith. If a person continues to step to the plate and swing at the pitches, ultimately he will hit a home run and win the game. This is the faith that must carry the community until economic justice is a reality. God bless and *keep your head to the sky!*

# Appendix I: Status of African-American Businesses

## *An Overview*

I hope there are no doubts in anyone's mind of the critical role that African-American entrepreneurs will play in the survival of the black community. As we move into the 1990s and the 21st century, black entrepreneurs will share an even greater burden to enhance the well-being of all Americans, especially Americans of African descent.

If black entrepreneurs are to assume this burden, it makes sense to understand their strengths and weaknesses. Consequently, a thorough analysis of the building of economic power through the rapid formation of business enterprises should begin with the current status of African-American businesses within the United States. Only after we've documented where we are and where we'd like to be can we begin to construct a workable strategy for focusing our resources intelligently to accomplish the economic power of which we speak.

They say that opinions are like hearts - everyone has one. I certainly do have mine, particularly when it comes to evaluating the current status of black businesses. In my opinion, the condition of black businesses is at best that they're surviving. Although we have seen significant growth in the number of businesses started, the depth and breadth of these new players tends to be somewhat limited.

Currently, 94 percent of all African-American businesses are sole proprietorship, which is good for the individual, but doesn't provide much leverage for the African-American community. According to a survey by the Commerce Department's Census Bureau, the number of African-American business firms in the United States has increased from 308,000 in 1982 to 424,000 in 1987. This equates to a 38 percent increase during a five-year period.

## Exhibit A. U.S. Firms

| | 1982 | | 1987 | |
|---|---|---|---|---|
| | Black Firms | All Firms | Black Firms | All Firms |
| a) # Business Firms | 308,000 | 12,000,000 | 424,000 | 13,700,000 |
| b) % Total | 3% | 100% | 3% | 100% |
| c) Receipts | $9.6 billion | $967.5 billion | $19.8 billion | $1,994.8 billion |
| d) % Total | 1% | 100% | 1% | 100% |
| e) Receipts Per Firm | n/a | n/a | $47,000 | $146,000 |
| f) % Firms in Service | n/a | n/a | 49.4% | 43.4% |
| g) % Firms in Retail | n/a | n/a | 15.6% | 16.4% |
| h) % Firms in Construction | n/a | n/a | 8.7% | 12.1% |
| i) % Firms in Transporation and Public Utilities | n/a | n/a | 8.7% | 4.3% |
| j) % Firms in Finance, Ins., Real Estate | n/a | n/a | 6.4% | 9.0% |
| k) % Firms in Mfg. | n/a | n/a | 1.9% | 3.2% |
| l) % Firms In Agricultural Svcs., Forestry, Fishing, & Mining | n/a | n/a | 1.8% | 3.5% |
| m) % Firms in Wholesale | n/a | n/a | 1.3% | 3.2% |

Source: Commerce Department's Census Bureau

As shown by Exhibit A, while the number of black firms was increasing, so was the total number of firms. All United States firms rose 14 percent, from 12 million to 13.7 million during the same time period. These 424,000 businesses constitute 3.1 percent of the total United States business base. Concurrently, these 424,000 businesses generate $20 billion ($19,763,000,000) in annual revenue, which comprises just under 1 percent of the nation's total receipts.

## Comparison to Mainstream Firms

In Exhibit A, the percent of the nation's firms owned by African-Americans remained at 3 percent from 1982 to 1987 and generated only 1 percent of total receipts for those years. Receipts per firm averaged $47,000 for black-owned firms, compared with $146,000 for all United States firms. Approximately 54 percent of

**Exhibit B. Industry Groups**

| 10 Industry Groups With Largest Dollar Volume of Receipts | Dollar Volume of Receipts ($ Billions) |
|---|---|
| a) Automotive Dealers and Service Stations | 2.2 |
| b) Business Services | 1.6 |
| c) Health Services | 1.4 |
| d) Special Trade Contractors | 1.3 |
| e) Miscellaneous Retail | 1.1 |
| f) Eating and Drinking Places | 1.1 |
| g) Trucking and Warehousing | 1.0 |
| h) Good Stores | 1.0 |
| i) Personal Services | 1.0 |
| j) Wholesale Trade, Nondurable Goods | 0.7 |
| Total Dollar Volume of Receipts | 12.0 |

Source: Commerce Department's Census Bureau

all black firms had receipts under $10,000; fewer than 2,000 had sales of $1 million or more. The 189 black-owned firms with 100 or more employees accounted for $2 billion in gross receipts or about 14 percent of the total receipts for all black firms.

## Industry Groups

As indicated by Exhibit B, the black firms in the industry group with the largest dollar volume of receipts in 1987 were automotive dealers and service stations. Business services was the second largest industry group in terms of dollar volume of receipts. More than one-half of all dollar volume receipts generated by black-owned businesses were generated in the automotive dealers and service stations, business services, health services, and special trade contractors industry groups.

## Metropolitan Area Breakdown

The ten top metropolitan areas with the largest number of black-owned firms accounted for 36 percent of the national total for all black owned businesses and 36 percent of gross receipts. It is interesting to note that of the top ten areas, seven (eight if you include the late Harold Washington, former Mayor of Chicago) have black mayors and a sizeable African-American population. Are these examples of political leverage being used to promote and support black enterprises? What do you think? The top ten metropolitan areas are shown in Exhibit C.

## Where Do We Go from Here?

Although I applaud the fact that the number of black businesses has increased by 38 percent from 1982 to 1987, the fact remains that

**Exhibit C. Top Ten Metropolitan Areas**

| Top Ten Metropolitan Areas | Revenue ($ Billions) | Number Of Black Businesses In These Areas |
|---|---|---|
| 1) New York | 1.2 | 28,063 |
| 2) Los Angeles-Long Beach | 1.3 | 23,932 |
| 3) Washington, D.C. | 1.0 | 23,046 |
| 4) Chicago | 0.9 | 15,374 |
| 5) Houston | 0.4 | 12,989 |
| 6) Atlanta | 0.7 | 11,804 |
| 7) Philadelphia | 0.6 | 10,249 |
| 8) Detroit | 0.5 | 9,853 |
| 9) Baltimore | 0.3 | 8,593 |
| 10) Dallas | 0.2 | 7,857 |

Source: Commerce Department's Census Bureau

94 percent of all black businesses are sole proprietorships and that black businesses as a whole make up only 3 percent of the nation's total firms. As mentioned earlier, these same firms generate only 1 percent of the total receipts of the nation's businesses. Although there does indeed seem to be some activity in initiating business enterprises among us, I'm afraid that the current direction will not ultimately lead to the community realizing any substantial benefit in terms of the number of jobs created and the additional influx of capital.

Some will ask: Well, how many black-owned businesses should there be to achieve some form of economic parity? What percent of the total receipts generated by America's businesses should black businesses contribute? What should be the make up of black businesses in the various industry groups and across legal structures (i.e., corporations, partnerships, sole proprietorship) to provide a foundation for further economic development? These are all very good questions. Unfortunately, I don't have an answer for most of them. However, we need to start somewhere. As an initial target, we should have representation in the number of businesses and in total receipts that are commensurate with our percentage of the population. Currently, African-Americans constitute 12.1 percent of the population. Therefore, it makes sense that 12.1 percent of total businesses be owned by African-Americans and that this same group, on average, generate 12.1 percent of the total receipts.

# APPENDIX II: THE MINORITY BUSINESS EXECUTIVE PROGRAM AT DARTMOUTH COLLEGE

**All** of the participants in this study are minorities and entrepreneurs, but there is one other common factor among them. The majority of them are alumni of the Minority Business Executive Program at the Amos Tuck School of Business Administration at Dartmouth College. This group of entrepreneurs was chosen because as a program facilitator at Tuck, I grew very close to some of them and was able to conduct thorough discussions with some on both their personal histories and business experiences. Since 1983, I have collected ideas, thoughts, concerns, and backgrounds of these individuals in preparation for writing this book. It seems appropriate that I provide a background on the very program from which it all started.

The Amos Tuck School of Business Administration at Dartmouth is the oldest graduate school of business in the world. Annually, the school conducts some of the most extensive executive training programs offered anywhere. One of those, which was the basis of this study, is the Minority Business Executive Program (MBEP). The Tuck School has conducted this program for senior executives of minority-owned and operated businesses since the summer of 1980.

Although the qualifications for participating in the program have evolved since the summer of 1980, the basic requirements remain the same. Currently, minimum qualifications for inclusion in the program suggest that the participating chief executives have been in business at least three years and have minimum annual revenues of $300,000 and employ no less than three people. If a firm is fewer than three years old, the executive must then have management experience in a Fortune 500 or large, minority-owned company.

Likewise, if a firm generates less than $300,000 per year but is an unusually successful venture or is unique in some way, exceptions can be made. The 1990 gross revenues of participating firms ranged from $100,000 to $80 million per year while the number of employees of these companies ranged from 1 to 320. Although the majority of the executives are African-Americans, the program usually attracts sizeable representation from the Hispanic, Asian, and Native-American communities.

## *The Early Days*

It was during the summer of 1980 that Paul Doscher, the director of conferences, negotiated a contract with the SBA to bring 48 presidents and owners of 8(a) companies to Hanover, New Hampshire for a "mini-M.B.A." seminar. The first MBEP faculty director, Willis Greer, and his Tuck colleagues offered a curriculum that included financial management, accounting, marketing, organizational behavior, and production. The participants also received a detailed briefing on recent legislation affecting minority business by speakers from both the government and private sectors. The program was administered through Tuck's conference office by Jan Bent until 1985, at which time Paula Graves took over as program manager. For many of the participants in the one-week residential program, it was the first opportunity to receive formal advanced management education, although most had several years of business experience.

In 1981, Tuck incorporated MBEP fully into its annual executive education programs. The school reached beyond the original 8(a) participants to admit a national group of participants along with minority alumni of Tuck's full-time M.B.A. program. The alumni of MBEP 1980 were encouraged to provide continuity as the program began the transition from year to year. Guest speaker Wallace L. Ford II, (D'70) then Assistant Secretary of Commerce for New York State, summed up the mood of the class saying:

It is important to point out that what the Tuck School is doing is extremely significant in serving as a model for what other business schools have to do and certainly what the private sector has to do in this country if we are to see some real progress and some substantive economic development in the American minority community.

## *The Transition*

This successful formula - Tuck faculty, a general management curriculum, outstanding minority guest speakers, and experienced participants - would become the program's framework for the next ten years. During that period, MBEP implemented progressive ideas and changed themes, but the original goals and vision of the program remained unchanged.

As word of this minority business program spread, the participant list for 1982 grew. This 1982 group included the core group of loyal alumni seeking continuing management advice along with new participants. In addition to the basic courses, MBEP began to offer new sessions on how to make a presentation for a bank loan, negotiation and bidding exercises, a communications class, and a lecture/discussion on the legal aspects of contracts for minority business owners, led by Edmond Noel (D'68, T'69).

A turning point for the program came in 1982 when the program began forging an alliance with National Minority Supplier Development Council corporate sponsors and regional councils. General Electric, through the efforts of Bill Chapman, former minority purchasing coordinator, paved the way for many corporations to sponsor minority suppliers' attendance at MBEP for the next six years. Along with direct sponsorship, Alcoa Foundation, ARCO, and Chemical Bank responded to the need for program development support the following year. The early support from these major corporations provided the framework for future corporate involvement.

In 1983, Faculty Director Hector Guerrero added operations, grievance negotiation, and a one and one-half day strategy simulation exercise to the program. Although MBEP was beginning to expand its scope and breadth, 1983 was also a pivotal point in terms of the program's survival. Enrollments in the program from 1981 to 1983 had been smaller than the original class. Consequently, it was uncertain if there existed a critical mass of minority entrepreneurs to support the program such that the resources expended could continue to be justified. At this point, Hector Guerrero, Paul Doscher, Jan Bent, and I developed a strategy to solidify the minority business community's commitment to a program such as this and to ensure the school's commitment to the program. By the end of the 1983 program, Tuck had given its full commitment to support the program over the long term.

The enthusiasm and commitment generated by the 1983 participants found its way into the 1984 session. That class included two individuals who would later have a significant impact on the program. Hollis Smith, executive director of the Southern California Regional Purchasing Council, and John Robinson, president of the National Minority Business Council, played an active role in developing Tuck's ties with the regional purchasing councils. Robinson, of the National Minority Business Council, and James Cossingham, president of Jayco Enterprises, a consulting firm, were forces behind the formation of the MBEP Alumni Association. That year, several representatives from supporting corporations participated in a Corporate Minority Purchasing Panel, co-moderated by Marlena Raimey (P&G) and Mike Johnson, president of Johnson Energy. Other panelists included Gary White, who was owner/president of Trans Jones, Inc., and John Haines of General Motors.

From 1985 to the present, the program has gained momentum. The MBEP alumni network has grown to over 400 strong and shows no signs of slowing down. The group has matured to the point where many are considering group projects, such as collaborating on joint ownership of businesses and monitoring potential minority business leaders through the public education systems. Some members have even developed internship programs for Tuck students to work at minority-owned companies between their first and second years of Tuck MBA studies.

One reason MBEP has obtained and maintains such momentum is due to the strong support provided by the large base of corporate and regional council supporters. Distinguished guest speakers in recent years have included U.S. Representative Parren Mitchell, former chairman of the House Committee on Small Business, The Reverend Leon Sullivan, author of *The Sullivan Principles,* Dean Sybil Mobley, Graduate School of Business and Industry, Florida Agricultural and Mechanical University, Ms. Harriet Michel, president of the National Minority Supplier Development Council, Mr. Philip E. Benton, Jr., President and Chief Operating Officer, Ford Motor Co., and U.S. Representative, Esteban Torres, Chairman of the House Committee on Small Business.

Given the diverse backgrounds of this group of minority entrepreneurs, it was an excellent group on which to base this study. With more than 400 MBEP alumni throughout the nation, it appears to be an excellent representation of minority businesses across the country. Tuck sponsors this week-long program every summer for minority business executives and in 1987, added a second program, the Advanced Program for alumni who choose to continue their formal management education. If you'd like to attend this program or desire more information about the curriculum, you should contact:

> Ms. Paula Graves
> Program Director
> Minority Business Executive Program
> Amos Tuck School of Business Administration
> Dartmouth College, Hanover, NH  03755

You may also contact the author:

> Robert L. Wallace
> President
> The BITH Group Holding Company
> 10227 Shirley Meadow Court
> Ellicott City, Maryland  21042

# APPENDIX III: GLOSSARY OF BUSINESS TERMS

**Affirmative Action** - Business actions undertaken by government and corporations in the hiring and employment of minorities, women, and other disadvantaged groups to remedy past abuses and discriminatory practices.

**Asset** - Something owned by a corporation or individual. Balance sheet classifications include:

> **Current Assets.** Assets that can be converted to cash within one year.

> **Long-term Assets.** Machinery, real estate, furniture equipment, etc.

> **Prepaid Assets.** Assets that represent expenditures to be used over a certain perion of time before being reversed or amortized.

> **Intangible Assets.** Assets whose value is placed on the books without a corresponding cash transaction.

**Asset Base** - The combination of assets that are owned by a company or individual and that serve to add value or can be used to generate wealth.

**Book Value** - The value of stock that is not based on market value but instead is based on actual tangible net worth of business. The book value is usually calculated by netting out intangible assets from net worth and dividing this result by the number of outstanding shares of common stock.

**Break-Even Analysis** - A calculation involving comparisons between fixed and variable costs to determine the volume of sales required to cover expenses, usually on a monthly or annual basis.

**Budget** - A summary of the anticipated costs and expenses a company or individual expects to expend over some predetermined period of time.

**Business Cycle** - A term that describes recession or inflationary trends in the national economy.

**Business Planning** - The process of predicting future events that could have impact on a business and concurrently mapping out a business plan of action to use the events to the company's advantage or minimize any possible negative impact from such events.

**Collateral** - Property pledged by a borrower to protect the lender in case the borrower defaults on transaction.

**Current Assets** - Assets that can be converted to cash within one year.

**Debt Service** - The total of principal and interest payments on a debt over some specified period of time.

**Economic Empowerment** - The process of making it easier, practical, and possible for a person or group to produce, market, and distribute goods and services to the marketplace.

**Economic Injustice** - The act of systematically preventing a person or group from freely and practically producing, marketing, and distributing goods and services to the marketplace. Group's economic progress is usually hindered through overt and subtle discriminatory practices.

**Economic Life** - The time period in which a capital asset is expected to remain in practical use. After this period, the asset is considered to be obsolete and has no economic value.

**Economic Value** - The current market value of an asset.

**Equity Capital** - Capital contribution made by equity participant in business start-up or expansion, which allows him or her to retain partial ownership of business.

**Factoring** - A financing strategy used to raise capital that involves utilizing accounts receivable as collateral.

**Financial Accounting** - Type of accounting that emphasizes the historical reporting of the operations and financial position of a business to external users on a periodic basis. It encompasses accounting for the company's revenues, assets, equities, and expenses.

**Financial Statements** - Set of financial reports that serve to summarize a business' financial condition. These reports include the balance sheet, income statement, statement of retained earnings, statement of changes in financial position, statement of changes in owners' equity accounts, and other notes.

**Fiscal Year** - The twelve-month period recognized by a company for tax purposes. The fiscal year does not have to follow the calendar year and can vary for different companies.

**Fortune 500** - The five hundred largest corporations in America.

**General Services Administration (GSA)**- Arm of Federal Government that coordinates service provision to the other arms of the Federal Government.

**Gramm-Rudman** - Bill passed by the Congress to reduce the federal deficit systematically.

**Hierarchy of Needs** - A widely adopted theory of human motivation developed by Abraham H. Maslow, that stresses two fundamental premises:

1) Man is a wanting animal whose needs depend on what he already has. Only needs not yet satisfied can influence behavior.

2) Man's needs are arranged in a hierarchy of importance. These five levels of need are (a) physiological, (b) safety, (c) social, (d) esteem, and (e) self-actualization. Once one need is satisfied, the next level of need becomes primary and demands satisfaction.

**Intangible Assets** - Assets whose value is placed on the books without a corresponding cash transaction.

**Leverage** - The use of borrowed capital to gain control over the most investments and property as is possible. Using someone else's money to acquire businesses.

**Leveraged Buy-Out (LBO)** - The takeover of another company by using borrowed funds or someone else's capital. The assets of the acquired company are usually used as collateral for the loan, and theoretically, the loan is re-payed from the operating capital of the target company.

**Long-term Assets** - Machinery, real estate, furniture, equipment, etc.

**Management Accounting** - Reporting of accounting information for the sole purpose of enhancing management's ability to maintain control of the operation.

**Mean Income** - The average income of a specified group. The number is calculated by adding the incomes of all members of the group and dividing by the number of members.

**Median Household Income** - The middle value of household income such that one-half of incomes are below this number and one-half are above. The median may be a more accurate measurement than mean when the data group under consideration has exceptionally high values at both ends of the distribution.

**Net Worth** - An entrepreneur's ownership in the business. Value is derived by subtracting all liabilities from all assets.

**Per Capita Income** - Income by or for each person.

**Prepaid Assets** - Assets that represent expenditures to be used over a certain period of time before being reversed or amortized.

**Private Sector** - That part of the national economy that invests in the production of new capital equipment, such as factories, warehouses, equipment, machinery, automobiles, or non-governmental services. These goods and services are usually sold in a market.

**Public Sector** - That segment of the national economy in which services are supplied by government and are not sold in a market. Consequently, in this sector, there is no price that can be used to value the productive activities of government. Therefore, government services are valued at the cost of providing them. The three levels of the public sector are federal, state, and local. This sector includes services such as national defense, health services, police, education, and fire services.

**S.W.O.T.** - Strengths, Weaknesses, Opportunities, and Threats. A strategic analysis tool used in the development of short-term and long-term strategic planning.

**Total Capitalization** - The combination of all debt capitalization and all equity capitalization. Debt capitalization includes all contracts, bonds, and notes. Equity capitalization includes all retained earnings, shareholder's equity, and paid-in capital.

**Unemployment Rate** - The number of persons without jobs who are actively looking for work divided by the total size of the labor force. Labor force here includes both the fully employed, the underemployed, and the unemployed.

**Working Capital** - The funds available to pay for current operating expenses such as labor and materials.

# Bibliography and References

Anderson, Dan Robert. Minority Enterprise Development Program. Madison, Wisconsin: Bureau of Business Research and Service, Graduate School of Business Administration, University of Wisconsin, 1973.

Ambry, K. Margaret. 1990-1991 Almanac of Consumer Markets: A Guide to Today's More Complex and Harder to Find Customers. New York: American Demographics Press.

Banner, David K. The Politics of Social Program Evaluation. Massachusetts: Ballinger Publishing Company, 1975.

Bates, Timothy Mason. Government Promotion of Minority Group Entrepreneurship. Wisconsin: University of Wisconsin, 1974.

Blackman, Courtney, Newlands McLaurin. Black Capitalism in Economic Perspective. New York: Irving Trust Company Economic Research Department, 1973.

Blagrove, Luanna C. Strategy For Minority Businesses. Connecticut: Blagrove Publications, 1980.

Bradford, Ernie. Hannibal. New York: McGraw Hill, 1981.

Brarda, Roger H. Personal Traits and Values Contributing to the Success of Spanish-Surname Entrepreneurs in the United States. California, [publisher not found], 1979.

Connolly, Peter. Hannibal and the Enemies of Rome. Silver Burdett, 1978.

Davis, Lenwood G. Black Businesses, Employment, Economics, and Finance in Urban America. Illinois: Council of Planning Librarians, 1974.

-- Black Capitalism in Urban America. Illinois: Council on Planning Librarians, 1974.

Dickens, Jr., Floyd, and Jacqueline B. Dickens. The Black Manager - Making It in the Corporate World. New York: Amacom Publishers, 1982.

Donnelly, H. James, Jr. Fundamentals of Management: Functions, Behavior, Models. Texas: Business Publications, Inc., 1975.

Dupuy, Jr., Trevor, N. The Military Life of Hannibal, Father of Strategy. Los Angeles: F. Watts Publishing, 1969.

Ewing, Samuel D. Minority Capital Resource Handbook. 2nd Edition. District of Columbia: Securities Industry Minority Capital Foundation, 1980.

Farr, Walter G. Minority Economic Development. New York: University School of Law, 1971.

Feingold, Norman and Dr. Leonard G. Perlman. Making It On Your Own. Acrpolis, 1971.

Fierce, Hughlyn F. Improving Minorities Share of Aggregate Income. New York: New York University, Institute of Afro-American Affairs, 1979.

Fromm, Erich. The Art of Loving. New York: Harper Collins, 1989.

Gilbreath, Larry Kent, Economic Diversification On The Navajo Indian Reservation, 1971.

Goldman, Peter. The Death and Life of Malcolm X. Chicago: University of Illinois Press, 1979.

Holliday, Thelma Y. Minorities In The Field Of Business. 3rd Edition. District of Columbia. Institute For Minority Business Education. Howard University, 1975.

Johnson, Ruth Ellen. The Development of a Unit On The Afro-American Entrepreneur In The United States Before 1866. Pennsylvania, 1979.

Lamb, Harold. Hannibal, One Man Against Rome. New York: Doubleday, 1958.

Light, Ivan Hubert. <u>Ethnic Enterprise in America.</u> California: University of California Press, 1972.

Perry, Bruce. <u>Malcolm X: The Last Speeches</u>. New York: Pathfinder Press, 1989.

Rummel, Jack. <u>Malcolm X: Militant Black Leader</u>. New York: Chelsea House Publishers, 1990.

Scott, William C. <u>Key Business Ratios of Minority Owned Businesses</u>. Texas: Center for Studies in Business, Economics, and Human Resources, University of Texas, 1981.

Sheffrin, M. Steven, <u>Macro-economics: Theory and Policy</u>. Ohio: Southwestern Publishing Company, 1988.

Soloman, Steven. <u>Small Business USA</u>. Crown Publishers, Inc.

Sowell, Thomas. <u>Race and Economics</u>. New York: Longman, Inc., 1975.

Stickney, Clyde P. <u>Financial Accounting: An Introduction to Concepts, Methods, and Uses</u>. New York: The Dryden Press, 1982.

Tideman, T. Nicolaus. <u>Efficiency In Minority Enterprise Programs</u>. Massachusetts: Harvard University, 1972.

Trower-Subira, George. <u>Black Folks Guide To Making Big Money In America</u>. 1st Edition. New Jersey: Very Serious Business Enterprises, 1980.

Venable, Abraham S. <u>Building Black Businesses</u>. New York: Earl G. Graves Publishing Company, 1972.

Yancy, Robert J. <u>Federal Government Policy and Black Business Enterprise</u>. Massachusettes. Ballinger Publishing Company, 1974.

*Ethnic Communities in Business*. Massachusetts: Cambridge University Press, 1984.

Other Sources:

An Analysis of How Eligibility Criteria Are Applied for Participation in the 8(a) Program. District of Columbia: U.S. General Accounting Office, 1978.

Business in the Ghetto. Illinois: Section of Corporation, Banking and Business Law, 1969.

California Utilities Utilization of Minority/Women Business. California: California Legislature Assembly, Committee on Utilities and Commerce, 1985.

Directory of Marketing Assistance for Minority Businesses. Washington, DC: American Marketing Association, Department of Commerce, Office of Minority Business Enterprise, 1976.

Effects of Government Regulation on Small Business and the Problems of Women and Minorities in Small Business in the Southwestern United States. District of Columbia: U.S. Congress, Senate Select committee on Small Business, 1977.

Franchise Opportunities Handbook. District of Columbia: U.S. Department of Commerce. International Trade Administration, U.S. Government Printing Office, 1984.

Guide to Doing Business with the Department of State. Rev. March 1985. Washington, D.C.: Bureau of Management, Office of Small and Disadvantaged Business Utilization, 1985.

Guide To Minority Business Directories. 10th Edition. Minneapolis: Minority Business Campaign, 1975.

Helping Small Business To Respond To Consumers' Needs. District of Columbia: U.S. Department of Commerce, 1982.

How The Law to Prevent Railroad Discrimination and Encourage Minority Participation in Railroad Activities is Being Implemented. District of Columbia: U.S. General Accounting Office, 1980.

Key Indicators of County Growth 1970-2010. District of Columbia: NPA Data Services, Inc.,

Major Problems With SBA's Section 8(a) Program For Disadvantaged Small Businesses. District of Columbia: United States Congressional House Committee on Government Operations, Commerce, Consumer, and Monetary Affairs Subcommittee.

Minority Business and Its Contributions to the U.S. Economy. District Of Columbia: Senate Committee of Small Business, The U.S. Congress. U.S. General Printing Office, 1982.

Money Income and Poverty Status in the United States. District of Columbia: U.S. Department of Commerce, Bureau of The Census, 1989.

Office of Minority Business Enterprise Could Do More to Start and Maintain Minority Businesses, The. District of Columbia: U.S. General Accounting Office, 1977.

Small and Minority Business Ownership in the Cable Television Industry. District Of Columbia: United States Congressional House, Committee On Small Business, U.S. Government Printing Office, 1982.

Source Book of Marketing Demographics. 5th Edition. CACI Marketing Systems, 1990.

Sourcebook of Zip Code Demographics. 7th Edition. CACI Marketing Systems, 1990.

State Of Black America, The. The National Urban League. 1988, 1989, 1990, 1991 Editions.

Statistical Abstract of the United States. District of Colimbia: United States Department of Commerce, Bureau of Census, 1991.

Strategies for Advancing Minority Ownership Opportunities in Telecommunications. District of Columbia: Advisory Committee on Alternative Financing for Minority Opportunities in Telecommunications, 1982.

Whatever Happened to Minority Economic Development? Illionois: Dryden Press, 1974.

# INDEX